**What the experts are saying about ⸜**
*The Concealed Handgun Manual...*

"Chris Bird's work on concealed carry comes at an appropriate time on this important issue. The book is well written, illustrated, and very informative." — **Clint Smith, director, Thunder Ranch shooting school.**

"An excellent guide to responsible, safe, and lawful exercise of the right to bear arms. Useful for persons who carry licensed firearms for protection, and for persons who want a better understanding of this controversial, important subject." — **Dave Kopel, author and research director, Independence Institute.**

"Mr. Bird has relied on his own years of experience and extensive research to compile an intelligent and well laid-out work. Detailed case studies have been used to validate theories and techniques. Not only does the book cover firearms and their safe and tactical use, *The Concealed Handgun Manual* also offers some interesting and poignant commentary on current societal views. Recommended reading material." — **Louis Awerbuck, president, Yavapai Firearms Academy.**

"After reading *The Concealed Handgun Manual* by Chris Bird, it is apparent that a book has finally been written that teaches the proper techniques needed to safely carry a handgun concealed. The techniques used and applied are both life-saving and practical. Survival is what this manual is about, and for that reason I personally recommend it to everyone who carries a concealed handgun, both civilian and law enforcement. . . . *survival is our number one objective,* and I believe that Chris Bird's number one objective is the same." — **Jerry D. Lane, law enforcement instructor, Heckler & Koch.**

# THE CONCEALED HANDGUN MANUAL

### Second Edition

## *How to Choose, Carry, and Shoot a Gun in Self Defense*

# THE CONCEALED HANDGUN MANUAL

## Second Edition

### How to Choose, Carry, and Shoot a Gun in Self Defense

### Chris Bird

Privateer Publications

San Antonio, Texas

Published by: Privateer Publications • (210) 308-8191
Post Office Box 29427 • San Antonio, TX 78229

Printed in the United States of America
First Edition 1997; Second impression 1998; Third impression 1999; Second Edition 2000.

**Publisher's Cataloging-in-Publication**
*(Provided by Quality Books, Inc.)*

Bird, Chris.
    The concealed handgun manual : how to choose, carry, and shoot a gun in self defense / by Chris Bird. -- 2nd ed.
    p. cm.
    Includes bibliographical references and index.
    ISBN: 0-9656784-6-6

    1. Pistols. 2. Pistol shooting.
    3. Self-defense. 4. Gun control--United States.
    5. Concealment (Criminal law) I. Title.

TS537.B48 2000                    683.4'3
                                  QBI99-1865

**Photo Credits:** Kemp Davis Photography, San Antonio; Smith & Wesson; Glock; SIG Sauer; Beretta; Browning; Milt Sparks; Galco; Dillon; Kahr; Kimber; and Thunder Ranch.

**Warning:** Neither the publisher nor the author assumes any responsibility for the use or misuse of any information contained in this book.

**Usage Note:** Use of the masculine personal pronoun is not intended to be discriminatory.

**Trade Names** appearing in this book are the property of their respective owners. Products and services are mentioned in this book for reference only. Nothing written or implied should be construed as an endorsement of any product or service.

Printed on recycled paper.

ii

*To Anita, whose idea this was and
who suffered through its completion.*

"Those who give up essential liberties to purchase a little temporary safety deserve neither liberty nor safety."

—Benjamin Franklin

# CONTENTS

# FOREWORD

Chris Bird and I became friends ten years ago, after meeting on a South Texas shooting range. As well as being avid handgun shooters, we shared a firm belief that everyone is ultimately responsible for his or her own safety. I was surprised that someone from England should share my thoughts on this, as I knew that handgun ownership is generally discouraged in that country. I have watched Chris adapt to our South Texas culture and notice that some of our colloquialisms have crept into his speech and even his writing style.

At the time Chris and I met in 1990, Texans had not been able to legally carry handguns for self defense for more than a century. A lot has changed since then. We watched with envy as other states passed concealed-carry laws in the early 1990s and experienced frustration when in 1993 our own governor, then Ann Richards, threatened to veto similar legislation here. I like to think that her threat was responsible for the end of her political career. The legislation finally passed in 1995 and was signed into law by our governor, George W. Bush.

The new law required applicants to complete a ten- to fifteen-hour training course, so qualified course instructors were needed. While I was among the first people qualified to teach the concealed-handgun course, Chris saw a need for a book that would go further than the mandatory course prescribed by the state. The result is *The Concealed Handgun Manual.*

As a long-time handgun shooter and a former crime reporter for a big-city newspaper, Chris is eminently qualified to write on this subject. In a way that no single expert might do, Chris has brought together the philosophies and tactics of many self-defense masters. He has provided a comprehensive overview simple enough for the first-time shooter to understand, and from which even experienced shooters can gain insight. I believe that in reading this book, many shooters can develop a mind-set to keep them out of trouble.

*The Concealed Handgun Manual* is a must-buy for anyone who considers carrying a concealed handgun for personal protection. Studying the text is a learning experience which will increase your awareness and understanding of the principles of pistolcraft and the mental discipline needed to win a gunfight. The book has valuable and potentially life-saving tips to incorporate into your training and dry-fire sessions. It is an outstanding, enjoyable, and very readable book.

Each chapter begins with a true-life account of actual shootings and events where handguns were used in self defense by private citizens as well as law-enforcement officers. These anecdotes are exciting, educational, and well researched. They provide examples of how others have faced deadly force and survived.

This is not just a book for those interested in the Texas concealed-handgun license. The text is of vital interest to anyone concerned with armed defense in a violent society. In addition, Chris has provided a summary of the laws and concealed-carry license statistics for each of the thirty-one states that allow law-abiding citizens to carry guns for protection. This book is for you, regardless of where you live.

*The Concealed Handgun Manual* ranks with the best publications available for making an educated and informed decision about legally carrying a handgun for personal protection. I highly recommend you add it to your library.

*Ted Bonnet*
*Twice World Champion, Standard Division*
*International Practical Shooting Confederation*

# INTRODUCTION TO THE SECOND EDITION

For this second edition, I was hoping to add at least two—Missouri and Colorado—to the list of states that have passed laws allowing any law-abiding citizen to carry a concealed handgun in public for protection. However, it was not to be. Since the first edition of this book was published, the nation has been rocked by a rash of multiple shootings at schools by students. The worst of these happened in April 1999 at Columbine High School in a suburb of Denver. Two students killed a dozen of their colleagues and a teacher before committing suicide. This happened just as the Colorado Legislature was about to debate and probably pass a bill that would have allowed residents of the state much easier access to concealed-carry licenses. The bill was withdrawn. Shortly before the Columbine tragedy, Missouri voters went to the polls to decide in the first referendum of its kind whether they too wanted the right to carry concealed handguns for protection. The referendum passed in 104 counties out of 114 in the state, but voters in the big cities, particularly St. Louis, managed to derail it after furious lobbying by the Clinton administration and other anti-gun activists.

We have also seen a volley of lawsuits, mostly by large cities, against gun manufacturers. Fresh from success in squeezing money from the tobacco industry, many of the same lawyers turned their sights on the makers of guns. The lawyers, and the cities they represent, contend that gun makers are responsible for the medical and law-enforcement costs the cities have borne when guns are misused. Nowhere in this equation has the benefit of handguns to law-abiding citizens who protect themselves from criminals been factored in.

Already, some gun companies have felt the pressure. It appears that Colt plans to reduce its exposure to these lawsuits by reducing its output to the civilian gun market.

I felt it important to address the school shooting issue, so have added a new chapter to show that guns and knowledge about guns have played a positive role in at least two incidents. I have considerably enlarged the last chapter, which deals with concealed-carry laws in the states which allow citizens to protect themselves effectively. Most of these states have their laws and regulations on the Internet, so I have included web sites. Many states are now recognizing licenses or permits from some other states, so where possible I have included these reciprocal agreements. In updating the numbers of license holders in each state, I discovered that in the last two-and-a-half years, the number of license holders has increased by about three hundred thousand.

The gun industry is making new smaller and lighter handguns specifically for the concealed-handgun market. I have also mentioned a new competitive shooting organization that meets the training needs of concealed-handgun carriers better than any other. Finally, I have added some new accounts of actual confrontations of criminals by armed citizens.

Stay safe and remain undefeated.

Chris Bird
San Antonio, January 2000

# ABOUT THE AUTHOR

Chris Bird has been a journalist for twenty-five years and a handgun shooter for more than forty. His love for shooting has steered him through the bureaucratic red tape of owning handguns in England,

 Canada, and Australia. As a commissioned officer in the Royal Military Police of the British Army in the 1960s, Bird was stationed in Berlin, West Germany, and Belgium, serving as company weapon-training officer and winning awards for shooting in competition.

An incurable romantic, Chris migrated to Canada after leaving the military, where he worked as a cowboy in British Columbia while shooting and hunting extensively.

Chris became a journalist and worked as a crime and investigative reporter for the Vancouver Province and the Canadian Broadcasting Corporation. He has also worked as a salesman, a private investigator, and a shotgun guard for an armored car company. In 1986 Chris competed in the Canadian Practical Pistol Championships.

The call of the sea lured him away from his Canadian career for a two-year voyage from Vancouver, Canada, to Sydney, Australia, aboard British Privateer, a twenty-seven-foot boat that he built himself. He sailed back across the Pacific to take up residence in the U.S.

Married to a native Texan, Chris has adopted the state as his spiritual home. He and his wife, Anita, live in San Antonio, where Chris has enjoyed working as a reporter for the Express-News. As a police reporter, he gleefully claims he has reported on more shootings and killings than Wild Bill Hickok had gunfights.

Given his choice, Chris would never be without a gun at hand. He has shot in practical shooting competition and at one point belonged to so many shooting clubs his wife complained she never saw him. He belongs to the National Rifle Association and the Texas State Rifle Association and is a director of the Texas Concealed Handgun Instructor Association.

# ACKNOWLEDGMENTS

This book would not have been written without the help and encouragement of many people. First, my wife, Anita, who had the idea, then encouraged, nagged, and supported me until I completed it, while the kitchen counter I had promised to rebuild remained unfixed. Bill McLennan, Greg Ferris, and Robert Butler unstintingly shared with me their time, skills, and expertise. I cannot thank them enough.

Other experts in the self-defense field provided information and experience. They include Clint Smith, Jerry Lane, Jeff Cooper, Terry Kenney, Harry Fleming, David Ham, and Bruce Siddle.

I would particularly like to thank those who shared the stories of incidents in which they were involved: Suzanna Gratia Hupp, Shayne Katzfey, Leo Arredondo, Domingo Moncada, "Joe Archer," Gordon Hale III, Jake Ryker, Joel Myrick, Marguerite Everheart, Laura Poldson, Jim Eichelberg and Pete Kanakidis.

Others who helped me in this project include: Marion Hammer, Chip Walker, and Bill Powers of the National Rifle Association; Jerry Patterson, Ron Wilson, and Ray Allen of the Texas Legislature; Al Cuellar and C.J. Havrda of the Texas Rangers; Jeff Page, Ray Torres, Joe MacKay, Joery Smittick, Jimmy Holguin, Andy Hernandez, and Al Ballew of the San Antonio Police Department; Jack Dean; Dennis McElroy; Gordon Hale, Jr.; Vincent Perini; David Kopel; Jean Souza; Gary Kleck; John Lott; Laureen Chernow; Ken Jorgensen; Richard Stengel; George Aylesworth; Eugene Cotton; Charlie Wells; Karen Beary; Jay Griffin; Chuck Dewey; Ted Bonnet; Bob Nagel; Denise Griffin; Charlie Johnston; and even Robin Terry. I thank you all.

In addition I want to thank all the manufacturers and their people who provided photographs and information, as well as all the state government employees who were so courteous and helpful in providing the information in Chapter 12.

Finally I wish to thank my editor and typographer, Susan Hughes; Bruce Hughes who incorporated the updates for the second edition; Kemp Davis, who took most of the photographs; Lisa and Luke Ham, who appear in the front-cover photo; Greg Ferris, Bill McLennan, and Dennis McElroy, who modeled for other photos in the text.

# Chapter One

## SCHOOL SHOOTINGS: ANOTHER POINT OF VIEW

Jake Ryker didn't know he had already been shot in the chest when he charged the shooter in the school cafeteria that Thursday morning, but it probably wouldn't have made any difference if he had.

It was Ryker's seventeenth birthday—May 21, 1998. He was just getting up from a table with his friends at Thurston High School in Springfield, Oregon. It was just before 8 a.m. and the students were getting ready for their first class. Ryker had a history assignment to turn in.

That's when Kip Kinkel walked through the cafeteria door and opened fire on his fellow students with a .22-caliber Ruger semi-automatic rifle with a fifty-round magazine. Kinkel had sawed off the butt of the rifle to make a pistol grip and to make it easier to conceal under his trenchcoat.

Kinkel, 15, had already murdered his parents—both teachers—before coming to school. And in the breezeway a few feet from the cafeteria door he had executed Ben Walker with a shot through the head.

*Jake Ryker, student at Thurston High School, Springfield, Oregon.*

1

At first, Ryker didn't see the gun as Kinkel came in, but he did hear the shots. When Kinkel started shooting at the students around his table from about twenty feet away, Ryker pushed his girlfriend, Jennifer Alldredge, to the ground. That was when he got shot. But he thought as he landed on the ground that the blow was from someone's arm or fist. He was unaware that a bullet had gone through his right lung and broken a rib. He looked up to see Kinkel approaching the end of the table where he and the others had been sitting.

"He grabbed my friend Mike, held him down and shot him in the head," Ryker said, referring to Mikael Nickolauson. "That's when I got up and started running. I tripped over this girl Christina and hit the ground. I hit my chin or my forehead or something. I remember my face bouncing off the floor."

Ryker looked up to see Kinkel pointing the rifle to fire again and heard the click as the firing pin snapped on an empty chamber.

"I knew when I heard that click that if anybody was going to hit him, now's the time," Ryker said.

Kinkel had fired all fifty rounds in the magazine and struggled to reload the rifle as Ryker came up off the floor and ran at him.

"When he saw me, he started backpedaling."

Ryker, a high-school wrestler six-feet four- inches tall, swept Kinkel's feet from under him in a wrestling tackle and the rifle went flying.

"I hit him hard enough that it knocked him over. His feet went up in the air, and I came down on top of him."

Another teenager picked up the rifle and several others joined in the attack on the shooter, including Ryker's brother Josh. But Kinkel was not ready to give up. Ryker could see Kinkel was armed with a knife but he also had a Glock 9mm semi-automatic pistol in his waistband under his trenchcoat.

"When he hit the ground, that's when he started going for that Glock," Ryker said. "I thought he was going for the knife. I put my hand on the knife and grabbed his face but then he took the gun out. That's when I grabbed the barrel of the gun. By that time, he had it up in my face so I was looking down the barrel."

The previous weekend, Jake Ryker, his 14-year-old brother Josh, and their father Robert had been shooting at a local range. They had been shooting a .45-caliber Colt Gold Cup semi-automatic. The pistol is a target version of the .45 semi-automatic that until recently was the standard issue for the U.S. military. Robert Ryker, at that time a chief petty officer in the U.S. Navy, knew all about the big pistol. He was explaining the safeties on the .45 to his sons. He told them that if you push on the muzzle or the slide of most semi-automatics they will not fire.

"If you push the slide back an eighth of an inch, it throws it out of battery. I said that if somebody stuck one in your face or pointed one at you, you could push back on the slide and it won't go off," Robert Ryker said. "But then I said, if he's still got his finger on the trigger and you release the slide, it'll shoot because it'll slam back in battery and the hammer will fall."

Jokingly, Robert warned his sons not to try this move except as a last resort. He said he never expected that less than a week later his oldest son would be fighting for his life with someone who had stuck a pistol in his face.

"I was taught that very same thing when I was in the Navy as a gunner's mate and when I went to gunnery school, they showed us that. Our chief told our class don't ever try this unless you know you're going to be dead anyway," Robert Ryker added.

When Kinkel stuck the muzzle of the Glock 9mm in Jake Ryker's face, Ryker grabbed the muzzle with his left hand. Remembering his father's advice, he tried to push the slide back out of battery.

"I figured that would be the best thing for me to do with that thing pointed in my face," Jake Ryker said. "If not, I was going to get a bullet between my eyes. So I grabbed the end of it. When I grabbed it, I guess I didn't grip it strongly enough, but I got it away from my face and it discharged."

The 9mm bullet went through the knuckle of Ryker's left index finger, burned the top of his thumb, ricocheted off the floor, then ripped through another boy's buttocks. But Ryker's grip on the slide prevented the gun from cycling and it jammed.

By this time several boys, including Adam Walburger and Josh Ryker, had piled on Kinkel and managed to get the Glock away from him.

"Adam was helping Jake, and I grabbed the legs because he was kicking and fighting," Josh Ryker said. "We kept fighting him until we got pulled off by the adults."

"I was beating on him as much as I could. They had to pull me off him," Jake Ryker said.

It wasn't until another boy, Chris, pulled him off Kinkel that Jake Ryker realized he had been wounded. Chris grabbed him where his rib had been broken, and Ryker felt a stab of pain. The boy rolled Ryker over and pressed down on his chest where blood was welling from his chest wound. Ryker noticed blood all over Chris's hands. He noticed his own left index finger hanging by a piece of skin from his hand. Chris told him he had also been shot in the chest.

When he was arrested, police found that, in addition to the .22-caliber rifle and 9mm pistol, Kinkel was also armed with another handgun and had more than a thousand rounds of ammunition on him.

Jake Ryker has been called a hero for his actions in the school cafeteria, but he plays this down, pointing out that he was not the only teen to charge Kinkel, just the one in front. He said he did not have time to be afraid.

"By the time I got to stop and think about what the hell I just did I was actually in the hospital," he said.

Ryker spent about a week in the hospital. Doctors were able to save his finger, and he was fit enough a year later to survive Marine boot camp. In November 1999, Kinkel was sentenced to 111 years in prison for murdering his parents and two Thurston students and for wounding more than twenty students.

Robert Ryker is a concealed-handgun license holder and life member of the National Rifle Association . He is proud of his sons' knowledge and ability with firearms. He believes this knowledge enabled Jake to take down the shooter and almost certainly save the lives of more students.

"He knew enough about guns, had been around them enough, so he respects them like anybody should," Robert Ryker said. "But he knew when he could make his move because he was familiar with them."

Jake said he remembers shooting with his grandfather at beer cans with a .22-caliber revolver when he was six or seven years old.

"I got my first BB gun for Christmas when I think I was eight," he added.

The country has been plagued by a rash of school shootings, starting in February 1996 in Moses Lake, Washington, when a 14-year-old student killed two other students and a teacher, as well as seriously wounding a third student. This was followed about a year later in Bethel, Alaska, when a 16-year-old student killed the principal and another student, while wounding two more students. With these incidents as a warm up, there followed five mass shootings at schools around the country in which seven youths killed twenty-three students and two teachers. They also wounded sixty-eight others.

- October 1, 1997, in Pearl, Mississippi, a 16-year-old student murdered his mother at home then went to school, where he killed two students and wounded seven.
- December 1, 1997, in West Paducah, Kentucky, a 14-year-old boy killed three students and wounded five.

- March 24, 1998, in Jonesboro, Arkansas, four girls and a teacher were killed when two boys, aged 11 and 13, opened fire from ambush with rifles. Ten others were wounded.
- May 21, 1998, in Springfield, Oregon, Kip Kinkel opened fire with a sawed-down rifle killing two students and wounding twenty-three. He was stopped by Jake Ryker and others. Kinkel killed his parents before starting his rampage at school.
- April 20, 1999, in Littleton, Colorado, two boys, aged 17 and 18, killed twelve students and a teacher at Columbine High School, while wounding another twenty-three. The shooters then committed suicide.

The media frenzy that followed each of these incidents has caused widespread paranoia among parents, students, teachers, and school administrators. Some politicians and other public figures have been quick to blame these shootings on the "easy availability of guns." They have pushed for more government control of both guns and law-abiding gun owners. President Clinton, Attorney General Janet Reno, and Vice President Al Gore have been leading this campaign. However, even those who are pushing for more gun controls generally admit that none of the proposed new laws would have prevented any of the school shootings. The proposals include the FBI's instant check system applied to all gun-show firearms' transactions; limiting gun purchases to one a month; and raising the age for legal possession of a gun from 18 to 21. With more than twenty thousand gun laws nationwide, passing more is likely only to disarm and inconvenience law-abiding citizens.

Blaming the gun for school shootings is like blaming the car for traffic accidents. Guns have been readily available in the United States ever since the country was founded, so this is not anything new. There are still many Americans who can remember taking guns to school. Former Texas State Senator Jerry Patterson, who helped push the concealed-handgun law through the Texas Legislature in 1995, is one.

"In 1959, I took a gun to school for show-and-tell, and nobody thought anything of it," he said.

Robert Ryker, Jake's father, said that when he was at school he took a gun to school to work on during shop class.

"In my school annual, there is a picture of a teacher with an actual six-gun on his hip that we shot blanks in. We had a quick-draw contest in the courtyard," he said.

While demonizing guns has been popular with many public figures in the 1990s, other factors are probably more to blame for recent school shootings: lack of discipline at home and at school, single-parent families, child abuse, the use of behavior-altering drugs such as Luvox and Ritalin, violent video games and films, and the Internet. Many people blame the media for sensationalizing these incidents.

Patterson argues that the First Amendment to the Constitution—the amendment that guarantees free speech and freedom of the press—is far more responsible for the shootings than the Second Amendment which guarantees the right to keep and bear arms.

"The press's First Amendment right to report as they see fit has killed children in this country," Patterson said. "It's unequivocal. You can't argue that these copy-cat killings would have happened without the press."

However, he would not support more restrictions on First Amendment rights any more than he would support further erosion of Second Amendment rights, he added.

Robert and Jake Ryker both agree the media is much to blame for the shootings. Jake feels that if the media didn't give so much publicity to the shooters, others would not be encouraged to do it. He also thinks the media made Kip Kinkel into a national hero.

"I received hate mail because of this guy, because there are people who like this guy and think he did the right thing," Jake said.

There is an Internet site for Kinkel groupies, he added.

"One of them wanted to know how she could marry him. She was madly in love with him. They're seeking that attention."

Robert Ryker believes the media has a right to report what's happening, he just wishes they wouldn't make so much of it.

"If the media would quit making a circus event out of these shootings, the damn performers would quit coming to the circus," he said.

Media celebrities have not been slow to voice opinions about school shootings, most calling for more restrictions on guns and gun owners. Talk-show personality Rosie O'Donnell said she thought all gun owners should be jailed. She then weighed into Tom Selleck for taking part in ads for the National Rifle Association. Selleck had appeared on her show to promote a movie. He seemed angry and uncomfortable at O'Donnell's attack, later calling her unprofessional. O'Donnell was a spokeswoman for K-Mart, which sells guns and ammunition. She apparently quit after gun owners started complaining to the stores and threatening a boycott.

In May 1999, actress Sharon Stone made a big production of turning in a shotgun and three handguns to the Los Angeles police as a result, she said, of the Columbine High School shooting. Stone said she was surrendering her right to bear arms and urged other gun owners to turn in their guns. This is a woman who has made a lot of money from violent films. In one of her movies, she portrays a character who murders lovers during sex with an ice pick.

While the Second Amendment has come under attack as a result of these shootings, so has the free speech guarantee of the First Amendment. A 13-year-old boy in Ponder, Texas, was jailed for five days after writing a scary Halloween story as a class assignment. Christopher Beamon's essay described shooting his teacher, Amanda Henry, and two students. The teacher gave him an "A" and had him read the story aloud in class. Parents named in the story complained, and Principal Chance Allen called police.

When Christopher appeared in front of Denton County Juvenile Court Judge Darlene Whitten, she ordered him imprisoned for ten days. He was set free only after the family's lawyer demanded his release and the district attorney declined to prosecute.

In November 1999, the Chicago public school system abolished rifle training with air rifles for some nine thousand cadets in the Junior Reserve Officer Training Corps. The move was another paranoid reaction to the school shootings elsewhere in the country. It took prompting from *The Chicago Tribune* to bring this harmless and useful form of training to an end. The newspaper published an article drawing attention to weapon training in Illinois schools, while schools nationwide are pondering how to prevent shootings.

Paul Vallas, speaking for the school district, said it didn't want to send a contradictory message to students, discouraging the use of violence and weapons, and at the same time supporting a marksmanship program. This evisceration of the JROTC is particularly troubling as there appears to be no reason for it other than a desire by officials to avoid controversy. This action was taken at a time when the media were reporting about plummeting rates of violent youth crime and gun deaths since the early 1990s.

According to the Centers for Disease Control and Prevention the number of gun deaths—homicides, suicides, and accidents— dropped 21 percent between 1993 and 1997, while gunshot wounds dropped 41 percent during the same period. Fatalities dropped from 39,595 in 1993 to 32,436 in 1997 as non-fatal injuries fell to 64,207 from 104,390.

Meanwhile, violent youth crime fell 30 percent from 1994 to 1998, according to Justice Department figures. The arrest rate for juveniles aged 10 to 17 was the lowest for murder, robbery, rape, and aggravated assault since 1988. However, a report by the National Commission on the Causes and Prevention of Violence found that these rosy assessments tell only part of the story. The report stated that violent crime in the larger cities has risen 40 percent since the 1960s.

It seems these school shootings and other multiple shootings around the country have given the national media, some politicians, and anti-gun activists a wonderful opportunity to brainwash the American people into believing that guns are bad and that the people who have them are evil. Their ultimate aim is the disarmament of America.

The shooting at Columbine High School came at a time very convenient for those to whom guns are an anathema. A bill that would have given law-abiding Colorado residents the right to carry concealed handguns for protection was before the state legislature. It would most likely have passed had it not been withdrawn in the furor that followed that shooting.

Many people who support the right of civilians to carry concealed handguns for protection seem to be in favor of allowing teachers to be armed. Jesse Ventura, the colorful governor of Minnesota, spoke for many when he suggested that if someone at Columbine High School had had a concealed-handgun license and been armed, lives would have been saved. He was widely criticized in the media for this statement, but at least he kept his job. The same cannot be said of John Varis, superintendent of Reading Community Schools in Ohio for 13 years. Reading is a suburb of Cincinnati. Varis was forced to resign after he suggested at a public meeting that teachers could be armed and trained to respond to a school shooting. He pointed out that guns can be used to save lives as well as kill people. Some parents circulated petitions calling for his removal. Varis said he was discussing school-safety options.

Most of the high-profile school shootings have occurred in states that give ordinary citizens the right to carry concealed handguns for protection. But in each of those states, concealed-handgun-license holders are prevented from carrying guns at schools. Is this an effective policy? Professor John Lott, author of *More Guns, Less Crime: Understanding Crime and Gun Control Laws*, thinks not.

"I understand the motivation behind it—to try to create safe zones—but what I think happens when you do that is, rather than making it safer for the good people, you make it safer for those who are intent on doing the harm," he said.

Lott has studied the effect of concealed-handgun laws on multiple shootings in public places. He concludes that in states where concealed-handgun laws have been passed, such shootings have been reduced more than 80 percent. Where they have occurred in those states, they have been in places—like schools—where concealed-handgun-license holders are not allowed to carry their guns.

"Allowing teachers and other law-abiding adults to carry concealed handguns in schools would not only make it easier to stop shootings in progress. It could also help deter shootings from ever occurring," Lott said.

*Joel Myrick, assistant principal at Pearl High School, Mississippi.*

One high-profile school shooting that was brought to an end by a civilian with a handgun occurred in Pearl, Mississippi, on October 1, 1997.

Shortly after 8 a.m., Joel Myrick, an assistant principal at Pearl High School, was walking back to his office with a cup of coffee in his hand. He was dressed as usual in a pinstripe suit, white shirt, and tie. He crossed a large area about the size of a basketball court with a high ceiling that was referred to as the Commons. About six hundred students were milling about in this vast area. They had just arrived and were waiting around for the school day to begin. It would be unlike any other school day they had ever experienced.

As Myrick reached his outer office, he heard a loud explosion. Immediately, he set down his coffee and stepped back out into the Commons.

There was another loud boom. Most of the children in the Commons ran for the exits, many of them screaming. As some ran towards Myrick, he held open the door and they flooded into his outer office. After fifteen or twenty children had run past him into his office, Myrick heard the third boom.

He realized someone was shooting. He started moving carefully out into the Commons looking for the source of the gunfire. His view of part of the Commons was blocked by a stairwell. By this time the area was almost empty of students. After moving a few steps, Myrick saw the barrel of a rifle, then as he moved further, a large youth wearing a long coat. He was walking, with the rifle pointed forward and down, towards the center of the common area where there were four columns, each about three feet thick.

As Myrick watched, he saw the shooter lift the barrel of the rifle slightly and fire another shot. Myrick saw chips of concrete fly from one of the columns as two girls fell to the ground. The shooter, later identified as 16-year-old Luke Woodham, kept walking towards one of the columns where several children were trying to hide. But one boy was left exposed.

"He pulled his book bag up to his chest, and he said: 'No, man, no.' And Luke shot him within about four or five feet," Myrick said.

The two other children behind the column turned and ran. Woodham worked the lever of the rifle, chambered another round, and fired at them. The bullet hit the floor behind them and broke up. They were hit by pieces of the bullet and went down. Woodham was walking away from Myrick thumbing rounds into the magazine through the slot in the receiver of the .30-30-caliber Marlin rifle.

"I was contemplating running [at Woodham] but I was scared. Because there was about forty or fifty feet between me and him, and I thought, if I start running and he turns around, I'm dead, because he's killing folks," Myrick said.

The assistant principal said he has been hunting all his life and knows what the .30-30 round will do to a deer.

Woodham turned and started to walk towards one of the halls that lead off the Commons. Myrick sprinted along the side of the Commons towards an exit that lead to where his truck was parked. In the truck he kept his .45 handgun.

"I knew I had to get to my gun, because I was defenseless and I couldn't do anything with him at that point. I knew there was no one else around that could do anything with him at that point," Myrick said. "He was king. He was God of that school, and he could take life whenever he got ready, and he was doing it."

About halfway to the exit, Myrick turned and looked back.

"This is the image I'll remember for the rest of my life. I looked, and I saw seven bodies laying around in various positions. I could smell gunpowder," he said.

Woodham was walking away from him down the hall with the rifle held diagonally across his chest. Myrick had his truck key in his hand even before he reached the back door. He sprinted across the parking lot to his pickup, opened it up, and reached under the seat for his gun. The .45-caliber Colt compact semi-automatic was in a soft case. Myrick undid the zipper and took it out. It had a full magazine but no round in the chamber. He paused a moment realizing that he was holding a loaded gun on school property, then he racked the slide, chambering a round, and put on the safety. Myrick said that once he had the gun in his hand he felt "unbelievably safe" during the rest of the incident.

He took off running with the gun pointed up in the air and

his finger alongside the trigger guard. He didn't want to enter the building through the door from which he had exited, so he started running clockwise around the building.

Myrick fondly remembers an elderly black custodian named Irene who summed up the whole situation in two words. She was standing in the next entrance with one foot each side of the door so she could run in or out depending on the threat. She looked at Myrick running past with a gun in his hand and she said: "Oh my."

Myrick turned the corner of the building and ran towards the front door. He figured that was the closest entrance to where he had last seen Woodham. He thought the shooter was probably searching classrooms, closets, and bathrooms looking for more unarmed victims.

When he was about forty yards from the front door, Woodham emerged from it still carrying the rifle. Myrick stopped and settled into a classic Weaver stance, pointing the gun at Woodham, and yelled: "Stop."

Woodham turned his head and looked at Myrick, but kept walking to his car, which was parked at the curb. Behind Woodham cars were leaving the parking lot and kids were running. Myrick didn't have a clear shot at him, and Woodham didn't point the gun at him.

"I made the decision not to shoot at him at that point. I safed my weapon again, and took off running towards his car."

Before Myrick could reach the car, Woodham had taken off, burning rubber as he accelerated away.

"I remember looking at the white smoke coming off his tires."

Myrick ran as fast as he could to cut Woodham off before he could escape from the parking lot onto the street. Woodham was slowed by traffic at an intersection on school property. Some cars were still bringing students to school, and others were trying to leave the area as fast as they could. A car was stopped in front of Woodham at a stop sign. Woodham backed up and went around the car, but the delay allowed time for Myrick to reach the exit ahead of him.

Myrick was standing with one foot on the road when Woodham turned the corner about thirty yards away. There was nothing on the other side of the road but trees, so this time the assistant principal would have a clear shot.

"I was going to shoot him as he came across my field of fire, because the junior high was right down the road, and that's where my son goes to school," said Myrick. "I don't know where he was heading, but I knew he had just shot up a bunch of folks with a high-powered rifle, and he was getting away. I just figured I needed to stop him."

When Woodham turned the corner and headed straight for him, Myrick took up his position, covering the shooter with the .45 in a two-hand hold. He clicked off the safety. When Woodham saw him, he swerved off the road onto the grass away from Myrick. The grass was wet, and the car spun out, coming to a stop across the road about fifteen feet away from him, Myrick said.

The assistant principal kept Woodham covered and told him not to move. Woodham's knuckles were white from where he was gripping the steering wheel and his glasses were askew on his face, but he didn't move. Still keeping him covered, Myrick walked quickly to the car.

"I knew I had him at that point. I moved right up to the car and held the pistol a couple of feet from the side of his head. I told him: 'If you do anything, I'm going to kill you.' And he never moved. He never said a word. In the seat next to him was the rifle lying muzzle down."

Myrick noticed that Woodham had black electrical tape around both of his hands. He found out later that Woodham had stabbed his mother to death before coming to school and had cut himself.

Myrick got the youth out of the car and made him lie face down on the grass. The assistant principal pulled Woodham's jacket up over his head, partly to immobilize him and partly to see if he had any other weapons on him. Myrick put his foot on the back of Woodham's head to make sure he didn't move, then asked why he had done this.

"Mr. Myrick, the world has wronged me, and I couldn't take it anymore," Woodham replied.

"I didn't think twice, I said: 'My God, wait till you get to Parchman,' which is the state penitentiary," Myrick recalled.

A few minutes later a police car pulled up, and the police officer took over, handcuffing Woodham. Myrick cleared his gun then ran back into the school. He found Woodham had killed two girls and wounded seven other students.

Although no one but Woodham knows for sure, Myrick believes he would have continued his murderous rampage if he had not been stopped. He still had two rounds in his rifle and thirty-six rounds on him at the time of his capture.

"I truly believe that he would have continued to do what he was doing."

In June 1998, Woodham was sentenced to life in prison for his rampage, which he tried to blame on the leader of a satanic group that he belonged to.

Like Jake Ryker, Joel Myrick has received hate mail. He has received more than twenty letters from around the country from people blaming him for what happened. Some of the letters were bizarre enough that he was concerned for his safety.

"The gist of what they were saying was that I was the problem. Luke Woodham was not the problem; that I created Luke Woodham because I'm a big bully that carries a gun."

Myrick has been a hunter and shooter all his life and is a member of the National Rifle Association. He is also an officer in the National Guard. He believes children are being desensitized to killing because of the graphic violence they see in movies and the violence they participate in when playing video games. This is the same sort of indoctrination that soldiers receive to enable them to kill an enemy.

He says kids need to feel a sense of belonging. If there is a common thread to the school shootings, it is that the shooters felt alienated from the student body.

"They were really not a part of the mainstream culture," he said. "They were a little bit outside."

In 1999, Myrick moved from Pearl to a job as the principal of a high school in northern Mississippi. He has been working to develop a sense of community in his school, so all students feel that they belong. If he sees a kid sitting alone, he will go and talk to him or her, he said. He also speaks to adult community groups to get them to become involved in the school and its students.

"I've really made a big effort to try to draw kids into the mainstream of the school, so everybody feels like they're part of the school and nobody is just left out."

Myrick is in favor of taking the initiative and trying to head off such incidents before they start. However, in a school situation, once someone has decided to go on an armed rampage, it is not easy to prevent them.

"You are not going to stop them by making the school into a prison, although I do believe an armed security guard is a great deterrent because some of these shooters are cowards," he said.

If these youths knew there was a good chance they would be shot or killed it would deter some, Myrick said. Under the current system, schools proclaim loudly with signs that they are drug- and gun-free zones.

"It's a shooting gallery. What better place to go and shoot than a gun-free zone," he said.

Myrick does not have a concealed-handgun license, though he could easily get one in Mississippi. He said it is legal for him to have a gun in his home and in his vehicle. He is usually not far from one or the other and does not want to carry one on his person.

He believes having teachers carry guns would create a problem. Teachers get jostled by students in crowded hallways. Female teachers with guns in their purses would be vulnerable because they have to put down the purses to teach.

"You're not maintaining a posture of keeping your weapon secured in a crowded hallway. That's why I think that an armed guard would be better."

Myrick did feel that with sufficient training, it would be an advantage to have a teacher or administrator with a gun locked inside the school building.

"I would love to have a gun loaded in my desk, drawer locked. It would be safe there; it would be inaccessible," he said. "It would really be safer than the one in my truck that's there now, because I'm not watching my truck, and if you wanted to take a pipe and knock my window out and snatch my gun you could."

He acknowledges that if he had had a gun in his desk at Pearl High School he could have reached it a lot quicker and perhaps saved some of the students from being shot. He stressed that whoever was allowed to keep a gun on school premises should receive training and have strict instructions about when it could be used.

Former Texas State Senator Jerry Patterson agrees that allowing teachers to carry guns in school buildings would pose serious security problems.

"I think a teacher who has a license to carry should be able to carry everywhere except in the building. Leave it in your car, like Myrick did," Patterson said.

Although the school shootings have received an enormous amount of publicity, they are quite rare. According to a Justice Policy Institute report in 1998, the chance of a student becoming the victim of a school-associated violent death is slightly less than one in a million.

Patterson believes such incidents run in cycles and that eventually they will peter out.

"Unfortunately, I think it's going to run its course," he said.

## Chapter Two

## *WHY CARRY A GUN?*
## *THE POLICE CAN'T PROTECT YOU*

It was a sunny fall day in central Texas when Dr. Suzanna Gratia walked into the Luby's Cafeteria in Killeen, Texas, with her mother and father. As they entered the restaurant, Gratia had no inkling that she would be the only one of them to leave there alive.

October 16, 1991, was Bosses' Day, and the cafeteria was packed with employees taking their employers to lunch. Gratia, then 32, was a chiropractor in nearby Copperas Cove. She and her parents were waiting for her friend, the restaurant manager, to return to their table. They had just finished eating and were dawdling over coffee.

The pleasant atmosphere was shattered when a pickup truck burst through the window into the restaurant, smashing into customers and showering them with broken glass.

*Suzanna Gratia Hupp.*

At first, Gratia thought it was an accident. She started to go over to help the people knocked down by the pickup.

Then she heard a flurry of gunshots.

Immediately, Gratia and her father tipped over their table and, with her mother, took cover behind it. Gratia decided it must be a robbery, but the shooting continued. Then she thought maybe it was a hit. Perhaps someone important was in the restaurant because it was Bosses' Day.

But the driver of the pickup was walking unhurriedly from one person to another shooting them.

"It took a good forty-five seconds, which is a long time, to figure out that the guy was just going to walk around and shoot people," Gratia said. "You kept waiting for him to stop and give some sort of explanation, but he didn't."

By this time, the gunman, later identified as George Hennard, was standing at the right-front fender of his truck, about fifteen feet from Gratia, still shooting people.

"I thought, I got this turkey. I reached for my purse. I had a perfect place to prop my arm; everybody in the restaurant was down; he was up. Then I realized that a few months earlier I had made the stupidest decision of my life. My gun was one hundred yards away, in my car, completely useless to me. I had made the decision to begin leaving it in my car because I was concerned about losing my license to practice chiropractic."

In 1991, Texas had no concealed-handgun carry law. Only law-enforcement officers could carry concealed handguns legally in the state.

Gratia was appalled. She groped for something to do to stop the carnage. She thought about throwing her purse at the gunman. She eyed the sugar container and the butter knife, but Hennard had two semi-automatic handguns and was in complete control of the situation. Any attack would be suicide.

Meanwhile, Gratia's father, Al Gratia, was getting increasingly frustrated.

"I've got to do something. I've got to do something. He's going to kill everybody in here," Gratia remembers her father saying, as he started to rise to his feet.

Suzanna grabbed him by the shirt collar and jerked him down, cursing at him and saying: "If you go at him, he's going to kill you, too."

But he shook her off and, when he thought he had a chance, tried to rush Hennard.

"I remember ducking down because I already knew what was going to happen. He didn't have a chance. The guy could see him coming a mile away. Dad probably covered half the space, and the guy turned and shot him in the chest. My dad went down in the aisle. He was still alive and still semi-conscious, but he was maybe eight feet from me. I saw the wound and, as horrible as it sounds, I basically wrote him off at that point."

After shooting Gratia's father, Hennard changed direction away from her and her mother. For the first time she looked at the gunman's face.

"You think the stupidest things. I remember looking at this guy, thinking, this is a good-looking guy—with a new truck. What could possibly be so wrong in this guy's life that he's doing this?"

Hennard reached the wall and fortunately turned away from Gratia. She and her mother were in the front part of the restaurant and were trapped until somebody broke a window near the back. Her first thought on hearing the crash of the breaking glass was that Hennard was not alone. Perhaps it was a terrorist attack. But she saw people escaping through the broken window and knew it was their only chance to get out.

Gratia kept peeking around the table, where she and her mother were crouched, until she saw an opportunity. She stood up with her back to Hennard who was still shooting people, expecting at any moment to be shot.

"I remember standing with my back to the guy, and I kept hearing the gunshots. I kept waiting to feel the impact. I remember feeling that so vividly."

Gratia grabbed her mother by the shirt, pulling her to her feet. "Come on, come on, we've got to run; we've got to get out of here," she urged.

Her feet grew wings and she ran, not stopping until she was through the window and outside in the sunshine. The restaurant manager, Mark Kopenhafer, met her outside and asked if she was all right.

"I said, 'Yeah, but Dad's been shot.' And I turned around to say something about Mom or something to Mom, and she wasn't there."

Her mother had not followed her out of the restaurant. Gratia learned afterwards from the police what had happened. When they arrived on the scene, the officers knew a man was inside the restaurant shooting people. Earlier, while Hennard had been systematically executing people, everybody was hugging the floor, and it was quiet except for the sound of the gunshots. But when the police arrived, people were scrambling to get out, and pandemonium reigned. The officers could not see who was doing the shooting.

"My mother, according to them, had crawled out into the open where my father was and was cradling him until the gunman got back around to her.

"According to the one cop, he didn't realize who the man was at that point, and he saw the guy look down at my Mom. He said, she looked up at him, put her head down, and then he put the gun to her head and pulled the trigger.

"My parents had had their forty-seventh wedding anniversary a week and a half before, and she just wasn't going anywhere."

Hennard killed twenty-three people and wounded another thirty-three before he put one of his pistols to his own head and pulled the trigger.

Since that day, Suzanna Gratia, now Suzanna Gratia Hupp since her marriage, has testified before Congress and numerous state legislatures, urging law-makers to allow law-abiding citizens to carry guns for self defense. She is acknowledged to be one of the most compelling witnesses in the gun-control debate. Hupp has been elected to the Texas Legislature and as a politician is a champion of gun rights.

"I'm not a crack shot, but I can definitely hit what I'm pointing at," she says.

When legislators ask her what would have happened if she had shot at Hennard and missed, she answers: "It's possible, but if nothing else, it sure would have changed the odds, wouldn't it? Because, as it was, I can't begin to get across to you or anybody else what it's like to sit there and wait for it to be your turn. I get very angry right now even thinking about that. Can you imagine not being able to fight back?"

Hupp's testimony in February 1995 before the Texas Senate committee looking at a proposed concealed-handgun carry law undoubtedly helped sway lawmakers to the reality that the police and the justice system cannot protect people. Although the justice system is supposed to deter crime, it hasn't been doing a very good job. While patrolling police officers do deter some crime, it is difficult to determine how much. Most often they take reports of crimes after they happen and then try to catch the perpetrators.

"I think you're living in Wonderland if you think the police are going to protect you," says retired San Antonio Police detective and firearms instructor Bill McLennan. "If anything, we're going to be there in the aftermath. Rarely will we be there to prevent anything."

Even when police catch the offender, the punishment seldom fits the crime. In the early 1990s, Texans were told that on average a convict spent less than one month in prison for each year to which he was sentenced. Convicts serve more of their sentences now, thanks to a prison-building program.

At a time when discipline at home and at school, as well as self discipline, are at an all-time low among teenagers, people are being killed at a high rate for fun and profit. And because no one seems to be successfully attacking the root causes, it will get worse before it gets better.

Attorney General Janet Reno was quoted in November 1995 as saying: "If the last decade's trends continue unchecked, juvenile arrests for violent crime will double by the year 2010."

But the trends turned around in the last years of the 20th Century, as mentioned in the previous chapter. Violent crime—particularly by juveniles—steadily decreased in the late 1990s, though it was still much higher than in the 1960s.

And still the fear of crime is there. Law-abiding people are afraid to walk the streets of their cities, particularly after dark. They are afraid to use automated teller machines or walk to their cars in shopping-mall parking lots. They are being told to bar their windows and lock the doors of their homes and cars when they are inside.

"I put an alarm on my car. I lock my doors when I ride around—I didn't use to," says McLennan. "I put a Club on my steering wheel, because I don't want anybody to take my car. I've got a kill switch on my car. I've got bars on my front door. I've got bars on my windows. I've got all kinds of deadbolt locks. I lock myself up like a prisoner, and I have an alarm on my house. The bad guys are running around free, and I'm locking myself up in jail. I think something is out of proportion here."

Few will argue against a law-abiding citizen taking these sorts of precautions, though most deplore the need for them. But when it comes to carrying a handgun for self defense, many people balk at the idea as somehow uncivilized.

"I think the problem here is that people are buying into the mythology that guns make us safer. The truth is that they don't, and there is no evidence to support that they do," says Robin Terry, communications director of Handgun Control, Inc.

Tell that to Greg Ferris, the San Antonio gun-store owner who was attacked in his store by three street-gang members in 1993. They did not charge into the store like coyotes after a jack rabbit just to rob. They were on a mission of murder to prove they were the toughest little gangbangers in the neighborhood. Only his custom handgun saved Ferris's life. His story is told in a later chapter.

Or tell it to any of the people featured in the "Armed Citizen" columns of the *American Rifleman*. The magazine of the National Rifle Association (NRA) scours the country's newspapers for incidents in which armed citizens win confrontations with criminals. Each month, the magazine relates ten or a dozen such encounters.

It's not just that members of the gun-control movement have chosen not to protect themselves, but in their elitist arrogance, they don't want you to either.

Listen to Robin Terry of Handgun Control, Inc., again: "We don't think that people should be walking the streets with a gun in arm's reach at all times, because we think that escalates the level of violence. Minor traffic altercations and minor arguments which could have turned into fist fights are now going to turn into gun fights."

In her statement, Terry betrays an attitude typical of many in the gun-control movement—a lack of trust in the average law-abiding citizen.

"Working to keep handguns out of the wrong hands," brags the letterhead of Handgun Control, Inc. Make no mistake, they mean taking the guns out of the hands of anyone who is not a law-enforcement officer.

Paxton Quigley was a founding member of the gun-control movement. Following Robert Kennedy's assassination, she helped found the first gun-control political-action committee—the National Committee for Handgun Control. After two of her friends were raped, her house burglarized twice, and her car stolen in front of her eyes, she changed her mind. Author of the book, *Armed & Female*, she now teaches women how to defend themselves with guns.

Members of the gun-control movement believe that there are far too many guns of all kinds in American society and that these guns are responsible for much of the violence. This is probably true. Guns facilitate violence. A killer can do in a fraction of a second by exerting a few pounds of pressure on a trigger what it might take him ten minutes and a lot of exertion to do with a baseball bat.

But it is also true that guns prevent violence. Many years ago, when my wife was about seventeen, she was stuck in a traffic jam in a San Antonio park. A man in his mid-twenties opened her door on the passenger side and got into the car. Anita pulled a small .25 semi-automatic out of her purse with her left hand and laid it across her right forearm. As she kept it trained on him, she told him to get out. He did.

"To this day, I don't know if he intended to chat me up or if he had something more sinister in mind," she says.

It was illegal in those days for her to be carrying a loaded gun for protection in Texas—it still would be for a seventeen-year-old—so naturally she never reported the incident to police.

Marguerite Everheart of New Mexico has twice been accosted in highway rest stops. On one occasion, she was driving north on Interstate 25 to Montana to shoot in a rifle match. She had her son, who was about six years old, with her in the car. While she was traveling through Wyoming it started raining so heavily she felt it was unsafe to continue. She pulled off into a rest area and decided to catch some sleep. Everheart opened the driver's window about an inch so the windows would not fog up and went to sleep. She woke to find a man in his thirties trying to push down her window and force his way into her car.

"He wanted me to open up the door, but I wasn't going to do that," Everheart said. "When I'm on the road I always carry at least two handguns with me. And I had my handguns very close to me."

Everheart pulled her Beretta 9mm from under the blanket and pointed it at the man. He realized the error of his ways and left in a hurry. When the rain stopped she drove on.

"If I hadn't of had the gun with me, I don't know, I may have lost my car and everything that I had in the car," she said.

On the second occasion, Marguerite Everheart was driving to another rifle match. She was on the highway between Santa Fe, New Mexico, and Las Vegas, Nevada, when she again pulled into a highway rest stop. Leaving her son asleep in the car, she went to the women's restroom. She had a Colt .380-caliber semi-automatic in her purse.

A man followed her into the restroom and tried to push his way into her stall as Everheart was trying to leave.

"Luckily I had my purse behind me in such a way that I could get to the gun, and I proceeded to explain to the man that it was loaded and that I knew how to use it," she said. "He left."

Everheart is not sure what the man had in mind, but without the gun, she may well have been raped or even raped and murdered.

Laura Poldson works for the Texas State Rifle Association in a Dallas suburb. One morning she was driving to work when she stopped for gas at a filling station she often used. She is a concealed-handgun license holder and was wearing a gun. Poldson was filling the tank of what she refers to as her "Mom-mobile," a dirty white Oldsmobile Cutlass Supreme, when an older model sedan with two men in it pulled in behind her.

One of the men pumped gas, while the other leaned on the hood of his car and said: "Nice car you've got."

As her car was in no way special, warning bells went off in her head. Laura replied in a noncommittal tone: "It gets me where I want to go and back."

"Nice car; maybe I should get one like it," the man said. "Maybe I should take yours."

"The tone of his voice wasn't threatening, but it was not kidding either," Poldson said.

She decided she was through filling her tank whether it was full or not. She put up the pump nozzle with one hand and reached for her keys with the other. Meanwhile the man had straightened up and was no longer leaning on his car, though he had not moved towards her.

"What are you, ten-foot tall and bulletproof?" Poldson retorted.

"Have you got a gun?" the man asked in alarm.

"That's for me to know and you to find out," she replied.

The two men immediately got into their car and drove off. Poldson got back into her car, locked the doors, and sat there shaking. After a few minutes, the manager came out of the convenience store and asked her if she was all right. She said she felt scared to death.

"I couldn't believe I just did that," she said.

Reflecting later on the incident, she said she probably wouldn't have shot the men over her car. She just reacted because she felt in danger. Poldson was wearing a .380-caliber semiautomatic in a holster in the middle of her back at the time, but never even had to draw it. None of these incidents were reported to the police, so they never showed up in any statistics, though these women may well have prevented serious crimes because they were armed.

Professor John R. Lott Jr. of Yale University Law School is author of *More Guns, Less Crime: Understanding Crime and Gun Control Laws.* He contends that a woman who defends herself with a firearm is 2.5 times more likely to survive a violent confrontation with a criminal than if she does not resist at all. If a woman resists a criminal attack with anything other than a firearm, she is four times more likely to be hurt than if she uses a gun. Men who resist crime with guns also fare better than men who do not resist or resist without firearms, but the difference is less dramatic. When a woman produces a gun the dynamic of the confrontation changes more radically than if a man defends himself with a gun.

"When you are talking about a male criminal attacking a female victim there is a larger strength differential than when you're talking about a male criminal attacking a male victim on average. The presence of a gun represents a much bigger change in a woman's ability to defend herself than it does for a man," Lott said.

Gary Kleck, criminology professor at Florida State University, conducted a national survey of nearly five thousand people in 1993. Extrapolating on the data he accumulated, Kleck estimates that about 2.4 million Americans each year use firearms to defend themselves in confrontations with criminals. Interestingly, guns were fired in only about a quarter of the incidents. In three-quarters of the cases, the threat of a gun was enough. Probably, in the majority of those cases where a crime was prevented and no one was hurt, the incident was not reported to police.

Even in cases where a shot was fired, the shooter may not have informed police, because only a third of them claimed to have hit anybody.

"If you believed what they said, they might have actually wounded somebody as much as 8 percent of the time maximum, but my impression is that they are probably guessing in a number of cases," Kleck says.

He thinks it more likely that only about 2 percent wounded or killed their assailants.

Before the Republicans took Congress like Sherman marched through Georgia, the Democrats rammed through federal legislation that mandated a five-day waiting period and a background check for a handgun purchaser, with the ridiculous expectation that it would keep guns out of the wrong hands. They also slapped a ban on some semi-automatic firearms of military appearance, as well as magazines holding more than ten rounds. But while the federal government was restricting firearms in the statistically suspect belief that it would reduce crime, a movement was sweeping the states like a South Texas brush fire. State legislatures passed laws to allow residents to carry concealed handguns for self defense.

As of 1999, thirty states had passed laws requiring officials to issue residents concealed-handgun carry licenses, provided they meet certain criteria. These states and their criteria are examined in the final chapter. In addition, one state, Vermont, has never required residents to have licenses to carry handguns, concealed or in the open.

This brush fire of legislation has produced an absolute furor in the gun-control community, which is doing everything it can to discredit the movement. While most of the states with "shall-issue" laws passed them in the 1990s, Florida's concealed-carry law went into effect October 1, 1987. As the first state in recent years to pass such a law, Florida has become the standard by which others are measured.

"In eight years, they have had a total of fifty-four revocations for committing a crime with a gun, which means roughly seven a year out of about 150,000 who have a permit at any one time," says criminologist Kleck. "If that were the violence rate of the United States as a whole, we'd be more peaceful than Switzerland."

The Metro Dade Police Department, which enforces law in Miami, Florida, is the only organization that has kept tabs on license holders themselves. From January 1, 1988, until May 31, 1990, Metro Dade police recorded any incident in which a license holder came to their attention. By 1990, more than eighteen thousand licenses had been issued to Dade County residents.

But in the 29-month period, only 57 incidents occurred, including 22 where the license holder was arrested. Eight of the arrests were for aggravated assault; the others varied from the serious—a license holder fired a couple of shots at a motorist who cut him off in traffic—to the less serious—the permit holder was arrested for drunk driving and his gun was found in the car. In other incidents, in which license holders were not arrested, they thwarted five robberies, interrupted four burglaries, and prevented one rape.

Despite claims by Handgun Control, Inc., that "law enforcement across the country has consistently opposed" concealed-carry legislation, Florida police chiefs and sheriffs don't oppose it. In December 1994, Charlie Wells, then president of the Florida Sheriffs' Association, admitted he had been "apprehensive as hell" about the law before it went into effect. But after seven years his fears had not been realized.

"The bottom line is that it's an absolute no-factor. There's no reason to be concerned about it," Wells said.

About the same time, Karen Beary, executive director of the Florida Police Chiefs Association, polled fifteen of her members. None voiced any problems with the concealed-carry law, she said.

At the other end of the country, Washington state has had a "shall-issue" handgun permit law since 1961.

"It's part of the way of life," said Eugene Cotton, executive director in 1994 of the Washington Association of Sheriffs and Chiefs of Police.

While the law is accepted with mixed feelings by some law-enforcement officers, "there are those of us that figure it's a constitutional right," Cotton said.

"The real problem is the crook who carries one [a gun] and has no permit," he added.

However, many supporters of stricter gun controls believe that any attempt to reduce the number of guns in society is good and that an unarmed society is a safe society. They contend that self defense is not a valid reason for keeping or wearing a gun.

The people who support this view tend to be people who know little or nothing about guns and are afraid of them. If nobody had guns, we'd all be safer, they reason.

This line of thinking was promulgated by Gregory Curtis, editor of *Texas Monthly* magazine. In the May 1995 issue, he addressed the pros and cons of the recently-passed law that would give Texans the right to carry concealed handguns for self defense. He acknowledged that those who carried guns would be safer than those who didn't. But if everyone carried a gun, nobody would be safer, Curtis claimed. He seemed to think it is unfair to all the potential victims out there for some individuals to improve their safety by carrying a gun. This is akin to outlawing burglar alarm systems because not everyone can afford one.

Some people say carrying a handgun and learning how to use it for self defense is a logical extension of being responsible for your own safety. This school of thought is represented most vocally by the NRA, whose officers and members generally feel that the Second Amendment to the Constitution guarantees Americans the right to bear arms, not just while hunting or target shooting, but for self defense against criminals and against government tyranny. That is one factor that proponents of gun control, like Handgun Control, Inc., and the Violence Policy Center, conveniently overlook. This country became an independent nation because a group of colonists used their arms against British tyranny.

The Second Amendment states: "A well-regulated Militia, being necessary to the security of a free State, the right of the people to keep and bear Arms, shall not be infringed."

Anyone who researches the context in which that sentence was written can hardly fail to realize that the framers of the Constitution intended that "the people" should have the right not just to own, but to carry, arms and that the first half of the amendment did not refer just to the National Guard. It was customary in the 18th Century for people to wear swords and handguns without restriction. The Second Amendment specifically affirms that right to "the people." Yet the gun controllers and confiscators try to twist that sentence to say it refers only to some kind of part-time army. It is well to remember that the amendment says "the people," not "the people who have never been convicted of a felony" nor "the people who have passed a training course." Just "the people."

However, the reality is that ever since the amendment was signed, judges and legislators have been whittling away at that right in the elitist belief that "the people" cannot be trusted with guns. And it doesn't happen just on the national level. Many states have similar clauses in their constitutions, only to find the right has been breached more than honored.

Former Texas State Senator Jerry Patterson thinks the law that has kept Texans from wearing guns since the 1800s has been unconstitutional.

He quotes Article 1, Section 23, of the Texas Constitution: "Every citizen shall have the right to keep and bear arms in the lawful defense of himself or the State; but the Legislature shall have power, by law, to regulate the wearing of arms, with a view to prevent crime."

Patterson says that in 1875, when the Texas Constitution was being debated, an amendment was offered to "prohibit" instead of "regulate" the wearing of arms.

"That amendment, to replace the word 'regulate' with the word 'prohibit,' was defeated, clearly showing the intent of the framers of the Texas Constitution that the legislature has the right only to regulate the wearing of arms," Patterson says. "The reason the amendment was defeated was because of recent experiences that many of the delegates remembered. General Cos, Santa Anna's general, came to San Antonio and started confiscating arms from Texas citizens."

Later, after the War Between the States, the Union occupiers of Texas and the carpetbaggers wanted to keep handguns out of the hands of two groups, Patterson says, former Confederate soldiers and recently freed slaves.

"So when we got rid of the Yankee army, and we decided to write the 1876 constitution, we wanted to make sure it said the Legislature could regulate the wearing of arms, not prohibit the wearing of arms," he says.

Patterson believes that all subsequent laws that prohibit Texans from wearing arms have been unconstitutional. He has tried, without success, to find a handgun violation in which the defense alleged that the whole statute was unconstitutional.

"Anyone caught after January 1 [1996] with a handgun would not be able to use that defense anyway, because the Legislature will have regulated the wearing, instead of prohibiting," Patterson said.

Both sides in the long-running gun-control debate support their positions with statistics and studies, and each side derides the other side's figures and conclusions with an almost Cold War fervor. The NRA says that the states with the most restrictive handgun controls, like New York, Illinois, and California, have the highest violent crime rates. Handgun Control, Inc., says states like Florida, which have allowed citizens to carry guns for self defense, have seen an increase in violent crimes.

Who's right? Both sides pick their statistics carefully, but the gun-control advocates seem to play fast and loose with the truth. In 1999, the Texas Department of Public Safety released figures on how many concealed-handgun license holders had been arrested in the license program's first three years and for what reasons. Based on these figures, the Violence Policy Center put together a report which it entitled "License to Kill, and Kidnap, and Rape, and Drive Drunk." Under this headline, the VPC trumpeted that license holders had been arrested for "nearly two crimes" a day and "more than one serious violent crime per month." The figures also revealed that fifteen license holders had been charged with murder or attempted murder. The report did follow up several of the more serious cases to show two license holders had been convicted of murder.

The media accepted the VPC report at face value and reported it without any attempt to put it into context. This irritated Bill Sturdevant, a chemical engineer from Navasota, Texas, and a concealed-handgun license holder, when he read an article on the VPC report in his local paper.

"I was really dismayed at the total lack of perspective in the article," Sturdevant said.

He decided to do something about it. During the next few weeks, he put together his own 75-page report entitled, "An Analysis of the Arrest Rate of Texas Concealed Handgun License Holders as Compared to the Arrest Rate of the Entire Texas Population (1996–1998)." His analysis put the arrests of license holders in perspective.

"The average Texan is eight times more likely to be arrested for violent crimes than the average concealed-handgun license holder is," Sturdevant said.

Violent crime rates are too complex to be much affected by a single law. So far, no one has proven conclusively that citizens carrying handguns for self defense are a major deterrent to violent crime, but there are certainly some strong indicators.

John R. Lott Jr. and David B. Mustard, then working at the University of Chicago, found that violent crime decreased significantly after passage by states of concealed-carry legislation. Their study, "Crime, Deterrence, and Right-to-Carry Concealed Handguns," published in July 1996, analyzed crime statistics from 1977 to 1992 by county before and after right-to-carry laws took effect. It is probably the most extensive examination of the subject yet undertaken.

When state right-to-carry laws took effect, murders dropped by 8.5 percent; rapes by 5 percent; and aggravated assaults by 7 percent, Lott and Mustard found.

They also found a substantial increase in the number of property crimes when states passed right-to-carry laws. Criminals appeared to change their behavior, switching to crimes where they were less likely to confront an armed citizen, Lott and Mustard said. Thus it seems that even citizens who choose not to carry guns benefit from right-to-carry laws.

License holders themselves are probably the most carefully screened group of people in the nation. This is particularly true in states that have passed right-to-carry laws in the last decade. The few states that have had "shall-issue" laws for many years tend to be comparatively relaxed about handing out permits. The cost of the permits or licenses is relatively cheap and often no training course is required. But applicants still have to pass criminal record checks.

In states where laws have been passed more recently, applicants have to jump through a lot more hoops and be prepared to shell out more money. It cost me about $300 to get licensed in Texas, including $140 for the license and $150 for the training course. The result is that the percentage of licensees whose permits are revoked for abuse is tiny. Despite predictions to the contrary, the sky has not fallen, and the streets are not running with blood in states that have passed concealed-carry laws.

Former NRA President Marion Hammer helped pass the Florida law.

"It gives law-abiding individuals the ability to choose whether or not to carry a firearm for protection. In effect, those people who refuse to be victims and want to be able to protect themselves can get licenses to carry and do not have to be concerned about being prosecuted for carrying a firearm," Hammer says.

Some states, like Maryland, Massachusetts, and New York—and like Florida before 1987—have a discretionary license system in which the politically connected and those showing need can get permits to carry handguns. The wealthy get to carry guns to protect their jewelry and the merchants to protect their cash.

"I find it most offensive that government would place a higher value on money or jewelry than the life of an individual, and that's exactly what they were saying," Hammer says.

David Kopel, research director of the Independence Institute in Golden, Colorado, has studied concealed-handgun licensing laws. He was asked what Texas could expect when its law took effect January 1, 1996.

"Based on what we have seen so far, we certainly are not going to get any increase in crime, and there's not strong enough evidence to show that there will be a decrease," he said.

Kopel found that in states which have "shall-issue" concealed-carry laws, only between 1 and 4 percent of the population bothers to get a permit. So the predictions of the doomsayers—that everyone will be carrying a gun and shooting each other at the least provocation—are just not true.

In the mid 1980s, long before the Killeen massacre, Ron Wilson was in Austin when he got a phone call that would have a lot to do with Texans' ability to carry handguns legally for self defense in the 1990s. At the time, Wilson was a Democratic representative for a Houston constituency in the Texas Legislature. His wife and children were temporarily living in an apartment while their new home was being built.

"I got a call, saying that my wife had been attacked," Wilson said. He got on the next plane and returned to their apartment in Houston.

"My wife had gone to take the trash out with my two-year-old son. When she returned to the apartment, someone jumped out of the bathroom—a guy, a black male—jumped on her."

The man tried unsuccessfully to rape her. When he asked her where her kids were, Mrs. Wilson fought like a lioness defending her cubs and drove him off. But not before he stabbed her in the head and chest. As he left, the man threatened to return.

It was that incident that started Wilson thinking about how to protect his wife from future attacks.

"That's where my interest came from," Wilson said of the bill that passed the 1995 session of the Legislature, giving law-abiding Texans the right to carry handguns for the first time in a century.

It couldn't be just his wife who was at risk, he thought. Other women are probably in similar situations.

"They ought to be able to protect themselves," Wilson said. "How can we, as policy makers, extend the right of self protection to individuals? I looked at a number of options: one is to put more money in the police force; another is hiring private security guards; another is requiring that individuals who own apartments provide on-site security. But those are all cost-prohibitive. And then I figured that the best way, after I looked at some other states, was just to give individuals a right to protect themselves, with deadly force if they had to. And that's where the idea came from. It took me about eight years to pass it."

Wilson says the first priority of a government in a democratic society is to protect its citizens. It provides military forces to defend against outside aggression and law-enforcement agencies to protect against domestic aggressors. Licensing citizens to carry handguns for individual protection is an additional step.

"It's just a logical extension. There's nothing abnormal about it," Wilson says.

Besides, in Texas, citizens have long had the right to carry rifles everywhere except where alcohol is served and into government buildings. "Even before this bill passed, it was totally legal for me to walk down Main Street in Houston with a fully-loaded AK-47 and not break any laws at all," Wilson says.

People who were taking the training to become licensed gun carriers in Texas gave different reasons, but all felt they could not depend on the government to protect them adequately. U.S. courts have consistently held that law-enforcement agencies have no duty to protect an individual citizen. It is fine for U.S. Senators Charles Schumer or Edward Kennedy to rail against private ownership of firearms. They have never had to walk a mile in the moccasins of a woman being stalked by an abusive former husband who has threatened to kill her. In 1986, a bodyguard employed by Kennedy was arrested for carrying two submachineguns, a pistol, and

146 rounds of ammunition into a Senate office building. It's okay for Kennedy to be protected by firearms, but not for you. What hypocrisy!

In Texas, many people applied for concealed-carry licenses to legalize what they had been doing for years. Gary, 49, who owns a wholesale distribution business in San Antonio, has been carrying a gun since he was fourteen.

"The police can't protect you; they're there to write the reports," he said. "I don't believe in allowing my safety or my family's safety to be handled by someone who has absolutely no concern about it."

Gary wears his gun almost all the time—except when he goes into an airport, courthouse, or anywhere there is a metal detector. "When I get out of bed, it goes on," he said.

Gary has been stopped by police officers who found a pistol in his possession. They let him go after checking and finding he had no criminal record.

"We've done it before, when it wasn't legal to carry concealed, but we've always done it," he said.

Most of the people taking training courses for a license are men. But many of the women are there because of previous incidents that have scared them.

Rochelle, 33, is office manager for a supermarket. She handles the money for the store and leaves work at 1 a.m. Ironically, neither of the incidents that prompted her to take the course occurred late at night.

The first happened about 2 p.m. in the parking lot of another grocery store. Rochelle had just come out of the store and was walking towards her car, when a man drove up next to her and ordered her into his car. When she refused, he drove beside her as she continued walking towards her car. As she reached her car, Rochelle pulled a can of Mace from her purse and sprayed it in the man's face. He wiped his eyes, then drove off, she said.

The second incident also happened in the afternoon. Rochelle returned home to find a pane of glass in the door broken. Undaunted, she entered the living room to find the television set had been moved and everything usually kept on top of it had been removed. Then she heard a noise upstairs.

"I realized then, they were still in the house," Rochelle said.

She coolly used the telephone downstairs to call the police. When the dispatcher learned she was still in the house, he said, "Would you please go back outside and wait for the officers."

She had been out at the range, so she had a .380-caliber semi-automatic pistol in her car.

"I got the gun out of the car and went back into the house," Rochelle said. A couple of minutes later the police arrived and found her in the house. "I'm walking through the house with this gun and they go, 'Ma'am, do you live here?' I said, 'Yeah.' They go, 'Please put the weapon down.'"

While Rochelle was getting her gun, the youths had escaped. A couple of weeks later, however, she got a call from the police, who had recovered a handgun and some other property the thieves had stolen, she said.

Joe, 51, is a San Antonio radiologist who has a weekend farm near Comfort in the Texas Hill Country. He carries a revolver in the car when he is going to and from the farm and wants to be legal. Joe is also concerned about going into the hospital where he works late at night. Texas law makers prohibited the carrying of concealed weapons in hospitals, even with a license.

"I'm also a little concerned about the way society in general is going. If it hadn't happened now, in the next twenty years it will, because we're all at the mercy of criminals. If they want to do something, they're going to do it," Joe said.

Another man concerned about the way society is heading is Gordon, a retired dairy farmer, who still keeps some beef cattle on his farm.

"I'm taking it [the course] for self protection. I live in the country, have all my life, and the country used to be a safe place," he said.

Recently a man was shot to death by an employee on a ranch near Gordon's home in Bandera County, he said.

Gordon, 63, grew up in an era when everyone had two parents at home. If he got into trouble at school, he got into worse trouble when he got home. "Nowadays, if a teacher touches a kid at school, he's got a law suit; the parents jump all over him. It's just turned backwards in my opinion," Gordon said.

Although I personally never made a habit of carrying a handgun in my car, except when I went to a shooting range or hunting, I recall one occasion when I took a gun along.

It was a Friday afternoon, and I picked up my paycheck from the San Antonio Express-News and promptly lost it. Later I learned that a man who lived on the west side of the city had the check. I called him, and he told me his small son had found the check lying on the ground in the parking lot where I had parked my car. About 7 p.m. on a dark winter's night I prepared to drive to the man's house.

The west side of San Antonio is not a particularly safe place after dark. It is the poor, Hispanic side of the city. As a police reporter, I could testify to its violence. I had covered domestic shootings, robbery shootings, drive-by shootings, and bar shootings there. I was mindful of all the cops I had heard at one time or another saying: "I'd never go there if I didn't have a gun."

I put a .40-caliber custom semi-automatic in the car and felt much safer. I passed the scene of a murder that I had covered a few months before, just before I turned onto the street where the man lived. I gave the man $20 for his trouble and honesty, then drove home.

I didn't need the gun, but felt safer for taking it. In Texas at that time, I had just committed a crime.

While no one expects the carrying of handguns by law-abiding citizens to be a panacea, former Senator Patterson, Texas Governor George W. Bush, the NRA's Marion Hammer, and others believe armed citizens will make the country a little safer.

"I think the first time a carjacker follows what he thinks to be a victim home in a nice expensive car, pulls up behind him, and the victim drops a couple of carjackers bloody in the driveway, there will be fewer carjackings," Patterson said. "Overall I think it'll have a minimal effect, but it definitely will not have a negative effect."

So far he has been proved right.

## Chapter Three

## STAYING OUT OF TROUBLE:
## NON-VIOLENT DISPUTE RESOLUTION

U.S. Customs Special Agent and firearms instructor Robert Butler was in Columbus, Georgia, when he visited the local outlet of Toys-R-Us with his father to pick up something for his children at home in Texas.

"I was walking in, and these three gangbangers drove by and almost hit me with their car," Butler recalls. "They said something, and I said something back: to watch where they're driving."

He had dealt with street-gang members before, both as a police officer and as a Customs agent, and knew how dangerous they can be.

The youths stopped, and Butler stopped. They stared at each other, then the youths drove off towards the parking lot. Butler and his father Grant entered the store.

"I thought they might drive down to the parking lot and wait for us to exit the store," Butler says.

He carries a Ruger SP101 snub-nosed revolver without a holster, tucked into his belt behind his right hip. If he isn't wearing a jacket—and

*How U.S. Customs Special Agent Robert Butler usually carries his five-shot Ruger SP101. It is usually hidden under his shirt or a jacket.*

he wasn't on this occasion—his shirt goes over it. He was concerned about what might be awaiting him and his father when they left.

"So while I was in the store, I moved my gun around inside my shirt to the front so I could just lift up my shirt for quick access to the weapon," Butler says.

"I was ready. When I walked down, I was looking both ways to see where they were. If they'd've driven up, that gun would have been in my hand."

As it turned out, the gangbangers were not in sight when Butler and his father left the store. But Butler was thinking ahead, planning for what might happen . . . and so should you, if you carry a gun and intend to protect yourself.

You have already reached adulthood, and some of you have even reached senior-citizen status, without getting killed or being convicted of a serious crime. You, therefore, possess certain life skills that have kept you safe up to now. The odds are that, whether you choose to carry a gun or not, you will die of what are generally referred to as natural causes—cancer, a heart attack, or just plain old age. Some readers may be destined to die in traffic accidents, others in fires, tornadoes, or earthquakes. A few may be murdered by felons wielding guns, knives, or clubs. The object of this book is to provide you with the knowledge and encourage you to acquire the skills to prevent you from becoming one of the latter—a victim of violent criminal attack.

Criminals generally are opportunists. They look for an easy target that has what they want—cash or valuables that can be converted into cash. The first step in taking charge of your own security is to become a less-attractive target. As Clint Smith, director of Thunder Ranch shooting school, says: "If you look like food, you will be eaten."

Few people look less like food than Robert Butler. He is more than six-feet tall, exudes self confidence, and is always alert. He has also survived one gunfight. The three little gangbangers were well advised not to mess with him. But had he been a five-foot tall, one-hundred-five-pound woman, they might have been waiting.

All self-defense instructors I have spoken to agree that a confident, alert demeanor will discourage most opportunistic criminals from choosing you as a target. If they do, you should have some warning and be able to take evasive action.

"You need to pay attention to your surroundings and to what's going on around you, primarily looking at people and evaluating what they're doing, how they're acting," says firearms instructor and former police officer Bill McLennan.

"We know that criminals size people up before they attack. They do this by watching a person's body language. They look for introverted people, people that aren't paying attention to what's going on. They'll prey on the weaker-looking people and the older people."

McLennan says we should be sizing people up and analyzing their movements. What seems out of place or unusual? A youngish man wearing a coat in an Arizona summer should set off the warning bells. It could be an undercover cop or it could be someone carrying a sawed-off shotgun under his coat with robbery on his mind.

I have watched journalists, who are supposed to be professional observers, walking from a newspaper building to where their cars are parked with their heads down, apparently staring at the sidewalk a few feet in front of them. Maybe they are trying to figure out a crossword puzzle clue or maybe they are afraid of stepping in something unpleasant.

You can wipe dog mess off your shoe; it's harder to erase the memory of a rape or purse snatching. Of course, if you are killed, after a few brief seconds of terror, the world will have to find someone else to revolve around. But it will devastate your loved ones.

# Color Codes

Colonel Jeff Cooper, one of the leaders in self defense and father of the "New Technique" of combat shooting, called it living "in yellow." One of his most valuable contributions was to adapt color codes for mental conditioning to overcome a normal person's reluctance to pull the trigger on another human being.

White is the condition of vulnerability. You are not paying attention to your surroundings. The ultimate Condition White is when you are asleep. You are not alert to anything that is going on around you. About the only place you can usually afford to be in Condition White, if you take your safety seriously, is when you are at home with the doors locked.

Yellow is the condition of being alert. Every time you step out of your door, every time you wear your gun, you should be in Condition Yellow. Your eyes are moving, scanning your surroundings, not just in front of you but also behind you. A stealth attack is usually made from the rear. When driving, keep your eyes on the rear-view mirrors for anyone following you. When you pull up to a stop light, be aware of the people and vehicles around you. Many attacks are made at stop lights. When you stop, leave enough room between your vehicle and the one ahead so you can pull around it and escape in an emergency.

When you get into your car, lock the doors as automatically as you put on your seat belt. Keep the windows rolled up so you cannot be reached. When Gordon Hale III, whose story you will read in a later chapter, was attacked, his pickup was surrounded by other vehicles stopped at a traffic light.

"He said he'll never run with his windows down and he'll never drive in the middle lane again," his father said afterwards.

Hale believes if he had been in the inside or outside lanes, he could have driven off on the shoulder or the median, and if he had had his windows rolled up, his attacker could not have reached him.

Some carjackers and criminals with other motives will deliberately bump your car from behind. When you stop and get out to inspect the damage and trade accident information, they will attack. If you don't feel comfortable about the situation, drive to the nearest police or fire station.

When approaching your car in a parking lot, glance under the car as you approach. Before you get in, look in the back to make sure no one is hiding there.

If you are walking, pay particular attention to bushes, doorways, and parked vehicles—anything that might provide cover for an attacker—and keep away from them.

Keep your back to a wall when you can. Take the seat against the wall in a restaurant or bar. Wild Bill Hickok ignored this rule, and it cost him his life in Deadwood, South Dakota, in 1876. He was playing poker when Jack McCall shot him in the back of the head. The cards Hickok was holding—two pairs, aces and eights—became known as the dead man's hand.

Be particularly alert when using automated teller machines. Many people have been robbed at gunpoint and forced to give up their personal identification number so their accounts can be looted. Sometimes they have been killed during these robberies.

Not being in Condition Yellow probably contributed to the death of San Antonio construction contractor Joe Ince on a January evening in 1994. Ince, 38, was lead trumpeter in the Trinity Baptist Church orchestra. He was returning home from music practice when he stopped to make a paycheck deposit at a bank teller machine. After putting the check into the machine, Ince was abducted at gun point by a seventeen-year-old youth and a thirteen-year-old girl. He was driven off in his own extended-cab pickup by Oscar Ortiz III, with the girl holding a .22 revolver to his head.

The pair forced Ince to give up his wallet, his ATM card, and his account access number. They drove around to several teller machines and made one withdrawal. At one point, Ortiz taunted Ince, asking him how it felt to have a gun to his head, according to the girl's testimony. The girl told a San Antonio jury that Ortiz grabbed the gun away from her, complaining she wasn't "doing it right." He then shot Ince once in the temple. After pushing the mortally wounded man out of the pickup, they drove to another teller machine and withdrew more of his money. In total they got about $600. Ortiz was sentenced to death by the jury in July 1995.

Most of the techniques used to avoid becoming a victim are available in pamphlets put out by police departments. The advice is generally good where it relates to alertness. However, beware of the advice not to resist that often accompanies these suggestions. As far as we know, Joe Ince did not resist his abductors. One such leaflet gives the following advice: "If the attacker is only after your purse or other valuables, don't resist. You don't want to escalate a property crime into a violent confrontation."

If a man demands that you hand over your purse with an implied threat that you will get hurt if you don't, that is already a robbery, a crime of violence. And how can you be sure that all he wants is your purse?

While Condition Yellow is the state of general alertness, once you have identified a specific person or set of circumstances as a possible threat, you move into Condition Orange. You may deal with it best by avoidance. It can be as simple as turning around and walking back into the building you have just left. Your self-defense tactics are most successful when you don't know what might have happened if you hadn't taken avoiding action.

The two teenagers with their gimme caps on backwards who are hanging around your car in the mall parking lot should prod you into Condition Orange. Now you have a specific threat. Your best course of action is to walk back into the mall and contact security. That may not fit in with your image of what an armed person should do, but it's good advice. As you will see in later chapters, shooting someone is often traumatic and expensive.

Even if they take a baseball bat to your windshield, you may do better to call the police rather than take them on. In some states, like Texas, it is legal to use deadly force in certain circumstances to prevent burglary or criminal mischief. In other states, it is legal to use deadly force only to protect yourself or another from serious physical harm. Know the laws regarding the use of deadly force in your state.

Even if it is legal to shoot someone smashing your car windows or running out of your front door with your television, it may not be wise. You may think I am advising you to wimp out. I am not. I am alerting you to the reality of today's America. If you have money or other assets like most middle-class citizens, you can be right and still lose everything. It is a lot cheaper to replace a windshield or a television than it is to pay a lawyer to defend your actions in court when the family of the kid you killed—or worse, crippled—sues you. This is something you should think about before it happens.

D on't think of a gun as your only salvation, even if you are carrying one. The mind, rather than the gun, is the weapon, according to David Ham, a third-degree black-belt aikido instructor. The mind can think of better ways of getting out of a tight situation than shooting your way out.

Several years ago, Ham, who is a businessman and advertising executive, was driving his Infinity Q 45 in downtown San Antonio. He was returning home from teaching a self-defense class to a group of law-enforcement officers when he pulled up at a red traffic light. Looking to his left he saw, stopped beside him, a brown Ford Mustang, about twenty years old, with a blue stripe and lowered suspension. Ham immediately identified the three teenage youths in the car as likely gang members. Sure enough, the youth in the front passenger seat looked at Ham and flashed a gang sign with his hands.

"I naturally turned to the right to see who he was signing, and there wasn't anybody there," Ham says. "I'm trained to look out of my peripheral vision, so as I'm turning back to the left, I see this guy take a sawed-off shotgun and place it on the window sill. I could hear the thunk of the barrel on the window sill."

At the time, Ham had been practicing aikido for more than a dozen years. Unlike karate or tae kwon do, aikido is a defensive art. There are no attacks in aikido and there are no contests or competitions. Aikido philosophy is to use the minimum force necessary to remain undefeated. In fact the ultimate use of aikido is to avoid a fight entirely. This is not to say it is an anemic art: it can be lethal. It is particularly useful to police officers, as it enables them to take a violent suspect to jail without stopping off at the hospital first.

Despite aikido's defensive philosophy, Ham's first thought was aggressive when he saw the youth pointing the shotgun at him.

"I thought, as I was rotating my head, 'you stupid son of a bitch, I can kill you.' That was my first thought off the top of my head," Ham says.

He was unarmed and the young hoodlum had the drop on him from about three feet away. It was not that he was able to kill the youth but rather that by pointing the shotgun the teenager provided him with justification to kill him.

"You're stupid to make this opening because the effect of that is: I could legally kill you. That was the logic," Ham says.

The muzzle of the double-barreled shotgun was so close that Ham could see the marks of the hacksaw that had been used to chop down the barrel.

"It looked like a howitzer, man; I could have driven through the tunnel. I mean, it was just big. Interestingly enough, I was never frightened during the incident. I don't know why. Maybe that's because of my training."

Even before he had finished turning his head, Ham decided to use the subtler side of aikido. He faced the youth with a wide grin on his face. He lifted a hand above the rolled-down window and gave the kid a thumbs-up sign and uttered one word: "Cool."

"Yeah," the kid replied and lowered the shotgun. The lights changed, and the Mustang drove off.

Ham followed, staying back to write down the license plate number of the car, then turned off and drove to the police station. He recounted the incident to the sergeant in charge of the gang unit and learned later that the youths had been found and the shotgun seized.

Ham feels that even if he had been armed he would probably have been killed or seriously injured if he had tried to shoot it out.

Some of the most vulnerable people in our society are those, usually women, who are involved in domestic disputes. Messy divorces, spurned lovers, sexual jealousies, all produce strong emotions that often result in violence. Again and again, police are forced to tell people in these situations that they can do little until they are attacked. Stalking laws help, but essentially these potential victims find they are on their own. If you are being stalked or threatened by someone, it is important to report each incident to police to show a pattern of threatening behavior.

When San Antonio barber shop owner Henry Gomez, 68, shot and killed a jealous lover in his home, he was not arrested. Gomez had recently broken off a relationship with one of his hairdressers. The woman started going out with Arthur Andrade Reyes, 54. But Reyes apparently felt his relationship with the woman was threatened as long as she kept working at Gomez's barber shop.

On July 10, 1996, Reyes came to Gomez's living quarters, behind the shop. He accused the barber of trying to make a fool out of him by letting the woman continue to work at the shop. Reyes told him that both he and the woman were going to die. Later the same day, Reyes returned, and Gomez told him the woman had agreed not to work at his shop any more. However, Reyes again threatened him. Wisely, Gomez told police of the threats, and officers took a report.

On July 13, Reyes returned. The barber saw a pickup pull up at the back of his house. He heard Reyes talking to one of his sons at the back door. At this stage, he was in Condition Orange, though he would probably not have known it by that name. He was faced with a specific threat. Gomez went into his bedroom and took a loaded .357 Magnum Taurus revolver from his dresser drawer, according to a police report. Reyes barged into the house. Gomez told him not to come any further, but Reyes took no notice. Gomez was now in Condition Red. He was ready to shoot if Reyes kept coming. Condition Red doesn't mean that you shoot, just that you have made the decision to shoot if necessary. If Reyes had stopped and backed off at that point, Gomez probably would not have pressed the trigger. But Reyes kept coming at the older man, keeping one hand in his pocket as though he had a weapon in it, Gomez later told investigators.

Reyes lunged at Gomez. Gomez fired one shot, hitting Reyes between the eyes.

It turned out that Reyes was unarmed, but Gomez fired when in fear for his life. It did not hurt that Gomez was an elderly man and that both his sons gave statements that supported his version of events. But the police report on file, alleging that Reyes had threatened Gomez previously, added valuable corroboration to the barber's story.

# Non-violent dispute resolution

When the Texas Legislature passed its concealed-handgun licensing law in the spring of 1995, it came with a lot of baggage. When the clock struck midnight on December 31 that year, Texas would allow—for the first time in this century—ordinary citizens to carry handguns. It was a big change. Unlike many Western states, Texas had no open-carry law and no previous concealed-carry licensing system at all. For decades, a majority of Texas politicians had shown they did not trust ordinary citizens to carry guns for protection. As with Florida in 1987, there were many organizations and individuals, including the state's leading newspapers, predicting carnage in the streets.

Consequently, Texans wanting a concealed-carry license have to jump through more hoops and put up more money than the residents of most other states. One of the requirements is to take a training course of between ten and fifteen hours that includes classroom time and a fifty-round range course.

This course, which covers the laws governing concealed carry and self defense, may be costly and inconvenient, but it is a good requirement. Giving someone a license to carry a handgun without a training course is like giving out driver's licenses without a road test.

One of the subjects taught in the Texas course is non-violent dispute resolution. The course was designed by the Texas Department of Public Safety, which adapted for civilians some of what it teaches Highway Patrol officers about understanding confrontation and preventing it from escalating into violence. It was taught to me by Greg Ferris, who has educated hundreds of Texans in the concealed-handgun course. Much of what follows is his interpretation of the required Texas training course.

According to Dr. Eric Berne in his 1964 best-seller, *Games People Play*, we all have three "selves" or "ego states" within us. These are parent, adult, and child.

Berne observed that people easily change viewpoints, feelings, and behavior during interaction with others. They exhibit behavior that he linked to parent, adult, and child ego states.

Parent-like behavior is authoritarian. Under stress we become angry and protective. We tend to give orders and make judgments about what others are doing. Our parents told us, "Brush your teeth" or "Do your homework," while we were growing up. In the parent mode, we behave like our parents did. We say, "Quit that" or "You should know better."

Anyone who is spoken to like that tends to react in a defensive or child-like fashion with replies such as, "I will if I want to" or "Screw you." This escalates the conflict, which, if allowed to progress into a slanging match, may end in violence. In stressful situations, such as traffic accidents, parent-like and child-like behaviors tend to become dominant. A person in the parent or child ego state tends to be emotional and to speak in the first person, lacing his speech with "I," "me," or "my."

Berne's way of deescalating a conflict was to speak and behave in an adult way. The adult ego state is objective and logical. It is based on reasoning and life experience. The adult ego state is able to effectively analyze a situation: what caused it and how to resolve it. It can put its analysis into words in a non-prejudicial manner. A person in the adult ego state uses "we," "us," and "our."

"We have two sides to an argument; the adult ego state can express both sides," Ferris says.

The parent and child ego states prove useless in deescalating a conflict. We want to be in the adult ego state when we're in a dispute. We want to be objective and able to analyze what's going on.

"The adult always leaves room for the second person," Ferris says. "And that's the best way to resolve a conflict. It prevents defensive reaction, does not embarrass the other person, and allows them to save face and maintain their dignity."

Most adults will recognize signs of emotional disturbance in a conflict situation from their own life experience. For most people they will be reminders rather than anything new.

They are tip-offs or warnings you should be watching for in a confrontation. The signs include:

*1. Eye Contact.* It occurs in different ways. The person won't make eye contact. He is watching you through his peripheral vision or is casting you furtive little glances. More dangerous is the guy who bores a hole right through you with his eyes, like you're not there. This person could be waiting for you to finish talking so he can speak his piece. He knows exactly what he's going to say, and he's waiting for his opportunity to say it. He is not listening to what you are saying. Alternatively, he may be planning his moves. He may be waiting for an opportunity to attack. Again, he's not listening. Last and most dangerously, he may be devaluing you as a human being. If he's looking through you like you aren't there, he could be moving into Condition Red, where he is breaking down his natural inhibitions against killing you. He's looking at you like a target rather than a person.

*2. Silence.* Silence can be interpreted in much the same way as eye contact. He could be waiting for you to finish talking, he could be planning, or he could be dehumanizing you.

*3. Crying.* The danger here is that when you see him burst into tears, you will assume that you have won the argument, that he has submitted to you. You relax your vigilance and may even move closer to him. But you may be misreading him. He may have decided that his only option is violence. He knows that he may get killed or injured. He may actually have gone into mourning for himself, losing any inhibitions he may have had against taking your life. By comparison, you have let down your guard and will be taken by surprise when he makes his move.

*4. Clenching Fists.* This, along with tensing muscles and body tremors, indicates the body is pumping itself up with adrenaline, preparing for a fight.

*5. Sweating.* Look for it particularly where it doesn't occur as a result of heat—on the upper lip, on the forehead, and on the palms of his hands. If he's wiping his palms on his pants or shirt, he's getting ready for action.

**6. Erratic Breathing.** He may be taking long, deep breaths or he may be panting. Either way, he is pumping up, oxygenating his blood in preparation for violent action.

**7. Increased Blood Pressure.** His face or skin may flush, or you may be able to see the blood throbbing in his throat. While increased blood pressure will make you bleed more from a wound, it will also keep you fighting longer. If you lose blood pressure, you can go into a coma.

**8. Violent and Abusive Language.** As an argument gets closer and closer to violence, the decibel level goes up. It gets louder. The words used get shorter and more blunt. Factual argument turns into a personal, emotional quarrel.

**9. Tantrums.** Adults can and do throw tantrums, stamping their feet, kicking tires, or throwing things.

**10. Stuttering Speech.** People who normally speak coherently start to stutter and stammer. They may be so preoccupied with what is about to happen that they don't pay attention to the words they are saying.

This list is by no means complete. There are other signs, such as rapid blinking and nervous tics. People under stress tend to exhibit one or more of these signs. Watch for them and try to get distance between you and anyone showing these signs. Back up or move to get something such as a vehicle between the two of you.

The Texas Department of Public Safety course recommends analyzing the elements of your confrontation by asking the following questions and others that may occur to you. Remember the four categories by using the mnemonic PACE:

**Problem.** What is the problem? What is the conflict about? What brought the two sides into conflict? What are the risks and gains?

***Audience.*** Who are the players involved in the conflict? What is their agenda? What do they have to gain and lose? How far are they willing to go? What are their cultural differences and similarities, their roles in the community? What signs of emotional disturbance are they showing?

***Constraints.*** What are the obstacles to effective communication? They include: the time of day—we usually feel more comfortable during daylight; the weather—tempers are shorter in hot weather; location—we may be on their turf; ego states—those involved may be in the parent or child ego state; their beliefs and value systems—the gang member is going to have a more macho code of behavior than the straight-A high-school student; bystanders or family members can boost a person's courage and make him less able to lose face; language—in Florida, Texas, or southern California, people confronting you may speak only Spanish, while in San Francisco or New York they may understand only Cantonese.

***Ethical Presence.*** The only person you can control in an argument or confrontation is yourself. Are you in control of yourself? Are you in the adult ego state? Are you speaking from the adult behavior perspective, not expressing parental or child-like emotions, personal feelings, opinions, or value judgments? Parent and child words and behavior only polarize and escalate the conflict.

Having used PACE to analyze the conflict, you need to deescalate the conflict. Use the mnemonic LEAPS to remember five techniques recommended to defuse a situation:

***Listen.*** In a conflict, we become very self-centered. We want to talk and force our point of view on the other person. If we listen and nod occasionally rather than argue, much of the heat will go out of the situation. Listening is a very important communications skill and should not be confused with just hearing another person.

*Empathize.* Put yourself in the other person's shoes; see things from their point of view. Be sure to empathize aloud so the other person can hear you doing it. Agree with the person where you can with honesty. However, do not sympathize or become emotionally attached to their point of view. If you do, you will lower your guard.

*Ask.* Question the other person about specific facts. Remember the Five Ws: Who, What, When, Where, and Why. Try them out. But go further by asking questions like: "How does this make you feel?" "What would you do if...?" "How would this affect you?" Asking questions builds rapport and solicits input from the other person rather than pushing your perspective onto him.

*Paraphrase.* Put the other person's meaning into your words and feed it back to him. This means that you are understanding his point of view and giving him a chance to agree with something you have said. It is the only way to interrupt someone in mid-sentence without generating more hostility. The other person becomes a better listener because it is his perspective that is being played back to him. It creates empathy and generates an atmosphere of fair play: you have listened to him and made an effort to understand his perspective, therefore, he will be obligated to do the same for you.

*Summarize.* When we summarize, we move towards conclusion. Our tone and words should be shaped with decisiveness and authority. For example, you might end with one of these: "Based on what you've told me, why don't we do this?" "Let's do this." "Why don't we do this?" "If you do this, I'll do that." Note the use of "we" and be sure to make the resolution a winning proposition for both sides.

When you strap on your concealed handgun, you should be aware of two things:

First, the legal system will likely hold you to a higher standard of behavior than your untrained, unarmed neighbor. You need to be able to show that you did nothing to start or escalate an argument. President Theodore Roosevelt was the advocate of the philosophy, "Speak softly and carry a big stick." These are words for the civilian gun carrier to live by. You have your big stick—actually a small stick, but with a lot of punch—now learn to talk softly. Don't get into heated arguments; walk away. It is no longer okay for you to flip the middle finger or yell "a--hole" at someone who cuts you off in traffic.

I recently met a man who had done some plumbing work for my wife and me when we bought a house in San Antonio. He told me he had gone through the training course and had a Texas concealed-handgun license.

"Then I discovered that I had a case of chronic road rage," he said.

If someone cut him off in traffic or did something else to anger him while driving, he was afraid he would lose his temper and shoot them. He said he had sold all his guns and did not plan to renew his license. I congratulated him on making a wise decision.

Second, be aware that when you start carrying a gun, your personality may change. You may become more confident, but also more aggressive. You may go to places that you would not have gone before simply because you are armed. You may think you are invincible, but you're not. Remember, step softly and don't go into places where angels fear to tread.

However, having encouraged you to avoid a shootout if it is possible, there may come a time when you are faced with a life-or-death—your death—situation. What are you going to carry, and how are you going to react? The next chapters will help answer those questions.

# Chapter Four

## CHOOSING A HANDGUN: SEMI-AUTOMATICS AND REVOLVERS

# STOPPING POWER

The call was for "Burglars in action."

When San Antonio police officer Bill McLennan and his partner arrived at the house, the homeowner told them he had just shot the burglar. He had come home from a hunting trip to find the burglar going out the door clutching his guitar. The homeowner had shot the thief with his hunting rifle, a weapon chambered for the .22 Savage Hi-Power, a high-velocity cartridge with ballistics close to the standard .223-caliber U.S. military round. The thief had dropped the guitar and run off.

"We knew the guy was hit, because there was blood on the guitar and there was a hole in it," McLennan said.

The homeowner told the officers the burglar was holding the guitar about waist level when he fired. The complainant gave them a description of the man, so while his partner took the report, McLennan started to prowl the area looking for a crook with a stomach ache.

He found nothing until he decided to check the bars in the area. More than half an hour after the shooting and half a mile from the house, McLennan was coming out of a bar when he saw a man walking towards him. The man seemed to fit the description of the burglar.

"But he seemed okay. As he approached me, it sounded like he was walking in water or his shoes were wet. It turned out, it was blood actually sloshing out of his shoes, and the guy was bleeding pretty good," McLennan said.

The burglar had taken a good hit from a high-velocity round, had walked half a mile, and was still standing half an hour later.

In most cases in which a homeowner shoots a burglar, the burglar flees, according to McLennan.

"Rarely do I recall finding one at the scene of the crime," he says.

If a high-velocity rifle won't put a man down with a single shot, a handgun certainly can't be relied on to do so.

McLennan, retired chief firearms instructor for the San Antonio Police Department, used to believe in the stopping power of a handgun bullet, but has changed his mind over the years.

"You have to destroy a lot of tissue; you have to make 'em bleed," he says. "They run out of oxygen, and they finally quit what they're doing."

Like many things in life, a handgun is a compromise. It is the least-effective firearm for self defense. Except at very close quarters—at arm's length—shotguns and rifles are much more effective in stopping a drug-hyped robber or rapist intent on making you pay for his lack of social skills. A handgun is the hardest firearm to shoot accurately, and, even when you hit what you are shooting at, your target doesn't vaporize in a red mist like on television.

I first learned this many years ago when I was working on a ranch in western Canada. I took a shot with a .45-caliber Smith & Wesson revolver at a coyote standing seventy-five yards away. At first I thought I had missed it, as I watched it run more than ten yards before keeling over. When I opened the coyote up, I found the bullet had ripped through its heart. It was a lucky shot, but that animal ran thirty or forty feet shot through the heart with a 260-grain, semi-wadcutter bullet. Imagine the coyote as a two-hundred-fifty-pound parolee armed with a butcher knife from your kitchen, and you're shooting at him across the living room.

Even if you hit him in the heart, he could still impale you on your own sausage slicer.

In choosing a handgun for self defense, remember that the gun has two functions. In some cases, presentation of the gun, coupled with a shouted order to "STOP, GO AWAY, BACK UP," will be enough to defuse the threat. It reminds the potential robber or rapist that he has urgent business in another county.

Keep the order short and loud. Don't say anything like: "Go ahead, make my day." It's too long, and it's not forceful enough. But more important, if you shoot and somebody overheard you taunting the person you just killed, a prosecutor or plaintiff's lawyer will make you look like some homicidal maniac. However, your expression should leave your potential attacker in no doubt that if he continues his intentions, you will shoot him. While any handgun will do, a large gun with a hole in the business end as big as a howitzer reinforces the seriousness of your intentions.

In cases where the threat is not enough, the gun is a delivery system for those little lead missiles, scarcely bigger than a cigarette filter, that rip and tear your attacker's anatomy. It is the bullet that stops the attack, not the gun. The size and weight of the bullet depend mostly on the caliber of the gun from which it is fired. So one of your first decisions in picking a gun is deciding on a caliber.

# CALIBER

Caliber is a confusing term. According to the dictionary, it is the measurement of the bore or internal barrel width of a gun in inches or millimeters. For example, a .45 barrel has a bore diameter of about 0.45 inches, and a 9mm has a bore diameter of about 9 millimeters. However, the measurement is not exact. A .44 Special or a .44 Magnum will have a bore diameter of 0.429 inches—closer to .43 than .44. The caliber which really upsets the system is the .38. A .38 Special has a bore diameter of 0.357 inches—about a .36 caliber. It shoots the same bullet as the .357 Magnum. In fact, a .38 Special round can be fired in a gun chambered for .357 Magnum. The reverse is not true, because the case of the Magnum is manufactured slightly longer to stop people shooting the more powerful round in a gun not built to withstand the pressure.

We tend to talk of a revolver being of .38 Special caliber or of .44 Magnum caliber, or a semi-automatic as being a 9 millimeter Luger or a .45 ACP (Automatic Colt Pistol). Strictly speaking, it is the number only that refers to the caliber. The following words or letters usually refer to the cartridge case the bullet is fired from and thus the length and shape of the chamber. It may also give some hint about the cartridge's velocity: Magnum denotes a heavier powder charge and higher velocity than standard cartridges. When we talk of choosing a caliber, we are talking of the cartridge that we want the gun to shoot.

In self-defense shooting, the object is not to kill your assailant, though this may be a by-product. The intent is to stop him from continuing his attack on you. As a former police reporter in San Antonio, I know many people get killed by .25-caliber, fifty-grain bullets fired from cheap semi-automatics. But the victims don't usually die quickly, and they are often quite capable of shooting back, even when mortally wounded by such pip-squeak artillery. The reason people carry these "poodle shooters" is because they are small, light, easily concealed, and cost less than $100.

At the other end of the handgun spectrum is Dirty Harry's .44 Magnum revolver with its six-inch barrel. It weighs almost as much as a six-pack and is about as easy to conceal. But a hit from a .44 Magnum bullet traveling at 1,350 feet per second is more likely than a projectile from any other handgun to end a gunfight in one shot.

The old rule of thumb was: the larger the caliber, the more effective the bullet is in stopping an attack. When asked why he packed a .45, the ol' time Texas Ranger replied: "Because they don't make a fifty."

But even a .45 cannot be relied upon to put a man down with one shot. An undercover drug operation a few miles south of San Antonio, in April 1991, erupted into a shoot-out that left as many dead as the gunfight at the OK Corral.

Domingo Moncada, 27, an undercover member of a narcotics task force had brought a ton of marijuana to "sell" to drug trafficker Ben Gonzales, 24, for $1.3 million. The sale was to take place in a fenced area occupied by a battery of oil-field tanks beside a ranch road in rural South Texas. Moncada was accompanied by his brother, Juan Moncada, 33, who was acting as an informant, and sheriff's Chief Deputy Ken Meister, 45. The plan was to arrest Gonzales and his companion, Vincent Vargas, 23, when they handed over the money.

But Gonzales didn't bring any money. He was going to "rip-off" these men he believed were drug dealers—rob them of their dope. Before the meeting, he positioned Vargas's uncle, heroin addict Juan Flores Vargas, 60, in ambush behind a log in the brush. He was armed with a .22-caliber rifle.

When Domingo Moncada, Gonzales, and the others drove up, they parked and got out of their vehicles. Gonzales told them he was waiting for the man with the money.

Without warning, Juan Vargas opened fire from ambush with his .22-rimfire rifle. He hit Chief Deputy Meister once in the chest and once in the back. Meister fell to the ground without firing a shot.

Meanwhile, Vincent Vargas and Gonzales pulled their guns and started shooting at Domingo Moncada—or that is how it appeared. Gonzales opened fire but Moncada thinks Vargas didn't get off a shot, though he was trying to.

"I think he had a single action. He didn't know he had to cock the hammer back and then pull the trigger. I think he was just working on the trigger part," he said.

Moncada pulled his .45 semi-automatic from his waistband and ducked behind the Fiero he had driven there. He bobbed up and fired twice at Vargas, hitting him once, between the upper lip and the nose. Vargas went down.

Moncada fired at Gonzales who was now running towards a barbed-wire fence, shooting over his shoulder as he ran.

"He was running away, twisting, pointing a gun at me, when I shot him in the ass."

Moncada hit Gonzales as he was diving through the fence. The .45 bullet ranged up through his vital organs and lodged under the skin of his chest. He ran and crawled 160 paces through the brush before he collapsed. He died shortly after he was found by another officer. He was clad only in his socks and underwear as the rest of his clothes had been ripped off him by the barbed-wire.

Moncada and his brother both fired several shots at Juan Vargas, the sniper, one of the bullets wounding him superficially in the side. Meister died on the way to a hospital, while Gonzales and Vincent Vargas were dead at the scene.

In summary, Meister, who was also armed with a .45 semi-automatic, was put out of the fight by two shots from a .22 rimfire. Vincent Vargas was dropped by one shot from a .45, but Gonzales managed to travel 160 yards mortally wounded by another shot from the same gun. Had he been more inclined to fight than run, he might have done a lot of damage before he expired.

Moncada told me he loaded his .45 with three rounds of ball ammunition on top of hollow points. He downed Vargas with one of the ball rounds, but doesn't know if it was a ball or a hollow point that hit Gonzales. He said he loaded the ball ammunition in case he needed the penetration, for example, when shooting through a car door.

Despite the thousands of words that have been written about stopping power, the truth is that the effect a bullet has on a human body in a gunfight is a crap shoot. There are too many variables for accurate prediction. However, most gun experts agree that larger-caliber bullets that expand and stay in the body are more effective than smaller-caliber bullets that go right through the body and three apartment walls.

The shape of the bullet and velocity are important. Modern jacketed or semi-jacketed hollow-point bullets are much more effective than round- or flat-nosed bullets. A hollow-point bullet is designed to expand to more than double its original diameter when it hits flesh, creating a larger wound channel and slowing the bullet down faster. Thus it tends to expend all its energy in the body and not come out the other side.

For reliable expansion, a bullet needs to be going close to one thousand feet per second. A round-nosed bullet, however, tends to go through flesh like a darning needle through an old sock. If it doesn't hit bone, it'll go through the bad guy and two innocent bystanders behind him. And the crook may not even be aware he has been shot until someone asks him about the ketchup stain on his shirt.

Some of the best hollow-point rounds available are Cor-Bon +P, Federal Hydra-Shok, PMC/Eldorado Starfire, Remington Golden Saber, Speer Gold Dot, and Winchester SXT.

Bullet placement is a variable that can be controlled to some extent. A hit in the body or the head is better than a hit in the arm or leg—or a near miss. This is why we train and practice.

The variable over which you have no control is your opponent's will to fight. Most criminals are cowards who tend to run rather than fight—which is why producing a gun is often enough—but you can't count on it.

Many criminals going about their business are doped up to the point where they feel no fear and no pain. In such a state, they are resistant to the damage done by a bullet or even several bullets. Domingo Moncada thinks that Ben Gonzales managed to cover 160 yards when mortally wounded because he was hopped up on cocaine.

Other crooks are just plain tough. They'll fight and die rather than give up—like Michael Platt, the bank robber who killed two FBI agents and wounded five more with a Ruger Mini-14 semi-automatic rifle in Miami in April 1986.

So, what caliber gun should you carry? By now, you have probably reached the inevitable conclusion that there is no simple answer. Many experts feel that a gun of .38/9mm caliber is the minimum that should be considered for self defense. I agree with the principle but not the dogma, on the basis that any gun, even a .22 caliber, is better than no gun.

The weakest of the .38s in general use is the .380 Automatic, but some excellent pistols are made in that caliber. They will fit in a purse or fanny pack as well as a regular holster, offering maximum convenience for the civilian gun carrier, particularly in South Texas or Florida shirt-sleeve weather.

Anything more powerful than the .380 is worth serious consideration as a concealed-carry handgun. For semi-automatics, the 9mm round is the standard military and police round for most of the world. For many years, it was considered, like revolvers in .38 Special caliber, to be under-powered. However, with modern hollow-points, its performance has been improved.

The .40 Smith & Wesson has become very popular with law-enforcement agencies in the U.S. The more powerful 10mm is less popular and more of a handful to shoot, while the old .45 ACP is considered by many to be the ultimate in

*These cartridges with hollow-point bullets are commonly used in handguns for self defense.*
*From the left: .45 ACP, .40 S&W, 9mm, .38 Special +P+, and .357 Magnum.*

self-defense rounds. The new .357 SIG apparently performs well in gunfights, according to the Texas Department of Public Safety, which has adopted it.

There may be some occasions when a really small gun is needed due to hot weather or other conditions. Some good semi-automatics in .22 rimfire, .25, or .32 calibers are available, but normally they should be considered only for a backup or second gun.

A multitude of snub-nosed revolvers is available in .38 Special caliber and some in the more-powerful .357 Magnum. More effective yet are the .41 Magnum, .44 Special, and .45 Colt. While these make good home-defense guns, they tend to be large and heavy for concealed carry. The .44 Magnum is too hard to control for all but the experts, and even they would probably do better with a lighter load for defense against anything short of grizzly bears.

## SINGLE ACTION OR DOUBLE ACTION?

Single action and double action refer both to how the gun works and the method used to shoot it. Sam Colt's percussion revolvers, invented in the first half of the 19th century, could be operated only one way. The shooter had to cock the hammer manually with the thumb before he could fire the shot by pressing the trigger. This is single action—cock the gun, squeeze the trigger. The Colt Peacemaker, the gun most seen in Western films, was a single action. But Sam Colt had competition from other revolver makers.

Robert Adams, a London gunmaker, manufactured a revolver which could be fired in two ways—one could thumb-cock the hammer and press the trigger or use a long pull on the trigger, which raised the hammer and dropped it to fire the shot. This gun was a double action—it could be fired in two different ways. While that is what double action originally meant, it has also come to mean shooting a gun by the long trigger pull, or trigger-cocking method, that raises the hammer and lets it fall.

# THE REVOLVER

The single-action revolver is not ideal for self defense. It is slow to fire and slower to reload. However, the gun that helped win the West has its followers. It was probably the best self-defense handgun of the last century, and well into this century many western lawmen carried the Colt Single Action Army model. But single-action revolvers are outdated for self defense. Double-action revolvers are more efficient; they can be loaded and fired much more rapidly.

A revolving cylinder that usually contains five or six chambers identifies the revolver. To load the double-action revolver, move the cylinder latch with the thumb of the right hand (for a right-hander). Swing the cylinder to one side, using the first two fingers and thumb of the left hand, palm up. This is also the way to see if the gun is loaded. Feed the cartridges into

*Main parts of a revolver.*
*Note: This is a Ruger SP101 in .22 caliber, six-shot.*

the chambers, then close the cylinder using both hands. Do not flip the cylinder into place using one hand, as is sometimes seen in the movies. It will damage the gun. We'll go into this in more detail when we discuss reloading.

Most modern revolvers are referred to as double action, but can be fired single or double action. In self-defense situations, the gun should almost always be shot double action. There will be no time to cock the hammer in most cases. To shoot a revolver double action, you just pull the trigger. The trigger will move about half an inch before the gun fires, and the pull will be much heavier than single action—eight to twelve pounds, instead of three or four. In addition to dropping the hammer, the long pull has to cock the hammer and turn the cylinder, so a new round or cartridge lines up with the barrel under the firing pin. Some pocket-size revolvers, like Smith & Wesson's Centennial, can be fired only double action because the hammer is enclosed so it won't catch on clothing during a draw from a pocket or concealment holster.

When the firing pin, propelled by the hammer, hits the primer in the base of the cartridge, the primer ignites. It sends a flame through the flash hole into the main body of the cartridge case, igniting the powder charge. Pressure builds up in fractions of a second. The only release for this pressure is to push the bullet out of the cartridge case, out of the chamber, and through the barrel. The rifling in the barrel starts the bullet spinning, stabilizing it on its course.

Despite the long and heavy trigger pull, the cylinder can be unloaded in a remarkably short time. The fastest double-action revolver shooter was Ed McGivern of Montana. In January 1934, he fired five shots from a .38 Smith & Wesson revolver into a target at fifteen feet. He was clocked at two-fifths of a second and the holes made by the bullets could be covered with a playing card.

In choosing a gun to carry, we have to compromise among convenience, power, and accuracy. Convenience means a small, light gun that is easy to conceal; power is a big, heavy, large-caliber gun with better stopping power; and accuracy is a function of barrel length and the user's ability. Major George Aylesworth of the Metro Dade Police Department in Florida is convinced that after the novelty has worn off, many of Miami's concealed-carry license holders leave their guns in their cars or at home. Carrying a gun is both uncomfortable and a big responsibility.

"It's a real pain in the butt," Aylesworth says. "It's heavy, it's bulky, and it jabs you in the side."

The smaller and lighter the gun, the more likely you are to carry it. A .25 in the hand is better than a .45 at home. The smaller and lighter the gun, the harder it will be to control or to shoot fast and accurately in the medium to heavy caliber desirable for self defense.

A revolver for civilian self defense doesn't need a barrel longer than four inches. Longer barrels add weight, are less concealable, and are slightly more accurate. But most gunfights take place at a range of less than fifteen feet and a civilian is unlikely to be involved in an exchange of shots at thirty or forty yards. Many police departments used to equip their officers with Colts or Smith & Wessons in .38 Special and .357 Magnum calibers. The patrol officers usually carried revolvers with four-inch barrels, while detectives used the two-inch models. There are many of these revolvers in good condition on the second-hand market and they make good carry guns.

If buying new, the same guns are available. Smith & Wesson's Model 19, or Model 66 in stainless steel, come with 2.5-inch and 4-inch barrels in .357 Magnum caliber, which will also shoot .38 Special rounds. Stainless steel is desirable in a carry gun, particularly in a hot or humid climate. The 2.5-inch barrel version is more versatile and can be carried more easily in a holster, fanny pack, or purse. It has more muzzle blast

*Smith & Wesson Model 19 in .357 Magnum/*
*.38 Special caliber with 2.5-inch barrel.*

*Smith & Wesson Model 65 LadySmith in .357 Magnum/*
*.38 Special caliber with 3-inch barrel.*

*Smith & Wesson Model 60 Chiefs Special in .357 Magnum/
.38 Special caliber with 2-inch barrel.*

*Smith & Wesson Model 640 Centennial in .357 Magnum/
.38 Special caliber with 2-inch barrel.*

than an elephant gun and is harder to control than a wildcat. But you won't notice it in a fire fight. The Model 65 LadySmith with a three-inch barrel is also a good choice. These guns are built on a medium frame and are not feather weights. They tip the scales at about two pounds.

In the smaller, J-frame Smith & Wessons, there are three options: the Model 60 or Chiefs Special, which has an external hammer; the Model 649 or Bodyguard, which has a shrouded hammer; and the Model 640 or Centennial, which has a completely enclosed hammer. The Chiefs Special also comes with a three-inch barrel which ejects empties more positively than the two-inch barreled version with its shorter ejector rod. However, it is less easy to fit into a pocket or small purse.

While any of these three models is excellent, the Centennial is my personal favorite. These guns are going to be fired at belly-gun range, double action, so the Centennial with its completely enclosed hammer makes more sense. There is nothing to snag on a pocket, jacket lining, or purse. It's as smooth as a cue ball.

The models mentioned above are the stainless-steel versions, but each has blued-steel and aluminum-frame counterparts. The steel-frame guns check in at about twenty ounces, but the aluminum frames knock about six ounces off that. The most recent innovation in the quest for less weight is the titanium cylinder. The new Centennial AirLite Ti Model 342 with

*Ruger SP101 in .38 Special caliber.*

aluminum frame and titanium cylinder tips the scales at eleven ounces. Its Chiefs Special counterpart is the Model 337.

Eventually I expect we'll see guns that are lighter than the bullets they fire. I've never been a big fan of aluminum, whether it's used for auto-engine blocks or handgun frames. The softer metal doesn't stand up as well to the thousands of practice rounds that should be fired through a self-defense handgun. However, honesty forces me to confess that I have been carrying around a Colt Defender of late—a semi-automatic in .45 ACP caliber with, yes, an aluminum frame.

Smith & Wesson has also introduced the Models 60 and 640 in .357 Magnum caliber, worthy additions to the line. If the new AirLite Tis are the Centennial and Chiefs Special on aerobics, these babies are J-frames on steroids. They compete with Ruger's SP101. This little five-shot .357 is slightly heavier than the Smith & Wessons and comes in several barrel lengths. For convenience and concealment the two-inch barrel length is the best choice. It is the personal favorite of Robert Butler, U.S. Customs special agent, competition shooter, and firearms instructor.

"This little Ruger will fit in your pocket completely," Butler says.

It'll fit in a fanny pack, a purse, or the console of your car.

"You can have it in your hand in your coat pocket in a situation when you think you might need it. It's much more versatile," Butler says.

With the small S & Ws and the Ruger, buy them in .357 Magnum caliber, but use them with .38 Special +P ammunition and the recoil won't be a problem, Butler advises.

"Using the +P in a stress situation, you'll never feel the gun go off."

Colt reintroduced its Detective Special in 1993. This is a two-inch-barreled version of the Police Positive and carries one more round than the small S & Ws in about the same weight. It was discontinued in the mid-1980s because it was priced higher than the Smith & Wessons. The newer version, priced around $400, is slightly cheaper than the competition. Unfortunately, Colt has recently announced it is dropping many of its handguns from production, including the Detective Special. This appears in part due to the rash of lawsuits filed by major cities against gun manufacturers.

While there are other revolver makers, Colt, Ruger, and Smith & Wesson are the best, and all have been in business for many years. If you are serious about your safety, always get the best. Your life depends on it.

All Colt, Ruger, and Smith & Wesson revolvers can be carried and fired as they come out of the box. However, a good gunsmith can improve them. He can smooth the double-action trigger pull, lop off a hammer spur, and round the sharp corners. He can also polish the chambers to make extraction of empty cases easier and bevel the edges of the chamber mouths to make reloading easier. In addition, you can install different stocks that may make the revolver fit your hand more comfortably. Hogue and Pachmayr both make stocks to fit most popular revolvers.

# THE SEMI-AUTOMATIC

Unlike the revolver, the semi-automatic pistol or auto-loader has no cylinder. It carries its rounds in a detachable magazine that fits into the butt. The butt is the lower part of the frame to which the stocks are attached. The frame contains the trigger and hammer. On top of the frame is the slide, which, as its name suggests, slides back and forth when the gun is fired. The slide also encompasses the barrel, which is a separate entity. The semi-automatic has a single chamber at the rear end of the barrel.

Semi-automatics are built in three styles—those that can be fired only single action, those that can shoot only double-action, and those that can be shot both ways. For anyone but an expert, the more modern double-action semi-automatics

*Main parts of a semi-automatic pistol.*

are best for concealed carry.

A typical double-action semi-auto is carried with a round in the chamber and the hammer down. The first time the trigger is pulled, it feels similar to a revolver being fired double-action. The pull is long and heavy. The trigger action has to raise the hammer to full cock before it can snap forward onto the firing pin. The firing pin hits the primer, which ignites the powder charge, pushing the bullet out of the barrel. However, some of that recoil power caused by the burning powder is used to push the slide to the rear. The backward movement of the slide drags the empty cartridge case with it, flipping it out through the ejection port. The backward movement of the slide also cocks the hammer. As the slide shunts forward, driven by spring pressure, it strips another round from the top of the magazine and rams it into the chamber. The gun is now cocked and ready to fire. The second and subsequent shots are fired by a lighter, single-action pressure on the trigger.

This double-action mode for the first shot, single action for subsequent shots, is not ideal and takes some getting used to. The trigger pull on most double-action semi-automatics is nowhere near as sweet and crisp as the double-action pull on a quality revolver.

When police departments across the country started replacing their revolvers with semi-automatics in the 1980s and early 1990s, some gunmakers, notably Glock and Smith & Wesson, produced semi-autos that replicated the long double-action trigger pull of the revolver in the automatic. By this time, police departments were teaching their officers to use their double-action revolvers only in the double-action mode.

The double-action-only semi-automatics replicate the double-action pull of the revolver for every shot, not just the first. They do not cock the hammer when the slide slams to the rear. Each shot is fired with the same long and heavy trigger pressure. This is not a noticeable problem at three feet when the shooter is crushing the trigger as fast as possible, expecting at any moment to feel the impact of a would-be carjacker's bullets. However, at twenty or thirty feet, it might be the difference between a disabling hit and a flesh wound.

Perhaps the best solution is the Glock. This space-age semi-automatic has a long half-inch trigger pull reminiscent of the double-action pull on a revolver, but it takes only 5.5 pounds of pressure to fire—barely more than the let off for a single-action semi-auto. A good double-action pull on a revolver is seldom less than eight pounds. The Glock has no separate safety or decocking lever to complicate things either. Its only obvious safety is a small lever in the face of the trigger which is depressed as the finger squeezes.

Bill McLennan, former chief firearms instructor for the San Antonio Police Department, is a fan of the Glock.

"It's simple; it's tough; you can abuse it," McLennan says. "I think it's the best fighting pistol in the world. Next to that, I would probably go with a Smith & Wesson, Beretta, SIG—something of that nature."

In addition to its full-size guns, Glock makes two subcompact semi-automatics: the Glock models 26 and 27 in calibers 9mm and .40 S&W, respectively. Like the larger models, these guns have polymer frames that are almost indestructible and come with the same constant double-action-style trigger pull of 5.5 pounds. The magazine capacity of the Model 26 is ten rounds while the Model 27 magazine packs nine. The only problem with these guns is that the butt is so short that for shooters with medium or large hands the pinkie finger tends to flap in the breeze.

McLennan still prefers the larger Glocks 19 and 23 and says they are easier to shoot—the longer butt makes them more

*Glock Model 17 (top) and Model 26, both in 9mm caliber.*

comfortable—and are almost as easy to conceal. There was the added advantage of extra rounds—the Model 19 magazine held fifteen rounds of 9mm while the Model 23 packed thirteen rounds of .40.

However, since the passage of the federal law banning some so-called assault weapons, magazine capacity on any new gun has been limited to ten rounds, except for those used by law enforcement. While there are still some of the old high-capacity magazines available, they are going to become scarce as black bears in Texas in the future. This restriction has led to a movement away from the double-column 9mm magazines with their thirteen- to seventeen-round capacity and back to the single-column .45s.

Smith & Wesson produces a good selection of compact, concealable semi-automatics with double action on the first shot or double-action-only operation. They range from the 3913 LadySmith in 9mm caliber with its alloy frame, through the 4000 Series in .40, to

*Smith & Wesson Model 3913 LadySmith in 9mm caliber.*

the chunky 4516 in .45 ACP. The company also manufactures the Sigma Series with polymer frames in .380, 9mm, and .40 calibers.

SIG Sauer turns out some excellent double-action first-shot and double-action-only semi-autos, from the P220 in .45 ACP to the P229 in 9mm. But the neatest and most concealable is the P230 in .380 caliber with its Walther-influenced profile. This brings us to the classic Walther PPK/S American with its steel frame and one less round than the P230.

Beretta makes some fine medium-frame semi-autos in its Cheetah Series in .380 caliber, as well as some holster guns in 9mm. The company also makes a line of vest-pocket autos in .22 and .25, if that is your taste.

Heckler & Koch makes the USP Compact line of conventional pistols. The company also makes a unique handgun in 9mm—the P7. This handgun, colloquially known as the "Squeeze Cocker," has a lever on the front of the butt. When the shooter takes a firm grip, the lever is depressed, which cocks the gun. This action is unique, but the P7 fits low in the hand and is very pleasant to shoot when you get used to it.

*SIG Sauer Model P230 in .380 caliber.*

Another choice might be one of the small double-action-only semi-autos from Kahr. They come in 9mm and .40 S&W caliber. They weigh around twenty-two ounces and have a sweet double-action trigger pull.

There will be times when concealing even one of the current crop of .380s may prove inconvenient. Or occasionally a civilian gun carrier may want to pack a backup gun, maybe in a pocket or an ankle holster. Far better than going down caliber to a .25 or .22, consider the .32 ACP. For some years now, the small firm of L.W. Seecamp has been making a fine little .32. The Seecamp .32 is not much bigger than a cigarette packet. Unfortunately, they are as popular as millionaires' daughters and as scarce. The manufacturer doesn't appear to want to expand and doesn't keep up with demand. As a result, gun stores seldom have any in stock, and the occasional Seecamp that turns up at a gun show often sells for several hundred dollars more than its $400 list price. The Seecamp was originally made in .25 caliber. I saw a pair—a .32 and a .25 with the same serial numbers—at a gun show. The asking price for the pair was $2,300.

*Kahr MK 40, in .40 S&W caliber.*

*A Seecamp in .25 caliber. The .32 is similar in size and shape.*

Perhaps to take up some of the slack in the demand for the Seecamp, Beretta has introduced a larger-caliber version of the Bobcat .25, called the Tomcat, in .32 ACP. At less than five-inches long and about a pound in weight, it should fit handily in a jacket or pants pocket. With Winchester Silvertips, the double-action Tomcat should pack a reasonable punch. With more and more states passing concealed-carry laws, other handgun manufacturers can be expected to follow suit with similar guns.

North American Arms has introduced a copy of the Seecamp called the Guardian. It looks like the Seecamp, feels like the Seecamp, but fortunately is much easier to get. It, too, is chambered for the .32 ACP, holds six rounds in the magazine, weighs about fourteen ounces, and is double-action only.

My favorite 9mm handgun is the CZ-75, which I bought to shoot in practical competition in Canada in the mid-1980s. I can't recall a malfunction ever. It is an engineering masterpiece and has been widely cloned. At that time, it was almost impossible to get in the U.S. because it was made in

*Beretta Model 3032 Tomcat in .32 caliber.*

*CZ-75 in 9mm caliber.*
*Originally made in Czechoslovakia but much copied.*

Czechoslovakia, then a communist country. The only modification I ever made was to lop off about half of the hammer spur which had a habit of biting me in the web between my thumb and trigger finger. The CZ-75 has a smooth double-action first shot. However my IPSC (International Practical Shooting Confederation) instructor, Murray Gardner, urged me to carry it "cocked and locked" like a single-action semi-automatic. The thumb safety is in such a good location that I have always carried it that way.

Carrying a single-action semi-auto for self defense is like single-malt Scotch—an acquired taste. After a tune-up from a master pistolsmith like San Antonio's Greg Ferris, the Colt Government Model and its clones are thought by many experts to be the best fighting handguns—but only for someone who is prepared to spend as much time training as a TV anchorman spends with his hair. They are not for the casual shooter who keeps a gun in his glove box and dusts it off once a year to go to the range.

For decades, the Colt Government Model .45—and in other countries the Browning Hi-Power 9mm—was carried by the military in flap holsters with a full magazine, but no round in the chamber. To fire the pistol, the shooter had to rack the slide (pull it to the rear and let it go) to chamber a round, then pull the trigger. This made for a slow first shot.

Texas Rangers unofficially adopted the Colt Government Model as their sidearm. They liked the capacity of the Colt— seven rounds in the magazine plus one in the chamber—and the caliber—.45 ACP. They also liked the ease and speed of reloading—slap another magazine in, rather than fumble with loose rounds. (This was in the days before speedloaders.) They carried the Government Model cocked and locked—that is with a round in the chamber, the hammer cocked, and the safety on. The shooter had only to slip the safety off during the draw for a very fast first shot—as quick as any double-action revolver or semi-auto. Texas Ranger Charlie Miller tied down the grip safety on his Government Model with a piece of rawhide to deactivate it. Asked if it wasn't dangerous to carry the gun that way, Miller reportedly replied: "It had better be."

Even without the grip safety tied down or pinned, cocked and locked is still considered by some to be a dangerous way to carry a handgun. Worried about liability, many law-enforcement agencies have prohibited their officers from carrying handguns that way. Jack Dean carried a Colt .45 cocked and locked for more than twenty years as a Texas Ranger. But when he retired in 1993 to become U.S. Marshal for the Western District of Texas, the Marshals Service would not permit him to carry a cocked-and-locked pistol.

Thanks to Jeff Cooper, the Colt Government Model and its clones became very popular among combat-style competition shooters. As a result, many gunsmiths became expert at altering and adding to the former U.S. military sidearm, making it a superb defensive weapon. Not that the competition guns are ideal for carrying. The trigger pull—usually about three pounds—is too light for a defense gun. In a life-threatening situation, it's too easy to fire an accidental shot with a trigger pull that light. A four-pound trigger pull is considered an absolute minimum on a defense gun.

One major problem with the Colt Government Model for concealed carry by civilians is that it is big and heavy. A better choice is the Colt Commander, which has a shorter barrel than the full-sized Government Model, or the Officers Model, which is smaller yet. Even smaller is the Colt Mustang in .380 caliber. Some of these models come with aluminum frames, which make them lighter. I've already expressed my personal bias against aluminum frames while discussing revolvers. It applies to semi-automatics, too. Remember: the lighter the gun, the more you will feel the recoil.

Many clones of various qualities have been made of the old Colt Government Model and its smaller offspring. Some of the better quality ones make good carry guns, including those

*Colt Mark IV Series 80 Combat Commander in .45 caliber, customized by San Antonio pistolsmith Greg Ferris.*

*Kimber Ultra Elite Special Edition .45 ACP*

manufactured by Springfield, Kimber, and Para-Ordnance. There are several smaller gun makers—like Bill Wilson of Wilson Combat and Les Baer—who produce top-of-the-line, single-action semi-autos for those who want the best.

The Browning Hi-Power is a favorite with many professional gun carriers in countries other than the United States, where 9mm is the standard handgun and submachinegun round. I carried one as an officer in the British Army's Royal Military Police in the 1960s. The only way to carry a single-action semi-automatic for self defense is cocked and locked. With the Browning and the Colt Government Model, the thumb safety is located too far aft and requires an extension for easy operation.

# REVOLVER VERSUS SEMI-AUTOMATIC

Which makes a better self-defense gun, a revolver or a semi-automatic pistol? More words have been written about that

*Browning Hi-Power Mark III in 9mm caliber.*

question than are written about Republicans and Democrats in an election year. The experts still disagree.

Bill McLennan, president of Small Arms Consultants, has trained thousands of police officers in defensive shooting and tactics. He thinks the double-action revolver is the worst choice possible, particularly for most women and people of small stature without a lot of hand strength.

"It's extremely hard to shoot in the double-action mode, and that's the only way that you should shoot it. Most of these people go for it because it's got a heavy trigger pull and they think they're not going to have accidents. That's not the way to prevent the accidents. For safety, the finger goes straight [alongside the trigger guard] until I get ready to shoot the gun," McLennan says.

More accidents do happen with semi-automatics than revolvers, but the reason is poor training. If you open the cylinder of a revolver, it is easy to see whether it is loaded or not. In fact, it's easy to see whether a revolver is loaded without opening the cylinder. The shooter can see the rims of the cartridge cases, and the shootee can spot the glistening hollow-point bullets staring unblinking at him from the muzzle end. This may indeed be an advantage if a gun is performing in the deterrent role.

U.S. Customs Agent Robert Butler and top gunsmith Greg Ferris think revolvers are better for the average civilian because of their simplicity of operation. Butler recommends a five-shot revolver such as Smith & Wesson's Chiefs Special or Ruger's SP101 loaded with a light 110- or 120-grain hollow-point bullet in a +P round. It'll fit in a purse, fanny pack, the console of your car, or in a pocket.

"A semi-automatic is too hard to operate in a stress situation," Butler says. "Is there a round in the chamber? Is it off safe? Is it a double action? Do you have to cock it? Quite often I see students, when I run them through stress courses, who will hit the magazine release by accident and drop the magazine. When a semi-automatic doesn't fire, or if for some reason it doesn't cycle or it jams or something, you have to go through a procedure."

Butler makes a good point. Semi-automatics are more complicated than revolvers. Many people have been killed and wounded because someone took the magazine out of a semi-auto and thought it was unloaded, forgetting there was a round still in the chamber.

"A properly maintained revolver will almost always fire," Butler says. "Very seldom do you have a problem with it. Usually when a revolver doesn't fire it's because you have run out of bullets or you have a misfire."

Butler does acknowledge that you run out of bullets more quickly with a revolver, but he doesn't think that will make much difference.

"It's not like TV. I've been doing this for twenty years, and the most I've ever shot was six rounds out of a gun."

Revolvers usually carry fewer rounds loaded than do semi-autos of similar size and power. The Smith & Wesson Chiefs Special and the Ruger SP101 in .38 Special caliber or .357 Magnum both carry five rounds, compared with the seven rounds of .380 in the Walther PPK/S American and eight rounds in the SIG Sauer P230. And once they are shot dry, revolvers are more difficult to reload. Even with speedloaders that carry five or six rounds ready to be inserted into the cylinder in one movement, they are slower to recharge. An expert can reload a revolver in three or four seconds, while a fresh magazine can be slapped into a semi-automatic in two or three seconds. That extra second is a long time in a gunfight. A trained shooter can get off several aimed shots in that time. Also, the stress of combat tends to coarsen motor skills, making those five or six rounds in a speedloader into extra thumbs as you try to coax them into the chambers.

Paxton Quigley, author and self-defense teacher, arms the women who attend her training seminars with revolvers. They are simpler and safer for beginners to operate and maintain. As she points out in her excellent book, *Armed & Female*, semi-automatics tend to jam if fired without a locked wrist. Racking the slide to load the gun or clear a jam may be difficult for a woman without a strong grip. Even on the range, it may result in frustration and broken nails. In a gunfight, broken nails may be the least of her worries.

Each year handgun manufacturers produce new models. With the explosion of state concealed-carry laws, they are catering to the civilian gun carrier. The models mentioned in this chapter are good, and their makers can be relied upon to produce quality guns. The best way to decide which gun to buy is to shoot as many different models as possible before making a decision. Choose a gun that fits your hand and feels comfortable.

## AMMUNITION MANUFACTURERS

Cor-Bon Custom Bullet Co., 1311 Industry Road, Sturgis, SD 57785; 800-626-7266; web site: http://www.corbon.com

Federal Cartridge Co., 900 Ehlen Drive, Anoka, MN 55303; 612-323-2300; web site: http://www.federalcartridge.com

PMC/Eldorado Cartridge Corp., P.O. Box 62508, 12801 U.S. Highway 95 South, Boulder City, NV 89005; 702-294-0025; web site: http://pmcammo.com

Remington Arms Co., Inc., P.O. Box 700, 870 Remington Drive, Madison, NC 27025; 800-243-9700; web site: http://www.remington.com

Speer Products, Division of Blount, Inc., P.O. Box 856, Lewiston, ID 83501; 208-746-2351.

Winchester Division, Olin Corp., 427 North Shamrock, East Alton, IL 62024; 618-258-2000; web site: http://www.winchester.com

## HANDGUN MANUFACTURERS

Les Baer Custom Inc., 29601 34th Ave., Hillsdale, IL 61257; 309-658-2716; web site: http://www.lesbaer.com

Beretta U.S.A. Corp., 17601 Beretta Drive, Accokeek, MD 20607; 301-283-2191; web site: http://www.berettausa.com

Browning Arms Co., One Browning Place, Morgan, UT 84050; 801-876-2711; web site: http://www.browning.com

Colt's Manufacturing Co., Inc., P.O. Box 1868, Hartford, CT 06144; 800-962-2658; web site: http://www.colt.com

CZ-USA, 1401 Fairfax Traffic Way, B-119, Kansas City, KS 66115; 800-955-4486; web site: http://www.czusa.com

Glock, Inc., 6000 Highlands Pkwy, Smyrna, GA 30082; 770-432-1202; web site: http://www.glock.com

Heckler & Koch, 21480 Pacific Blvd., Sterling, VA 20166; 703-450-1900; web site: http://www.hecklerkoch-usa.com

Kahr Arms, P.O. Box 220, Blauvelt, NY 10913; 914-353-5996; web site: http://www.kahr.com

Kimber Manufacturing. Inc., 1 Lawton Street, Yonkers, NY 10705; 800-880-2418; web site: http://www.kimberamerica.com

North American Arms, 2150 South/950 East, Provo, UT 84606; 801-374-9990; web site: http://www.naaminis.com

Para-Ordnance Manufacturing, Inc., 980 Tapscott Road, Scarborough, Ont., M1X 1C3, Canada; 416-297-7855; web site: http://www.paraord.com

L.W. Seecamp Co., Inc., P.O. Box 255, New Haven, CT 06502; 203-877-3429.

SIG-Sauer, Sigarms, Inc., Corporate Park, Exeter, NH 03833; 603-772-2302; web site: http://www.sigarms.com

Smith & Wesson, 2100 Roosevelt Ave., Springfield, MA 01102; 413-781-8300; web site: http://www.smith-wesson.com

Springfield, Inc., 420 West Main St., Geneseo, IL 61254; 309-944-5631; web site: http://www.springfield-armory.com

Sturm, Ruger & Co., Inc., 200 Ruger Rd., Prescott, AZ
86301; 520-541-8820; web site:
http://www.ruger-firearms.com
Wilson Combat, P.O. Box 578, Berryville, AR 72616;
800-955-4856; web site: http://www.wilsoncombat.com

## HANDGUN STOCKS

Hogue Grips, P.O. Box 1138, Paso Robles, CA 93447;
800-438-4747; web site: http://www.getgrip.com
Pachmayr, 475 Smith St., Middletown, CT 06457; 860-632-
2020; web site: http://www.pachmayr.com

## Chapter Five

## *HOW TO CARRY:*
## *HOLSTERS AND OTHER ACCESSORIES*

Gordon Hale III is a 42-year-old master electrician who spends much of his working day in the less savory industrial areas of Dallas and Fort Worth. He works for a welding company and drives his pickup from job site to job site, repairing electric welding machines. He carries a lot of expensive electronic gear, including a radio to keep in touch with his company.

"He's the perfect kind of person to be carrying a concealed handgun," says his lawyer, Vincent Perini. "At least if you agree with the concealed-handgun law, he's a perfect example of the kind of person who needs it."

In October 1995, Hale took the concealed-handgun course at the Academy for Firearms Training in Grand Prairie, the Dallas suburb where he lives. The concealed-handgun license became effective in Texas on January 1, 1996. Hale received his license early in January and started carrying his gun, a .40-caliber Beretta Centurion Model 96D, in his pickup.

"It's like buying insurance: you hope you never use it," said his father, Gordon Hale Jr.

About 10 a.m. on February 21, Hale was driving his Dodge pickup westbound on Mockingbird Lane. He had made one call in the Mockingbird area and was returning to Kennedy Air and Gas where he worked. Despite its rustic name, Mockingbird Lane is a major urban thoroughfare with three traffic lanes in each direction. Hale was driving in the middle lane when his pickup and a van on his right brushed mirrors.

Hale is a neat, fastidious man who takes a lot of pride in his truck. The Dodge and the equipment it carries are his livelihood. The mirror was on the passenger side, and he couldn't see what

95

*It was a Beretta Centurion like this that Gordon Hale, III, carried on the seat of his pickup.*

damage it had sustained. He sped up and tried to wave the driver of the van to the side of the roadway so they could check for damage.

The driver ignored him. After several attempts to get the van driver to pull over, Hale dropped back behind the van. He wrote down the license number of the vehicle and the courtesy phone number. His sister worked at an office about half a mile further on, so he decided to go to her office, check for damage, and call the police from there.

Hale stopped in heavy traffic for a red light a few blocks before he reached his sister's office. The van now pulled in behind him. The van driver, a muscular Pacific Islander weighing about two hundred fifty pounds, approached Hale's open window.

As Hale's father recounted it, the conversation went somewhat as follows:

"What did you want?" asked the van driver, 33-year-old Kenny Tavai.

"Well, you hit my vehicle, and I wanted to stop and look, see what was the trouble," replied Hale.

"I didn't hit you; you hit me," Tavai argued.

"No, you hit me."

"No, you hit me."

"Well, regardless, I'm going up to my sister's place of business, and I'm going to check my truck out and call the police," Hale said.

"Don't do that."

Tavai had moved from Seattle about two weeks before and apparently had a Texas identification card but no Texas driver's license. He was a trainee driver for Marquis Messengers, Inc., and had been on the job for two days.

"I've got to do that," Hale said. "If there's damage, I've got to do it to collect the insurance."

"Don't do that," Tavai repeated.

"Yeah, I'm going to do that."

Tavai reached in through the open pickup window and grabbed Hale by the neck of his polo shirt and started smashing him with his fist. The first blow hit Hale on the side of the face and head. Hale was strapped in by his seat belt and boxed in by traffic in front of him, on each side of him, and by Tavai's van behind him. He couldn't go anywhere, so he tried to duck below the window as Tavai continued to pound his head with a large fist.

"Stop, stop," Hale yelled, but Tavai kept hitting him.

According to lawyer Perini, the only thing witnesses differed on was how many times Tavai hit Hale.

Hale had his semi-automatic in its usual place, on the seat of his pickup under his jacket. He reached back behind him and grabbed the gun.

Still begging Tavai to stop beating him, Hale brought the gun up towards his assailant's chest and fired once. The Winchester SXT jacketed hollow-point bullet hit Tavai under the heart.

The man stopped hitting him immediately, walked back to his van, and leaned up against it. He slid down the side of the van until he was sitting on the ground. Tavai was rushed by ambulance to Parkland Memorial Hospital, where he died several hours later.

When the police arrived at the scene, they arrested Hale and charged him with murder. He suffered some eye damage from the pounding he took and needed glasses prescribed. He was later no-billed by a grand jury.

Texas State Representative Ray Allen taught the training course that Hale attended at the Academy for Firearms Training as a prerequisite to getting his license. Allen says he doesn't give advice about where or how people should carry their handguns. However, he does tell his students that, if they choose to carry their guns on the front seats of their vehicles, they have to be concealed.

"We certainly tell people that it's legal to carry a firearm on the seat of your car, if it's concealed with a newspaper or a jacket or something of that nature. But we didn't give Gordon, for example, any advice about carrying it in his car," Allen says.

Wearing a gun is a hassle, especially for a civilian. The gun is heavy—at least a pound and often more than two. Then you must conceal it and keep it concealed, not just in front of the mirror, but when you work or go to the store or collect the kids from school. When you first start wearing a concealed handgun, you feel about as self-conscious as a teenage girl wearing her first mini-skirt. Depending on where you are wearing your gun, you learn to bend your knees instead of your back when you pick things up; you avoid stretching to reach something on a high shelf with your gun hand; and you sit down and get up carefully.

Finally, there are all the places a civilian, by law, is not supposed to carry a gun. For example, in Texas the current law states that a concealed handgun cannot be carried into a school, college, hospital, nursing home, church, court, racetrack, sporting event, polling place, amusement park, prison, or the secured area of an airport. In addition, many businesses, local government buildings, and public transit authorities display signs prohibiting the carrying of firearms. Employers may also prohibit you from carrying a gun while you are working. In some states, the validity of many such prohibitions has yet to be tested in court; however, it seems that many business owners and public officials do not trust their customers, employees, and voters to defend themselves. They would apparently prefer them to die passively like Post Office supervisors rather than resist violent criminals.

These restrictions have helped make carrying a concealed weapon so inconvenient that after the newness has worn off, many license holders will leave their guns at home or in the glove boxes of their cars. As firearms instructor Bill McLennan puts it: "Most people will quit doing it because you have to want to do this. If you're a gun carrier, you're not going to be concerned about how big the gun is. You know that it's a pain, and you'll put up with it."

If a concealed-handgun license holder finds that wearing a gun is too much trouble, he or she often decides to keep it in the car. In the glove box, in the console between the front seats, or under the front seat are favorite places. The glove box is particularly difficult for the driver to reach without making a production out of it.

Gordon Hale's father is convinced that if his son had kept his gun in the glove box of his pickup, he would not have been able to reach it when he needed it. Leaving it on the passenger seat under a jacket or newspaper worked well for Hale. It's invisible but instantly accessible. However, if the driver stops suddenly, the gun can slide off the seat onto the floor. This is what happened to one of the FBI agents during the shoot-out with bank robbers in Miami in 1986. He spent most of the gunfight scrabbling on the floor, trying to find his gun. McLennan says his father carried a gun in a holster attached to the front of his seat. He covered it with a towel when he got out of the car. You might want to rig up something similar.

However, wearing a gun is still the best way of ensuring that you'll have it when you need it. A man will most often wear his handgun in a holster, while a woman will usually carry hers in her purse.

# Hip holsters

Many people spend several hundred dollars buying a gun, then buy a generic holster for it at a gun show for $20. This, as McLennan says, is like buying a Cadillac and equipping it with the cheapest tires you can find. A good gun requires a good holster, a good belt (if it is a belt holster), and a good pouch to carry a spare magazine or extra rounds.

Alessi, Bianchi, Galco, Kramer, Don Hume, Mitch Rosen, Safariland, and Milt Sparks all build great holsters. There are other holster makers who are probably just as good, but you won't go wrong with these. Most of them, such as Bianchi and Galco holsters, can be bought off the rack in good gun stores, while others, like Sparks, make them to order. The best holsters are still made of leather, though Safariland is known for using space-age plastics.

The ultimate in concealment for a full-sized gun is an inside-the-waistband holster such as Milt Sparks's Summer Special, the Galco Royal Guard, or Bianchi's Pistol Pocket. All these holsters have leather loops that snap around the belt, rather than spring clips to hold them in place. My own favorite of this type is Milt Sparks's Executives Companion, which is almost rectangular in shape. This breaks up the outline of the gun and is comfortable.

The best of the inside-the-waistband holsters have a strip of steel sewn around the top to keep them from collapsing like an empty grocery bag when the gun is drawn. If the holster keeps its shape, the gun can be reholstered easily with one hand. A medium-sized handgun can be well hidden in an inside-the-waistband holster under a short jacket, vest, or

*Milt Sparks' Heritage Model is an updated version of his classic inside-the-waistband Summer Special.*

*The Executive Companion by Milt Sparks (below) is a comfortable way to carry a large semi-automatic.*

loose shirt. In summer weather, a T-shirt with an unbuttoned sports shirt over it will conceal an inside-the-pants rig quite successfully. The gun is less likely to be seen inside the waistband, say on a windy day or if the shooter is running, than if it is carried in a regular belt holster. The only part of the gun exposed is the butt. Remember that when wearing a gun inside the waistband, you'll need to buy your clothes a size or two larger in the waist, or eat less.

That is not to say a hip holster, worn outside the pants or skirt, is not a good carry. It is excellent in temperate

*Galco's Avenger (at left). Note the tension screw and the way the leather is molded to the gun.*

*Galco's Speed Paddle (below). The plastic paddle fits inside the waistband.*

*Galco's Yaqui Slide (at right, opposite).*

or cooler climates where jackets are heavier and bulkier. The regular hip holster is probably a fraction of a second faster to draw from than the inside-the-waistband type. The gun carrier is also less likely to grab a handful of shirt along with his weapon. Some hip holsters, such as Galco's Avenger, have tension screws that can be tightened to hold the gun more securely. Others, like Bianchi's Shadow, have a thumb-break retaining strap for security. As a general rule, if the holster is worn outside the waistband, it needs some type of retaining device to keep the gun from falling out when you bend over or run or during other physical exertion. Pressure between the belt and the body should keep the gun in an inside-the-waistband rig.

The outside-the-waistband hip holster has several configurations. The more traditional type of hip holster has its belt slot on the back of the scabbard, like Bianchi's Thumbsnap models. The pancake holster, like the Shadow, has belt slots fore and aft of the gun, giving the leather a more circular, or pancake, outline. Other holsters, such as Galco's Speed Paddle, have a curved plastic plate or paddle that fits inside the pants, while the leather scabbard hugs the outside over the belt. Some holsters are held to the belt by a spring clip. This makes them easy to remove for putting gun and holster in the glove box when you have to enter a building, like a courthouse, where guns are prohibited. Cheap holsters of this type can come off the belt with the gun during the draw, but this won't happen with holsters from reputable makers.

Then there are the bikinis of holsters, like Milt Sparks's and Galco's Yaqui Slide, that cover the trigger guard, the adjacent part of the slide, and little else. While some police officers are fond of these, they are not the best solution for the civilian. If you are going to carry your gun in a holster on the outside of your belt, choose a model that covers the barrel completely. If you inadvertently expose the bottom of your holster for a moment, an observer may be unsure that what he has seen actually contains a gun. It might contain a camera, a cell phone, or a pair of glasses. However, he will be in little doubt if he can see the black snout of your .45 auto protruding from beneath your shirt.

The secret of carrying a large gun in a belt holster is to use a heavy belt at least 1.25 inches wide. A thin trouser belt will cut into your midriff like a cheese wire and won't anchor the holster well.

Of course, there is also Special Agent Robert Butler's solution mentioned at the beginning of Chapter Three: just tuck a small revolver like the Ruger SP101 or a J-frame Smith & Wesson into your belt, butt forward, behind your hip. It is not a position for a fast draw, but it is comfortable, relatively secure, and convenient. Instead of the hassle of putting on and taking off a holster, it takes only a moment to tuck the gun into your waistband.

# OTHER HOLSTERS

While hip holsters seem to be the favorite way of carrying, there are many other ways of packing a concealed handgun.

Cross-draw belt holsters do not conceal well under a jacket, as they need to ride close to the navel for easy access. They are easier for an attacker to grab, as the butt of the gun is pointing towards him. A hip-draw requires a vertical motion of hand and gun; a cross draw is a horizontal movement and is more difficult to stop on target. However, a cross-draw is very fast to get into action. The weak hand pulls the coat to one side while the strong hand scoops out the gun and sweeps it onto the target.

Some of the same problems are evident with a holster riding on the belt in the appendix position. It may be faster than a hip holster, but does not conceal the gun as well unless it is worn under the shirt. But the main thing I have against the appendix position is that the gun is carried with the muzzle pointing at the family jewels. One of the men who competes at a local shooting club carries a .45 cocked and locked in an appendix holster. I can never look at where his muzzle is pointing without inwardly cringing.

A small-of-the-back holster, such as Galco's appropriately named S.O.B., is a better option for a belt holster that will conceal a small revolver or semi-automatic comfortably. With these holsters, don't bend over at the waist or the gun will "print" against the back of your shirt or jacket. If you have to pick something up, squat down, bending your knees rather than your back. This is the best way to pick up a heavy load anyway, as it is less likely to damage your back.

A belly band is an under-the-shirt belt with a built-in holster. It is usually a nylon and elastic belt about four-inches

*Galco's S.O.B. worn in the center of the back.*

wide worn just above the waist. Some are equipped with a shoulder strap which helps carry the weight of the gun. In addition to a built-in holster, the Bianchi Ranger belly band has pockets for such essentials as money. The belly band can be worn so the gun can be reached through the shirt front in a cross draw. The draw is easier if one shirt button is left undone or if the shirt has snaps instead of buttons. The gun can be worn for a cross or side draw under a shirt that is not tucked in. One hand pulls up the shirt while the other goes for the gun.

Shoulder holsters are another option. I have never liked the type that hold the barrel of the gun horizontal and pointing aft. The Miami Classic by Galco, worn by actor Don Johnson in the "Miami Vice" television series, is one of these. Detectives in one small South Texas city have a penchant for this type of holster, and in the police station often wear their rigs without jackets. Walking behind one of these officers and looking down the barrel of a .45 semi-automatic is downright

*Galco's Miami Classic positions the barrel of the gun horizontally—disconcerting for the person walking behind you.*

disconcerting. It also breaks one of Jeff Cooper's safety rules: "Do not point your gun at anything you are not willing to destroy." These holsters may influence people, but they don't make friends.

Another problem with these holsters is positioning the gun. Except with the smallest of weapons, your gun butt either dents your suit coat in front or the muzzle pokes your jacket out at the back.

Other shoulder rigs, such as Bianchi's Special Agent, carry a small handgun upside down with

*Bianchi's Special Agent (above) points the muzzle into your armpit. Note the belt slots on the side; it can also be used as a hip holster.*

*A traditional shoulder holster by Bianchi holds a large revolver with the muzzle pointing down. The bottom of the holster attaches to the belt.*

the barrel pointing directly into the wearer's armpit. Again, I tend to recoil from these styles as I think they send a bad message about muzzle direction. The traditional shoulder holster which carries the gun muzzle pointing down is more acceptable. The rigs that carry the gun horizontal or muzzle up often tend to flop about making them more difficult to draw from than the vertical models that are attached at the muzzle end to the pants belt.

While many people like shoulder holsters, and they do conceal a gun reasonably well, many ranges and shooting schools ban them along with cross-draw rigs because of a tendency to endanger your neighbor on the firing line with your gun muzzle during the draw.

Ankle holsters are not too practical except for perhaps carrying a backup weapon. Most good holster manufacturers make them. Alessi makes a good one. However, a gun on your ankle is going to be inconvenient during any vigorous physical activity such as running or fighting. It is a poor choice for a main gun, but acceptable for a secondary weapon, though it does tend to become exposed when the wearer sits down. Be sure to practice getting it into action. This sort of rig cannot be worn with tight pants.

Moving up the leg from the ankle, we come to the thigh holster. Women can carry a small revolver or semi-automatic on the inside of the thigh. The holster is mounted on a wide garter that holds it to the thigh. A garter belt around the lady's waist with a suspender leading down to the holster provides additional support. No lace in sight on the Galco example, but drawing the weapon certainly requires some provocative skirt hiking.

For those people carrying a very small weapon, whether it be as main armament or backup, there is the pocket holster. It beats just shoving the gun into a pocket. A holster holds the gun in a constant position in the pocket so the butt is easily accessible. It will make the outline of the gun less obvious and reduces

*Galco's Front Pocket model.*

pocket wear. If you anticipate trouble, you can have your gun in your hand before exposing it. A hand in your pocket is natural and non-threatening. You can even shoot through the pocket if you are attacked at close range.

# Fanny Packs, Purses, and Other Carrys

When choosing a fanny pack, purse, or briefcase in which to carry a concealed handgun, get one designed to do the job with a built-in holster in a separate compartment.

Fanny packs are popular, particularly in the Sun Belt, as a casual alternative to a purse for a woman and to serve the same function for a man. They carry keys, coins, wallet, street map, sunscreen, almost anything you might carry in your pants or jacket. And they will carry a bigger gun than anything you can carry in a pocket. Some fanny packs have a tag or loop which can be pulled diagonally downward with the left hand (for a right-handed shooter), unzipping two sides of the gun compartment and exposing the butt of the gun to the right hand. Fanny packs, such as Galco's Escort, also have compartments and pouches for anything else you wish to carry. I know one

*Galco's Escort, a fanny pack with built-in holster.*

FBI agent who carries his service semi-automatic in a fanny pack, at least during the summer months.

Gun carriers can also conceal their weapons in women's purses and briefcases that have special compartments built into them. A purse with a shoulder strap and an opening in the side closed by Velcro allows a woman to slide her hand onto the gun without drawing it. The disadvantage of packing a concealed handgun in a separate container rather than wearing it is that purses and briefcases can be

*Galco's Le Nouveau Sac purse with built-in holster.*

detached from their owners. They can be snatched or they can just be left and forgotten in a store, car, or office. This is also true of daytimers and books with built-in compartments to conceal a handgun.

With more and more people carrying concealed firearms, manufacturers are coming out with new and innovative ways of packing them. Thunderwear, Inc., makes a pouch that is worn between the pants and the underwear in the same place a kangaroo carries her offspring. It is not a very fast draw, but a small revolver or semi-automatic can be carried discreetly in hot weather, when wearing a jacket is a burden.

Another innovation is the Pager Pal. This pancake-shaped flap of leather has a holster sewn to one side and a dummy pager clipped to the top on the other side. The flap slips down between shirt and pants with the pager hooking over the top of the belt. A real pager can be substituted for the dummy. For a right-handed shooter, it is best to position the holster between the left hip and the belt buckle for a cross draw. To draw the gun, grasp the pager with your left hand and pull upwards until the butt of the gun appears above the belt. You can then draw the gun with the right hand. The Pager Pal comes in two sizes. The smaller holster will take some of the small semi-automatics such as the Colt Mustang .380 and the Beretta Tomcat .32. The manufacturer claims the larger holster will carry some of the double-column magazine semi-automatics like the Glock 23 and the CZ-75. However, concealment would obviously be better with the single-stack semi-autos like the SIG Sauer P230 or the Colt Officer's Model. The larger model will also carry a small-frame revolver with a two-inch barrel such as the Smith & Wesson 640.

# MAGAZINES AND SPEEDLOADERS

Most semi-automatics are sold with two magazines: one in the gun and a spare. While two magazines are enough for most

*A magazine pouch like this (above) can hold an extra thirty rounds of 9mm ammunition.*

*An H.K.S. speedloader (left) containing five rounds of .38 Special ammunition ready to insert into a revolver cylinder.*

*A Bianchi Speed Strip (below).*

civilian gun carriers, an investment in a couple more is wise. Modern metallurgy has produced springs that can stay compressed for months or even years without weakening. However, I like to keep two magazines full and two empty, and change them around from time to time. Damaged magazines are often a cause of malfunctions in semi-automatics, so having spares on hand is a good policy. You will also need the extra magazines if your practice routine extends to any form of combat competition. More on that later.

If your semi-automatic was originally designed for a magazine that packed more than ten rounds, you will want to get your hands on as many of the pre-assault-weapon-ban kind as you can. In 1994, Congress banned manufacture for civilians of semi-auto magazines containing more than ten rounds. New double-column magazines are partly cut through and have dents in them, limiting them to ten rounds. However, pre-ban magazines still turn up at gun shows and elsewhere.

In addition, you will want some means of carrying your spare magazines. Depending on the number of rounds your gun carries and your own personal preference, you will need a single- or double-magazine pouch. Most of these fit on the belt, either outside or inside the pants. Some shoulder holsters have double mag pouches built into the harness on the opposite side from the holster to balance the weight of the gun.

The fastest re-load is from a single or double pouch mounted on the belt on the side where the left hand drops naturally to it. The magazines are positioned vertically, bullets pointed forward, and the pouch does not have a flap and a snap. A good mag pouch should have enough friction to keep the magazine from falling out, but should allow an easy draw with the left hand.

A single pouch with a flap and snap might be mistaken for a sheath for a folding knife, which could be an advantage. Flaps also protect the jacket lining from the sharp corners of some double-column magazines. Most of the good holster manufacturers also make magazine carriers to match their holsters.

The fastest way to reload a revolver is with a speedloader, like those made by H.K.S. Products. However, unlike a spare magazine which is flat and easy to conceal, a speedloader is bulky and awkward to pack. Speedloaders can be mounted on the belt in pouches or on the harness of a shoulder holster. The pouches will require flaps and snaps. Several holster makers provide much flatter pouches carrying five or six loose rounds that dump into the hand when opened. Galco has a belt-slide cartridge pouch holding six rounds in pairs, which makes for easier reloading, particularly in the dark. No fumbling with six rounds in your hand, trying to get them into the cylinder without dropping some. Another solution is the Bianchi Speed Strip which holds six rounds to a flexible plastic band. The rounds can be loaded two at a time and fit flatly into a pocket or pouch.

# OTHER ACCESSORIES

Having shelled out for gun, leather, and ammunition, you need two more pieces of gear before you head for the range— eye and ear protection. If you need glasses to see the sights and the lenses are made of plastic rather than glass, your prescription glasses will probably do fine. However, if you are in your 40s or 50s, you may have noticed a deterioration in your eyesight. When I was in my early 50s, I found I could not get a crisp sight picture. My solution was to get a special pair of trifocals. Most trifocals have the bottom of the lenses for reading, the middle for intermediate distance, and the top for long distance. I had the optometrist change the prescription so the long distance parts of the lenses were in the middle and the intermediate distance segments were at the top. The intermediate segments were made so I could see my handgun sights clearly at arm's length. Now when I shoot, I tilt my head down slightly until I have the sights in focus and the target is slightly out of focus. This seems to be compatible with a normal Weaver or isosceles stance (see Chapter 7). These glasses take a little getting used to, but I wear them all the time. The optometrist told me he occasionally ordered similar prescriptions for pilots who have to see dials and gauges above and below the plane's windshield.

If you have 20:20 eyesight, you will need to get a pair of glasses to ensure you keep your eagle-like vision. Most ranges require shooters to wear eye protection, and even if they don't, you should. It is as wise as wearing a seat belt in a car. It won't guarantee to save your eyesight from a lead shaving or an exploding barrel, but it sure improves the odds.

I started shooting handguns in the 1950s when ear protection meant rolling up gun-cleaning patches and sticking them in your ears. It wasn't until the late-1960s, when I was taking a physical examination, that I realized I had lost some of my hearing. Nowadays we are much more conscious of the importance of protecting our hearing. Remember, once lost, it doesn't return.

The simplest and cheapest ear protection is foam ear plugs such as those used by workers around noisy machinery. These are much better than nothing, but not as good as a pair of ear muffs of the type made by Peltor or Silencio available for around $20. You can also buy hearing protectors that electronically filter out the noise of gunfire but allow voices through for normal conversation. These are a lot more expensive, about $170, but are particularly good for hunters.

## HOLSTER MANUFACTURERS

Alessi Holster Distributors/R & F, 37 Stone Rd., Rochester, NY 14616; 800-724-8923; web site: http://www.rfholsters.com

Bianchi International, Inc., 100 Calle Cortez, Temecula, CA 92590; 909-676-5621; web site: http://www.bianchiinternational.com

Galco International Ltd., Aztec Business Park, 2019 West Quail Ave., Phoenix, AZ 85027; 602-258-8295; web site: http://www.usgalco.com

Don Hume Leathergoods, Inc., P.O. Box 351, Miami, OK 74355; 800-331-2686.

Kramer Handgun Leather, P.O. Box 112154, Tacoma, WA 98411; 206-564-6652.

Pager Pal, 200 West Pleasantview, Hurst, TX 76054; 800-561-1603; web site: http://www.pagerpal.com

Mitch Rosen Extraordinary Gunleather, 300 Bedford St., Manchester, NH 03101; 603-647-2971; web site: http://www.mitchrosen.com

Safariland Ltd., Inc., 3120 East Mission Blvd., Ontario, CA 91761; 909-923-7300; web site: http://www.safariland.com

Milt Sparks Holsters, Inc., 605 East 44th St. #2, Boise, ID 83714; 208-377-5577.

Thunderwear, Inc., P.O. Box 372460, Satellite Beach, FL 32937; 800-375-4433.

## OTHER ACCESSORIES

H.K.S. Products, 7841 Foundation Drive, Florence, KY 41042; 606-342-7841.

Peltor, Inc., 41 Commercial Way, East Providence, RI 02914; 401-438-4800.

Silencio/Safety Direct, 56 Coney Island Drive, Sparks, NV 89431; 800-648-1812; web site: http://www.silencio.com

# Chapter Six

## *AVOIDING ACCIDENTS: SAFETY AND HANDLING*

When five-year-old Candelario Balderas III crumpled and fell to the ground in his grandparents' back yard, family members thought at first he had just tripped and hit his head on a rock. But when his aunt picked him up, she found blood gushing from a wound in his head.

It was fifteen minutes into New Year's Day 1996, and the extended family was celebrating on the west side of San Antonio. Candelario's mother tried to call the city's Emergency Medical Services but the line was busy. So she bundled the little boy into her car and started to drive him to the hospital.

When he arrived at University Hospital, surgeons discovered Candelario was suffering from a bullet wound.

"The bullet came down and hit him on top of the head, leading us to suspect he was hit by someone who was firing a weapon into the air to celebrate the New Year," explained homicide Sergeant Joe MacKay.

Candelario suffered brain damage but survived. He was not the only San Antonian to suffer from the thoughtless action of some New Year's reveler who fired a gun in the air without thinking about where the bullet was going to land. Nine years before, David Gomez Vega, 16, was hit by a bullet in the last few minutes of 1986. He died forty minutes into the new year.

A gun is a tool, but like a car, it can do a lot of damage if not used correctly and treated with respect. It doesn't have a brain, and it can't shoot by itself. Therefore, to shoot it, somebody has to pull the trigger, either by accident or on purpose. As firing a gun by accident can lead to serious injury or death, it is important to follow a few simple safety rules. As with most rules, there are exceptional circumstances where they may not apply, and I'll point out some of them. But the following rules are a good guide.

# Safety Rules

### 1. TREAT ALL GUNS AS THOUGH THEY ARE LOADED.

Guns that people thought were unloaded are the biggest cause of firearms accidents. If you handle all guns as though they are loaded, you will avoid such tragedies. All defensive weapons should be kept loaded and handy all the time. An empty gun or a loaded gun kept locked in a gun safe is not going to be much good if you need it in a hurry. However, you must ensure that children and other adults do not have access to your guns. Their handling habits may not be as safe as yours.

### 2. NEVER POINT A GUN AT ANYTHING YOU ARE NOT WILLING TO SHOOT.

That means keeping the gun pointed at the backstop when on the range and in a safe direction at all other times. Pointing the gun at the ground is usually fairly safe, but remember that walls, particularly apartment walls, are not necessarily bullet-proof. Always practice drawing your weapon and dry firing it in a safe direction. If you shoot enough, you will almost certainly fire a shot by accident at some time, but if you always keep the muzzle pointed in a safe direction, the result will do no more than scare the daylights out of you. In a shooting career that has spanned more than forty years and many thousands of rounds, I have fired three shots accidentally. Two of the bullets went harmlessly down range. The third one left a .45-caliber hole in a window before burying itself in a stream bank outside. I had been practicing the draw and thought the gun was unloaded. In each case, the gun was pointed in a relatively safe direction, and in each case I was shocked and embarrassed. Develop safe habits. Don't let the muzzle cover anybody when you are turning or passing a gun to someone. I have seen people who should know better wave their guns around, casually covering anyone in range when they "know" the gun is "empty." As mentioned above, it's only "empty" guns that kill people by accident. I make no apology for repeating it. Imagine that your gun has a wooden dowel or a laser beam extending from the barrel. This way you will always be conscious of where the muzzle is pointing.

### 3. KEEP YOUR FINGER OUTSIDE THE TRIGGER GUARD UNTIL YOU ARE READY TO SHOOT.

When I was taught to shoot in International Practical Shooting Confederation (IPSC) competition in Canada, we were taught to load, reload, unload, and move from one firing position to another with the trigger finger lying alongside the trigger guard—not on the trigger; not inside the trigger guard. I remember being ordered off the range during the first string of a match for reloading with my finger on the trigger. I learned, and now whenever I pick up a gun, my finger automatically slips into position alongside the trigger guard. It touches the trigger only when I am ready to shoot. A couple of decades ago, most holsters carried the gun with the trigger exposed. Today almost all of them enclose the trigger so that finger cannot reach the trigger until the gun is drawn. Get into the habit of putting your finger on the trigger only when the gun is coming onto the target.

### 4. BE SURE OF WHAT YOUR BULLET WILL HIT BEFORE YOU SHOOT.

Trick shooter Ed McGivern fired thousands of rounds at aerial targets in rural Montana in the 1930s. I shot tin cans thrown into the air in the wilds of British Columbia in the late-1960s. However, there are fewer and fewer places where this can be done safely anymore. It is certainly unsafe to shoot into the air in a city, as the hideous example of Candelario Balderas shows.

But bullets fired horizontally can also take unexpected paths if they hit a hard surface and ricochet. Remember skipping flat rocks across a pond as a kid? Bullets can also bounce off water in the same way. Imagine being attacked by a mugger in front of the polished granite wall of a bank. You fire three shots at your assailant. Two hit but the third strikes the granite wall and ricochets, striking a woman standing half a block away at a bus stop. Now, you almost certainly face a civil suit. If your life was in danger, your decision to shoot was right. It's better to be alive and facing a civil suit than dead and facing the undertaker. But it is something to think about. Remember, most apartment walls and many house exterior walls are not bullet-proof. I have seen many houses with stucco walls that have been shot up by gang members armed with rifles, shotguns, and handguns. Many of the bullets went in through the front wall, pierced several interior sheetrock walls, and went out through the back wall. Invariably the reason I was there was because someone, often a sleeping child, had been wounded or killed and I was reporting the story.

## 5. EVERY TIME YOU PICK UP A GUN, CHECK TO DETERMINE WHETHER IT IS LOADED.

With a revolver, open the cylinder to see it is unloaded. With a semi-automatic, first remove the magazine, then lock the slide back and look into the chamber. I also recommend looking into the slot from which you removed the magazine in case a round is somehow stuck there and could be kicked into the chamber when the slide goes forward. Gunsmith and firearms instructor Greg Ferris thinks making shooters chamber conscious is as important as making them muzzle conscious. He instructs them to check "what is in the chamber, what can be in the chamber, what has access to the chamber." If someone checks to see the gun is unloaded, then hands it to you, don't accept that it is unloaded, go through the procedure of checking for yourself. When you are on the range and you are going forward to check the targets, lay the gun down on the bench, unloaded, with the cylinder open or with the magazine removed and the slide back. Lay a semi-automatic down with the ejection port uppermost so people can see at a glance that the gun is safe. After having checked for yourself that a gun is unloaded, still treat it as though it were loaded.

## 6. DON'T HAND A LOADED GUN TO ANYONE, AND DON'T ACCEPT ONE.

Handguns should be passed from one person to another unloaded and with the muzzle pointed in a safe direction. This is a good general rule, but I can think of some exceptions to it. A range officer or instructor may accept, very carefully, a loaded gun from a student on the range if it jams or malfunctions and the student can't clear it. The muzzle should be pointed down range with fingers outside the trigger guard during such transactions. In another situation, you might want to hand a second gun to an ally during a gunfight. Otherwise, always transfer unloaded guns.

## 7. DON'T DRINK OR USE DRUGS BEFORE OR DURING SHOOTING.

There are exceptions to this, but it is a good rule of thumb. Some people are permanently on drugs for medicinal purposes. There is no reason they can't enjoy shooting. Just don't shoot or handle firearms when you are impaired. People tend to do stupid things after a few drinks, so if you know you are going to a party or function where you are going to drink, leave your gun at home.

## 8. DON'T LEAVE A LOADED GUN UNATTENDED.

An exception, of course, is when the gun is left in a strategic position for self defense at home, at the office, or in the car. People, particularly children, are curious, and a gun is a curiosity for many. You cannot assume that others have been schooled in gun safety. If someone shoots himself, herself, or someone else with a gun you have left unattended, you might avoid being charged criminally, but you will certainly be paying legal fees and jury judgments limited only by your ability to pay.

## 9. ALWAYS USE EYE AND EAR PROTECTION WHEN SHOOTING.

The only exception to this is when you have to use your gun in self defense. Otherwise wear shooting glasses or prescription glasses with lenses made of plastic. As I mentioned earlier, I lost some of my hearing by shooting with inadequate ear protection.

## 10. AVOID LEAD CONTAMINATION.

Ingestion of lead particles through the skin or by eating with unwashed hands after a session at the range can cause brain damage. (This may be why seasoned shooters are often regarded as weird by non-shooters.) Wash your hands and face after leaving the range and certainly before eating anything. Shower and wash your clothes as soon as conveniently possible. Also wash your hands and face after cleaning your gun. You will minimize your exposure to lead contamination by shooting bullets totally jacketed in copper. Most major bullet manufacturers now make bullets of this type. However, be sure to observe the precautions mentioned above, as other people may be shooting less safe bullets, and most primers contain heavy metals that can do you harm with prolonged exposure.

# TRAFFIC STOP SAFETY

Most of us don't often meet a police officer face-to-face. Frequently when we do, it is because we have become the subject of a traffic stop. This is usually not a pleasant experience for the person being stopped. He or she is usually accused of committing some infraction of the traffic laws, and the experience is probably going to be costly in terms of a ticket. It is not a particularly pleasant experience for the police officer either. Many police officers are killed during traffic stops. So they are often edgy when they stop us. How should you, the driver, behave during a traffic stop if you are a concealed-handgun-license holder and have a gun?

Different law-enforcement organizations have different ways of handling a traffic stop, and you might do well to ask your local police what their procedure is and how you should respond. Most police officers will approach you in your car, though some will order you to get out of the car.

When you pull onto the shoulder of the highway or to the side of the street and stop, you should immediately lower your window then put your hands on the steering wheel in the 10 minutes to 2 o'clock position. This enables you to talk to the officer when he approaches you and reassures him because he can see your hands. Officers are trained to watch hands because only by the movement of your hands are you likely to be a threat. Never at any time during the stop make any quick or furtive movements with your hands. If you are stopped after dark, turn on your dome light so the officer can see you more easily.

As soon as the officer speaks to you, tell him you have a concealed-handgun license and tell him where the gun is. If you have the license but are not carrying a gun, it is good policy to tell him so, because in most states when he checks your driver's license he will know that you have a concealed-handgun license. It is better that he hear it from you rather than find it out on his own. In Texas, the law stipulates that if a police officer asks you for any type of identification, you are required to give him your concealed-handgun license without specifically being asked for it. In many other states you are required to show the license only if asked for it. However, it is good policy to volunteer your license wherever you are.

Once you have told the officer that you have a license and are armed, follow his instructions and cooperate with him as fully as possible. Police have the right to disarm you if they feel you are a threat. Some officers realize that if you have a license you are more likely than the average person to be law abiding. Some officers, particularly the young and inexperienced, may view you as a threat. Whatever the attitude of the officer, be polite and pleasant.

# CHILDREN AND GUNS

In November 1997, a Denver television station—KMGH TV—and the Lakewood Police Department conducted an experiment to see how children would behave when they found guns. Lakewood is a suburb of Denver only a few miles from Littleton and Columbine High School. The experiment resulted in a three-part series on Channel 7 news called "Kids and Guns."

Two empty and disabled handguns were hidden in a room among various toys. Groups of two or three children were put into the room and left to explore, while their parents watched what they did from another room by means of two hidden cameras.

Two mothers watched in horror when their sons picked up the guns, pointed them around, and repeatedly pulled the triggers. Both mothers said they hated guns and would not let their children have anything to do with them. They acknowledged afterwards that perhaps their children needed to be taught about guns.

Reporter Susan Parks said that several other children had picked up or touched the guns. One mother seemed certain her son and his cousins would play with the guns. But they were the only kids who did the right thing. They didn't touch them and went to tell an adult. These kids knew about guns because family members had been jailed for using them, said Parks.

Lakewood Police Chief Charlie Johnston is a strong advocate of formal gun safety training for children. He said parents need to be aware that most children, at one time or another, will come across a gun.

"Shying away from it, avoiding it, or feeling that: 'I don't want guns in my house,' isn't going to work because kids will find guns," Johnston said.

He urged parents to expose their children to guns and allow them to shoot under supervision as part of an education process. This will alleviate their natural curiosity. In the experiment, the kids who had been exposed to guns behaved more responsibility when they found the guns, he added.

Johnston said it is also important to show children the damage guns can do. This can be effectively demonstrated by shooting a plastic bleach jug full of water, a watermelon, or a large, unopened can of tomato juice.

"We teach our kids very young that when a stove is hot, it burns you," Johnston said. "We say, 'Here, this is what hot means, and if you touch it it will hurt you.' We need to do the same kinds of things with kids as it applies to guns."

If you intend to keep a gun or guns ready for self defense and you have children in your house, you have a problem. You have two conflicting priorities. You don't want your children or their friends to hurt themselves or anyone else with your guns. But a gun kept for self defense must be kept easily accessible and ready to shoot at a moment's notice.

Some states, such as Texas and Connecticut, have passed laws making it a criminal offense to allow an unsupervised child access to a firearm. In Connecticut, the owner of a firearm is guilty of a Class D felony if a child gains access to the gun and causes injury or death to himself or another person with it. In Texas, the same offense is a Class A misdemeanor.

Just allowing a child (younger than seventeen) unsupervised access to a "readily dischargeable" firearm is a Class C misdemeanor in Texas. However, regardless of whether it is against the law, you don't want the sense of guilt that comes with a tragedy caused by your negligence. Even if the guilt doesn't get you, the civil lawsuit will likely bankrupt you.

What to do? One leaflet, called "Dealing with Gun Violence" and funded by the U.S. Department of Justice, makes the following recommendation: "If you choose to own firearms—handguns, rifles, or shotguns—make sure they are unloaded and securely stored. Invest in trigger locks, gun cabinets with a lock, or pistol lock boxes. Lock up ammunition separately."

This advice is given in a leaflet, sponsored with your tax money, that urges you to consider removing guns from your home altogether and urging your children "to organize against handgun violence," by which they probably mean gun ownership.

However, the advice is fairly standard: lock up your guns unloaded in one place and the ammunition somewhere else. Even Smith & Wesson in its instruction manual states: "Store your unloaded firearm and ammunition separately and in places inaccessible to children and unauthorized persons." Good advice when referring to a hunting handgun or a target pistol. Also good advice to absolve the manufacturer from lawsuits. But not very practical for keeping a gun to save your life.

How do you keep a self-defense gun instantly ready for action, but safe with children around? Police officers face this quandary every day. They have some advantages over most civilians. When they go to work, the gun goes with them. This is not always true with civilian gun carriers. Their employers may forbid them to take a gun to work. Most states with recently enacted concealed-carry laws allow employers to prohibit their employees from carrying a gun at work. This is true for all non-law-enforcement employees of the federal government. Many people don't want to leave expensive guns in their cars in unsecured parking lots, so they will leave the guns at home.

Another difference between law-enforcement officers and civilians is that in many jurisdictions the officers are required to carry their guns even when off duty. However, they may carry a smaller, lighter, and more convenient gun off duty rather than their service weapon. This means they may leave their service handgun at home when not at work and their off-duty gun at home when they are working. They still have the same problem. What to do with the gun when it's not readily at hand?

I asked several police officers how they cope. Most of them say they make it clear to their children that their guns are off limits and say they haven't had any problems.

"Being on the police department, I've seen so much tragedy," homicide Sergeant Ray Torres says. Torres comes from a police family. His father was a police officer and so was his older brother. He has a girl aged seven and a four-year-old boy.

But it is an accident involving his brother's wife and his infant niece that has made him particularly conscious of gun safety. It happened in the early-1970s at a holiday home on Lake LBJ when his brother's family was visiting. Someone had carelessly left a revolver on the counter where a five-year-old boy got hold of it. The gun went off and the bullet hit Torres' sister-in-law's wedding ring—on her hand—while she was holding her baby daughter. The bullet shattered and pieces of it embedded themselves in her arm. Luckily, Torres' niece was unhurt.

Torres says his daughter has recently asked him to teach her to shoot, and his son, who is not as disciplined, has started showing an interest in his father's gun. Torres is thinking of buying a gun safe or a trigger lock.

Homicide Detective Jimmy Holguin keeps his gun locked in his briefcase most of the time when he's at home. At night, he keeps the case unlocked and close to the bed. "I want the gun accessible," he says.

Holguin has two boys, aged seven and nine. He has let them hold the unloaded gun to satisfy their curiosity. On one occasion, a teacher at school told one of the boys that guns were bad. This confused the boy who worried that his father must be bad if he carried a gun.

"I had to tell him: guns aren't bad; they are dangerous," Holguin says.

Sergeant Joery Smittick and his wife have three daughters, ages twelve, eight, and two. When he arrives home from work, Smittick takes off his issue .40-caliber Glock semi-automatic.

"First thing I do, I unload it, take out the clip, take the round out of the chamber, and separate them," he says.

Smittick keeps his gun and another handgun high up on the dresser in his bedroom. He keeps the gun and the loaded magazine near each another. If he needs the gun in a hurry, all he has to do is grab it from the dresser, slap in the magazine, and rack the slide.

"It's still convenient enough that I could get to it and use it if I have to," Smittick says.

His daughters have shown little interest in the gun, though Smittick is thinking of taking the oldest to the range sometime soon. "I told my daughters they don't touch that thing; I put the fear of God into them," he says.

That may work well for girls, but boys tend to develop a fascination for guns when they see them on television.

As Lakewood Police Chief Charlie Johnston says, the best way to make a child safe around firearms is education. When they start reacting to firearms they see on television, it is probably time to teach them about guns and take them to the range. Former police officer and firearms instructor Greg Ferris says you have to satisfy their curiosity and show them what a firearm can do.

Ferris recalls as a youngster watching a television series about the FBI. He remembers totally unrealistic stunts such as seeing "Efraim Zimbalist Jr. go into the old FBI crouch, fire from the hip with a two-inch revolver .38 Special, hit a car doing sixty miles an hour; it flips over, explodes, and burns everybody inside to death."

"They do things on TV with firearms that firearms cannot do," Ferris says. "Children need to understand that what they see on TV is not the way it works in the real world."

Children must be taught a healthy respect for guns but they must be given a realistic appraisal of what a firearm is capable of. Teach them how to operate the gun, then take them out to the range and let them shoot it. This might be a good time to show them something spectacular by firing at a plastic jug full of water or a watermelon.

You will get one of two reactions. The child will be afraid of the gun and not want to shoot anymore or, like Ferris' son, he'll call for more ammunition. Either way, you have satisfied the curiosity. If he or she enjoys it, you can have some good parent/child time together whenever you go to the range. If they hate it, don't make them shoot. Come back in several years and try again. Ferris took his son to the range the first time before he was four. As a parent, it is up to you to decide at what age to take a child shooting.

Sergeant Tim Rupp, who is a strong advocate of education in making children and guns compatible, makes this suggestion when taking a child to the range: load the gun with only one round. That way, once the gun is fired, it is no longer in a dangerous condition.

The National Rifle Association has taught firearm safety to millions of children through its Eddie Eagle Gun Safety Program. It teaches children who find a gun to "STOP! Don't Touch; Leave the Area. Tell an Adult." The program is taught in schools and has wide support from law enforcement, with many officers involved in teaching it. The NRA estimates the program has been taught to more than ten million kids. Certainly due in part to the Eddie Eagle program, accidental firearms deaths among children are half what they were in the mid-1970s.

The best way to keep your self-defense handgun out of the hands of children and others is to wear it. If you are not wearing it and it isn't under your direct control, it must be made secure. Putting the gun on a high shelf will keep it out of reach of a toddler, but not a teen. Hiding it is also not a good approach. Remember when you were a kid? Was there anywhere in your house that you hadn't explored? I remember, as a kid, finding a .32 semi-automatic and ammunition in a drawer in my father's dressing room.

One of the best ways to secure your guns is to invest in a gun safe. Pick up any gun magazine and you'll find half a dozen advertisements for gun safes, or your local gun store may carry a line of them. They are big and heavy—five- or six-feet tall, two- or three-feet wide, and eighteen-inches to two-feet deep. They will store rifles and shotguns vertically in racks and have shelves for handguns, ammunition, and anything else of value you may have from cameras to jewelry. They vary in price and sophistication from about $700 to several thousand. In addition to being child- and burglar-resistant, some safes are advertised as being fire-resistant. Get a safe that you can bolt to the floor, as burglars sometimes arrive equipped with a dolly and wheel out the unopened safe to a waiting vehicle. When robbers walked into a retired pawnbroker's house, they tied up his wife and wheeled the safe, containing twenty-six firearms, as well as nineteen Rolex watches and other valuables, out on a dolly they had brought with them.

A gun safe is a good place to keep guns that are not likely to be used for self defense—your hunting rifles; your shotguns for doves, ducks, or sporting clays; or your hunting and competition handguns. Whether you keep them loaded in the safe or unloaded and whether you have another safe or hiding place for the ammunition is up to you. Personally, I am of the Elmer Keith school and believe that all guns should be kept loaded all the time. If everybody in the house knows this, there should be no accidents. A gun safe is also a good place to keep self-defense handguns that you leave at home when you go out.

If you can't afford a gun safe or if it is too bulky, several companies make handgun security chests that are much smaller and usually quicker to get into if you need the gun in a hurry. GunVault, Inc., makes two security chests for handguns, one with one shelf and another with two. The smaller one costs about $170 and measures 12 x 8 x 5 inches. The advantage of the GunVault is that it has a combination lock that can be operated by feel in total darkness. The top side has finger grooves with raised buttons in them. By placing your hand in the grooves, you can operate the buttons in sequence and the door pops open. It is not as fast as a holster, as its advertising claims, but it's a lot faster than a regular gun safe and much more secure than leaving your gun in a closet. Palmer Security Products also makes a line of small handgun safes under the name Pistol Pal. These security chests have a spring-loaded drawer that opens with a combination lock. Extra mounting plates allow

*GunVault's MiniVault for keeping a handgun secure at home or office.*

*A trigger lock.*

*A bore lock (below).*

the Pistol Pal 5500B to be secured in more than one place such as your bedroom and your vehicle.

There are various other ways to disable a handgun, but they are not particularly suited to your defensive handgun. A trigger lock, as its name suggests, is a clamp that goes over the trigger guard enclosing the trigger and locking into place. It requires a key to unlock it, but the price, about $10, is very reasonable. Another way of disabling a handgun is a bore lock. It is a rod that goes down the barrel of a revolver or semi-automatic and locks into place. Bore locks cost about $20.

## HANDGUN SECURITY CHESTS

GunVault, Inc., 7339 East Acoma Dr., Suite 7, Scottsdale, AZ 85260; 800-622-4903; web site: http://www.gunvault.com
Palmer Security Products, 2930 North Campbell, Chicago, IL 60618; 800-788-7725; web site: http://www.palmersecurity.com

## FIREARMS SAFETY PROGRAM

Eddie Eagle Gun Safety Program, National Rifle Association, 11250 Waples Mill Road, Fairfax, VA 22030; 800-231-0752; web site: http://www.nra.org

## Chapter Seven

## *BASIC HANDGUN SHOOTING: WATCH THE FRONT SIGHT*

Sergeant Robert Butler was irritated. The officer who had used the patrol car before him had not replaced the field contact cards he had used.

At the time, Butler was a patrol sergeant with the Terrell Hills Police Department. Prior to joining that department, he had been a Highway Patrol trooper with the Texas Department of Public Safety. Butler had just stopped a man he suspected was a burglar, and he wanted to fill out a field contact card on him.

Terrell Hills is an upscale suburb of San Antonio with its own small police department. It is mostly residential, containing some of the most expensive homes in the area—attractive targets for a burglar.

It was a November night about 9:30 and foggy. Butler had the man's identification and had patted him down lightly before rummaging through the patrol car looking for a contact card. He checked above the sun visor where they should have been; he checked in the glove box, but found nothing.

"It took my mind off him. I was mad at the officer who used the car with me 'cause he always used things and he never put cards back and so forth, left things dirty," Butler recalled.

As he got back out of the patrol car, the suspect fired at him six or seven times with a .25 caliber Raven semi-automatic, then ran off up the street. Initially Butler didn't realize he had been hit. A car drove by about the time the suspect opened fire, and Butler thought someone had tossed some firecrackers from the car.

It wasn't until he tasted blood that he realized he was wounded. One bullet had gone in under his right arm, through his right lung, bounced off his breast bone, and through the other lung. Both lungs were bleeding and were starting to collapse.

"Then it dawned on me that I might die," Butler said.

He was building a house at the time, and the thought flashed through his mind that he might never see it completed. As quickly as the thought came, it went, and he was back on the street with a felon running from him.

"I thought, I'm going to kill him. I figured if I was going to die, he was going with me."

Butler called in on the radio, telling the dispatcher he had been shot. He walked around the car and saw the suspect running along the street, going uphill.

"I drew out my service revolver, and I shot at him four times and missed him."

Suddenly Butler felt the presence of the man who had taught him how to shoot, Texas Department of Public Safety range instructor Reeves Jungkind, there beside him.

"I remember him talking to me, standing to my left, telling me, sight alignment, trigger control, basic functions, basic things that you use for shooting a handgun. And so on the fifth round, I pulled the hammer back, in single action, and aimed for his shoulders, slowly squeezed it off, and I shot him.

"The bullet went in the back of the left knee, almost dead center and blew out his whole kneecap. They said all that was left was ends of the bone. And I shot another round into where he fell. I remember he yelled at me, 'Stop shooting, you've shot me.' And I remember thinking, tough."

Automatically, Butler reloaded his revolver before calling again for the ambulance.

"What you are trained to do is what will come out," he says.

When they measured off the distance, Butler had hit the fleeing man at a range of 422 feet. Butler recovered to become a U.S. Customs agent, a competitive shooter, and a firearms instructor in his own right.

Bill McLennan, former chief firearms instructor for the San Antonio Police Department, says seven officers over the years have told him that they heard his voice while they were involved in a gunfight. They heard him saying: "Step to cover and shoot," or "Slow down and shoot accurately."

Most firearms instructors agree that in a gunfight you will do what you have been trained to do. That is why it is so important to develop good shooting habits. Two of the most important aspects of shooting a handgun accurately are the things Butler heard Reeves Jungkind say to him on that November night. They are sight alignment and trigger control.

If you grew up on a diet of film and television Westerns, you will have a quite false impression of what a gunfight is all about. Remember the scenes where the good guy in the white hat downed the bad guy with one shot fired from the hip at fifty yards; or the hero shot the gun out of someone's hand? While action scenes became somewhat more realistic as time went on, we were still subjected to Clint Eastwood wasting several gunmen at twenty yards or more, fanning a single action Colt from the hip. All this is fantasy.

The old-time gunfighters of the West, such as Wild Bill Hickok and Wyatt Earp, raised their guns to eye level and used the sights, or at least squinted along the barrels, of their six-shooters.

In his biography of Hickok, Joseph G. Rosa quotes Luther North, whose brother Frank North used to shoot at targets with Wild Bill near Cheyenne, Wyoming. Luther later wrote that Hickok "was very deliberate and took careful aim closing his left eye. If he could shoot from the hip he never did it there."

As one old gunfighter put it, "Speed's fine but accuracy is final."

That lesson is still being taught to police officers and civilians at shooting schools such as Gunsite and Thunder Ranch.

"Watch your sights; watch your sights," is the refrain hammered home to students by the staff throughout the Defensive Handgun I course taught at Thunder Ranch.

One film that gets the shooting right is John Wayne's final movie, *The Shootist.* Wayne plays a gunfighter who is dying of cancer. Rather than die in agony of natural causes, he arranges to meet three antagonists in a saloon. All the shooting in the film is done with revolvers held at arm's length and at eye level.

The only difference between the old gunfighters' style of shooting and modern technique is that we have learned that getting both hands on the gun provides a more stable mount.

However, there is still a place for unsighted fire with the gun held close to the body below eye level. But only at very close range.

Frank Hamer, the Texas Ranger Captain who tracked down and killed Bonnie Parker and Clyde Barrow, was eminently qualified to speak on the subject.

According to his biographers, H. Gordon Frost and John H. Jenkins, Hamer was said to have killed fifty-three men in close to one hundred gunfights.

He believed that shooting from the hip was a lot of nonsense invented by Hollywood. Hamer once told a friend he shot from the hip only when his assailant was so close "I didn't have room to raise my gun and point it properly."

However, there are certain things common to shooting with or without sights. One of these is the grip.

# THE GRIP

The way a person picks up a handgun gives a good clue to how familiar and proficient he or she is with it. When an expert picks up a gun, the barrel is automatically in line with the forearm and the forefinger is lying alongside the trigger guard.

To get the grip right, start with the hand empty. Open the hand so that the thumb and forefinger form a vee with each about forty-five degrees off a center line extended from the fore-arm. Take the gun by the barrel in the left hand, for a right-handed shooter, and push the top of the stocks firmly into that vee or web of the right hand so that the barrel is an extension of the forearm. Now wrap the three lower fingers around the stocks. The trigger finger should lie along the outside of the trigger guard. Every time you pick up the gun, fit it into your hand like this until that grip becomes automatic.

It is important to get a high grip on the gun to reduce the torque produced by the recoil. Firearms instructor Greg Ferris likens a handgun in recoil to an L-shaped teeter-totter. The lower your grip, the more the gun will rise in recoil. With a high grip, you are holding the gun closer to the axis of the barrel, and recoil will be absorbed by the arms and body.

On a revolver, the thumb should be pointing down toward the trigger. On a semi-automatic, there are two options, depending upon the gun and the shooter. Some people like the thumb down, pointing toward the trigger, particularly when shooting a double-action semi-automatic. With a single-action semi-automatic of the Colt Government type, most shoot-ers like the thumb to ride on top of the safety. Your grip should be as high on the stocks as possible.

When raising the gun to eye level, the finger enters the trig-ger guard and rests on the trigger. If shooting single action, the pad of the trigger finger should rest in the center of the trig-ger. If shooting double action, the trigger can be pulled with the pad or the first joint, as this gives better leverage for the heavier pull.

This is the correct grip for the right hand of a right-handed shooter, whether firing with one hand or two. When using the two-handed grip, the fingers of the left hand wrap around the fingers of the right hand. The forefinger of the left hand should rest on top of the second finger of the right hand just under the trigger guard. Some semi-automatics, such as the Glock, have the forward end of the trigger guard shaped

*Semi-automatic grip (at left): Hold the gun by the barrel with the weak hand (not shown here) and push it back into the vee of the shooting hand so the barrel is in line with the forearm.*

*Wrap the fingers of the strong hand around the butt, finger alongside the trigger guard and thumb resting on top of the safety, if using a single-action semi-automatic. (With double-action pistols, the thumb can be curled down toward the middle finger.)*

*Wrap the weak hand around the strong hand.*

*When the sights are on the target, the right thumb presses off the safety (below) and the trigger finger enters the trigger guard.*

*Revolver grip: Curl the thumb down toward the fingers of the strong hand for strongest grip. Some shooters prefer to let the thumb rest on the cylinder latch.*

*Wrap the fingers of the weak hand around the strong hand under the trigger guard. Squeeze the trigger with the first joint of the finger.*

like a finger rest to take the first joint of the left forefinger. Ignore it. Keep your left forefinger under the trigger guard. The heel of the left hand should press into the stock in the gap between the heel and fingertips of the right hand. If the right thumb is pointing down at the trigger, the left thumb rests on top of it. If shooting a single-action semi-auto with the right thumb riding the safety, the left thumb rests underneath the right thumb. The grip should be like a politician's handshake—firm but not vise-like.

Where possible, always bring the gun up to eye level and use both hands. You will recover more quickly from recoil with both hands on the gun. I found that recovery time between shots on a .45 Colt Commander with full loads using two hands was about a quarter of a second. Using one hand, recovery was about a third of a second from shot to shot. However, it is important to practice shooting with one hand, using left and right hands, in case one hand is disabled or you are hanging onto something with the other hand.

# The Stance

Two types of standing body position are currently favored for shooting a handgun with both hands: the Weaver stance and the isosceles stance.

The Weaver stance was invented by Los Angeles Deputy Sheriff Jack Weaver, one of the early contestants in practical shooting in southern California in the late-1950s. With a right-handed shooter, the left foot is a short step forward of the right and points toward the target or just to the right of it. The right foot points up to ninety degrees to the right of the target. The knees are slightly bent but the body is erect. The trunk of the body is turned about forty-five degrees to the right of the target. Some say the right arm should be locked straight, but photos of Weaver show both arms bent. The left arm is noticeably bent downward. The right hand pushes against the pull of the left hand.

*Weaver stance:
Turn the legs and body
at an angle to the target;
tilt the head to the side;
bend the left arm
downward.*

The gun is held slightly below normal eye level so the head is canted to the right side to bring the right eye down to the sights. The Weaver is almost a rifle stance.

In the isosceles stance, the shooter faces the target squarely with the feet side-by-side at least shoulder-width apart. The legs can be locked straight or be very slightly bent, but otherwise the stance is erect. The arms are extended evenly, forming an isosceles triangle. It is necessary for the shooter to lean more into the gun with this stance to prevent being thrown off balance by the recoil.

*Isosceles stance: Stand with the legs and body square to the target; extend the arms out straight, forming an isosceles triangle with the chest as its base.*

Some research indicates that the isosceles stance is more natural and is more likely to be used in the stress of combat. Bruce Siddle, of PPCT Management Systems, states in his book, *Sharpening the Warrior's Edge*, that even police officers trained in the Weaver stance revert to the isosceles stance under stress. Siddle and other authorities say that facing a threat squarely is a natural human reaction. Jerry Lane of Heckler & Koch has trained thousands of police officers in the Weaver stance, but has changed to teaching the isosceles stance as a result of the research done by Siddle and his colleagues.

*Author's modified-isosceles stance: Right foot back for stability but body square to the threat, head erect, and arms almost straight.*

Most people develop a shooting stance that is a mixture of the Weaver and the isosceles. I prefer a stance with the left foot forward, knees slightly bent but facing the target squarely, elbows bent slightly but left elbow bent more. Experiment and settle into the stance that suits you best. But remember, when the gangbanger screams at you that he's "gonna kill yore ass," your feet may not be planted in the perfect stance. You will have to draw and fire from where you are. So practice drawing your gun and shooting from different positions.

The legs should be bent enough to enable you to turn your body from the hips, not the shoulders. When you move the gun from one target to another, turn from the hips or by swiveling on the balls of your feet if the targets are widely separated.

Massad Ayoob, director of Lethal Force Institute, teaches what he calls a turret stance, which is an isosceles above the waist but with the legs in whatever position you find yourself when you have to shoot.

Bill McLennan teaches a modified Weaver that he calls a boxer stance: feet about shoulder width apart with one foot forward and one back. It gives you greater stability than the pure

*A one-handed shooting stance can vary from turning the body almost ninety degrees away from the target, as shown at left, to facing the target squarely. Note that the shooter is leaning aggressively into the weapon.*

isosceles. Most gunfights take place at very close range, and you may be fending off the robber with your left hand while you are trying to shoot him with the right. If you need to kick, you can kick from this position, McLennan says. He prefers certain aspects of the Weaver stance, in part because turning your body at an angle to the threat helps to keep your holstered gun away from your attacker when you are within grappling range.

Try the Weaver and isosceles stances. Have someone push you backward when your feet are in the isosceles stance. Then change to the Weaver—one foot back, one foot forward—and have them try to push you back. You'll soon see which foot position is more stable.

On the practice range, while waiting for the signal to shoot, hold the gun in both hands, elbows bent and muzzle pointing down range at the bottom of the target. The safety is on with a single action, and the trigger finger is straight alongside the trigger guard. This is the "ready position." On the signal to fire, bring the gun up to eye level, push off the safety, extend the arms into your usual shooting stance, place your finger on the trigger, acquire a good sight picture, and squeeze off the shot. The ready position is also good for checking out a real-life threat. You don't want to check out a threat in your house or anywhere else with your finger on the trigger. Anything that startles you is likely to result in an involuntary contraction of your trigger finger and an accidental shot.

When shooting with one hand, you can face the target squarely and raise the gun to eye level in the center of the body, as recommended by such experts as Captain W. E. Fairbairn, of Shanghai Police fame, and competition shooter J. Michael Plaxco. Or you can shoot with the shoulder of your gun arm extended toward the target and the body turned from forty-five to ninety degrees away from the target. Bill McLennan prefers to turn about forty-five degrees from the target, as he finds it easier to move, particularly backward. Practice shooting one handed using either hand.

# Sight Picture

Achieving a proper sight picture means getting the front sight centered in the notch of the rear sight with the tops of both sights level and with the top of the front sight right where you want to hit on the target. If you do that and your trigger control is perfect, you will hit what you are shooting at every time. Sounds easy, doesn't it?

*Correct sight alignment.*

It is, but there are some complicating factors. First, you need to determine your master eye. Extend one of your arms. It doesn't matter which one. Lift your thumb up, and with both eyes open line it up with some mark on the opposite wall. Close your left eye. Does your thumb appear to move in relation to the mark? If it stays anchored to the mark, your right eye is master. Try closing your right eye. If your right eye is master, your thumb should move to the right. If your left eye is master, your thumb will stay still.

If you are right-handed and your right eye is master, you are in good shape. If you are left-handed and your left eye is master, that's okay too. If you are right-handed but your left eye is master or vice versa, you should still be able to handle a handgun without a problem, but you may have trouble shooting a rifle or shotgun. Always align the sights using the master eye.

It is better to shoot a handgun with both eyes open, particularly in a defensive situation, because two open eyes can see more than one, and you don't want to be outflanked on your blind side. If you have trouble shooting with both eyes wide open, try half closing your weak eye. After some practice, most people are able to shoot with both eyes open.

No one can hold a gun absolutely steady. Whether you are an Olympic contestant shooting a free pistol at fifty meters or an average Jill or Joe trying to fend off a street-wise scumbag, you are looking for an acceptable sight picture, not a perfect one. The only difference between a tyro shooter and a pro is that the pro's front sight wobbles over a smaller area on the target than the beginner's.

Many instructors in combat shooting teach their students to concentrate on the front sight. The human eye can focus on only one thing at a time. If you focus on the target, the sights will be fuzzy and your accuracy will suffer. If your focus is on the front sight, the rear sight will be a little fuzzy and the lettering on scumbag's T-shirt twenty feet away will be blurred.

Anytime you are shooting at something or someone more than a few feet away, you need to get that front sight on the target. Think front sight. Concentrate on the front sight. Focus on the front sight.

Greg Ferris teaches his students to keep the front sight in focus, but to concentrate on making equal the bars of light on either side of the front sight within the frame of the rear sight. If you find this approach helpful, go for it.

When that juvenile gangbanger is pointing a sawed-off 12-gauge at your just-eaten dinner, it's really hard to get your eyes to focus on the front sight. Only constant repetition in practice will overcome your natural reaction to focus on that drain-pipe-sized barrel. Frequently people are mesmerized by their assailant's weapon and actually shoot at it rather than at the person wielding it. Aikido Sensei David Ham refers to that as "the mind captured by the weapon." Train yourself to focus on that front sight, though in a shoot-out you may not be able to tear your attention from your attacker.

Bill McLennan puts it this way: "If you don't look at your sights when you practice, you're not going to do it in the field. We say look at your sights. Realistically, you may be looking at the target, but you're aware of the sights. You've spent thousands and thousands of repetitions learning to use your sights, so that one time you didn't use your sights you still went to that learned position. You did everything exactly the same. Probably for all practical purposes you were using your sights, but it was a muscle-memory thing."

He says he used to shoot at close range by indexing the cylinder of his revolver against the target. He was persuaded by colleague Richard Stengel to use the sights.

"Until I started using the sights, I never had rounds that were almost touching each other on the target, and Richard was always doing that," McLennan says.

"The problem with my cylinder indexing, like all point-shooting techniques, was that it fell apart when one or more of the indices—distance to target, target size, target angle, time allotted—were significantly changed. You may not be able to control target distance, size, or angle, but you can and must control the speed at which you shoot. There is only a split second between deadly accuracy and a miss; you must not shoot any faster than you can be sure of hitting your intended target."

# Sights

Sights on self-defense handguns will usually be improved with a little color to draw the eye to them, particularly in low light. Sights with three white dots, one on the front sight and one on each shoulder of the rear sight, are popular. Some people like red or fluorescent orange on the front sight. You can use model paint or you can get sights specially colored from makers like Millett. Some also outline the rear sight in white.

For a self-defense gun, use a ramp front sight that will not snag on clothing whether you draw it from a pocket, a fanny pack, or an ankle holster. For the same reason, the rear sight should be non-adjustable. In fact, most sights on self-defense guns can be adjusted by drifting them laterally in their dovetail notches. Smith & Wesson semi-automatics come equipped with Novak's fixed sights, which have a low, clean profile that would be hard to snag on anything.

Some people swear by night sights—those luminous inserts that make your sights glow in the dark. Most gunfights take place in conditions of poor light, so they can be an advantage. Bill McLennan is a great believer in night sights.

"I think they're excellent. Probably one of the most innovative and best pieces of equipment that I've seen come along in my thirty years in law enforcement as far as guns go," he says.

However, night sights are no substitute for learning to shoot using a flashlight. You always have to identify your target, and night sights aren't going to do that for you.

Shooting instructor and gunfight survivor Greg Ferris dislikes night sights and recommends this experiment to show why. After dark in a lighted room, take a very unloaded gun with three-dot night sights and point the gun near the door where the light switch is located. Your partner in this experiment should be armed with a pen-sized flashlight. Without getting in line with the door or your muzzle, have him turn out the light. After getting accustomed to the sudden darkness, you will be able to line up the dot on the front sight between the two dots on the shoulders of the rear sight. Have your partner briefly flash the pen light at you to simulate an assailant's muzzle flash or your own. Suddenly, you will see at least six dots instead of three, making it almost impossible to get a good sight picture.

Night sights with luminous inserts are expensive. Some people swear by them, others don't. However, anything that gives you an edge in poor light is worth considering, even if they only help you land the first shot on target. The first shot is the most important, as gunfights tend to be won by the person who makes the first hit.

# Trigger Control

The purpose of trigger control is to squeeze the trigger and fire the shot without disturbing the sight picture or moving the gun. The way to do this is to steadily increase pressure on the trigger until the gun goes off. The let-off should be a surprise to the shooter, even though the time period with practice can be compressed into a few hundredths of a second. With a double-action revolver or semi-automatic, this means a long squeeze against anything from five to twelve pounds of resistance over about a half inch of travel. With a single-action semi-auto, it means taking up the slack in the trigger, then pressing to a sharp break at around four pounds. The double-action trigger should be pulled by the first joint of the trigger finger. The end pad of the forefinger squeezes the trigger of a single action. In all cases, the pressure on the trigger should be straight back and not to one side or the other.

With both types of action, the trigger should return forward under control of the finger. Do not allow the trigger to go all the way forward but just enough for the sear, which holds back the hammer, to reengage. You will feel the click. The finger should not come off the trigger when going forward; keep a little pressure during the release.

It is important to grip the gun the same way, with the same amount of pressure, and to squeeze the trigger identically each time you fire a shot, because the gun starts to recoil before the bullet is out of the barrel. Therefore the recoil pattern must be the same from shot to shot.

Greg Ferris teaches his students to allow the gun to recoil until it runs out of energy, and if you are relaxed, it will quickly settle back to where it was when it fired.

"You don't fight recoil, you ride it," Ferris says.

In fact, experienced shooters need that recoil to develop a rhythm to their shooting cycle. The shooting cycle starts with the sight picture and the trigger pull. The trigger breaks in the middle of the cycle.

"The end of the shooting cycle is when the gun has reached its apex in recoil," says Ferris. "Once it does that, now your cycle starts again. You release the trigger as you come down and start your trigger take-up as your sights come back onto the target."

You should keep your eye on that front sight even while it is rising in recoil. Of course, if one shot puts your attacker down, you will never develop a rhythm; but as long as he is a threat, you need to keep shooting.

Even if you fire only one shot, you need to bring your sights back into line with the target after you break the shot. This is called follow-through.

At some stage, most shooters will flinch or anticipate the recoil of the gun. It usually produces a low left shot on the target for a right-handed shooter. To test for this, have someone else load your gun or magazine with a dummy round among the live cartridges. When you get to the dummy, the click of the hammer will be accompanied by an embarrassing and noticeable dip of the front sight as you anticipate the recoil. Continued shooting with live and dummy rounds will usually cure the problem.

Bill McLennan thinks that trigger control is more important than sight picture in close-range defensive shooting. Despite deteriorating eyesight which affects his sight alignment, he still shoots better than most of us.

"Consequently I think the trigger is what's most important," he says.

When you start practicing, don't hurry. Shoot deliberately and strive for accuracy. Speed will come later. You might start with a figure target at twelve feet if you have never fired a handgun before. It is better to make hits at four yards than misses at twenty-five. If possible get a professional instructor to teach you the basics. This is important because an instructor can teach you the proper technique and correct any bad habits before they become ingrained. There is nothing more frustrating than unlearning a bad habit.

# T HE DRAW

Most people who carry handguns on a regular basis wear them in holsters. The ability to draw your gun from a concealed holster and fire an accurate shot at close range in less than a second is a skill worth acquiring. It could save your life. But remember, the fastest draw is to have the gun in your hand.

We'll start with the draw from a hip holster on the right side, for a right-handed shooter, concealed by an unbuttoned jacket. The holster can be inside or outside the waistband. Most shooters go to the range to practice without a jacket and wear the gun exposed. Practice drawing the gun from the position it will be in on the street, that is, with the gun hidden under a jacket or under a shirt that is not tucked in.

Thunder Ranch teaches an effective five-step draw. When the individual steps are mastered they should be combined into a smooth, flowing whole. Do not try for speed; concentrate on relaxed smoothness. Speed will come later. When reholstering the gun, reverse the cycle as exactly as you can, as this will help with muscle-memory training. Experts say it takes three thousand repetitions of an action for it to become a reactive response. When you draw, do not look at the gun. Keep your eyes on the target, and shift your focus to the sights only when the gun appears on the line of sight between your eye and the target. Also, do not look at the gun or the leather when you reholster. You should keep your eyes open for any other threats. Felons often travel in pairs or packs.

Assume a relaxed stance with hands at your sides. Later you can practice with your hands up or on top of your head. These hip-draw instructions are for a right-handed shooter:

**STEP 1—HAND TO GUN.** To clear the coat, bring the gun hand up and place it flat on your sternum, fingers pointing diagonally downward. At the same time, bring the left hand, with fingers horizontal, to a position just in front of your belt buckle. Move the right hand around your ribs toward the butt of the gun, the fingers turning toward vertical as the edge of the hand cuts under the coat. Grasp the gun in a perfect shooting grip. The thumb breaks the thumb snap if there is one, and the forefinger extends downward on the outside of the holster where it covers the trigger guard. With a single-action semi-automatic like the Government Model, the thumb should ride on the top of the safety, but don't take it off safe yet. This should be the slowest and most deliberate step in the draw. How well you shoot when the gun reaches eye level depends largely on how good a grip you get on the gun when it is in the holster. Also, if you start your draw slowly, it will take your attacker just a little longer to realize what you are doing. If you make a quick snatch at the gun, your opponent's reaction will be quicker.

**STEP 2—CLEAR HOLSTER AND ROTATE MUZZLE TOWARD TARGET.** Lift the gun upward until the muzzle clears the lip of the holster. Rotate the muzzle forward and upward until it is horizontal and pointing at the target. The forearm rests against the ribs or pectoral muscles. The gun can be fired from this position at an assailant who is at arm's length and crowding you. This position keeps the gun back from your assailant's grasp and is accurate enough to hit him. If you are fending off an attacker with your left hand, don't shoot him through your own arm. It has happened, according to Thunder Ranch's Clint Smith.

**STEP 3—HANDS TOGETHER.** The gun hand moves the gun to the front of the body at mid-chest height, where the left hand rises to cup the gun in a two-hand grip. The hands come together about six inches in front of the sternum, with the insides of the forearm resting against the ribs. At this point the safety is still on, and the trigger finger is pointing straight alongside the trigger guard.

**STEP 4—GUN TO TARGET.** Punch the gun forward with the gun hand against a slight restraining pull of the left hand. With a single-action semi-automatic, the thumb of the gun hand slides the safety off and the finger goes into the trigger guard while the gun is traveling forward. The trigger finger takes up the slack on the trigger as the gun reaches the end of its forward movement. The gun stops when the gun arm is almost straight and the gun is between you and the target at eye level. With a double-action revolver or auto, the trigger stroke is started as the gun goes forward into battery, meaning it is capable of being fired. If you do not need to shoot immediately, the draw ends here. If you need to shoot, continue with the next step.

**STEP 5—SIGHT PICTURE AND TRIGGER SQUEEZE.** As the gun reaches the firing position, shift your focus from the target to your front sight. Do not try for a perfect sight picture. You should start your compressed trigger squeeze on an acceptable sight picture. Keep steadily increasing the pressure on the trigger until the gun fires with a surprise break.

Practice your draw extensively with an empty gun, striving for smoothness. Speed is the economy of motion and will come

*Steps in the hip draw:*
*1: Hand to gun.*

*2: Clear holster*
*and rotate muzzle to target.*

with practice. You want to be very certain of the mechanics of your draw before you start doing it with a loaded gun. This applies to any draw.

In hot weather a vest such as those worn by photographers will cover the butt of an inside-the-waistband holstered gun. The vest is cleared in the same way as a coat.

*3: Bring hands together.*

*4 and 5:*
*Push the gun forward,*
*raising it to eye level.*
*Open fire if necessary.*

*Shooter lifts his shirt with his left hand to reach the gun with his right.*

You may choose to wear a T-shirt and an unbuttoned sports shirt to cover the gun. Again, clearing the clothing is done in the same way. However, if the shirt is buttoned but outside the pants, clear it by grasping the hem of the shirt with your left hand and lifting it above the gun. Once the gun is out of the holster and in front of the sternum, the left hand comes down and across to take its grip. Be careful not to allow the left hand or arm to get in front of the gun muzzle.

Drawing from a shoulder holster or cross-draw belt rig starts with the left hand pulling open the jacket. The right hand moves to the gun and secures a solid shooting grip. The thumb breaks the thumb snap if there is one, or the hand pulls against the spring if there is not. Bring the muzzle down in a vertical arc, trying not to point the barrel at you or anyone else until the gun is in front of your chest, where the left hand can wrap around the fingers of the right hand. From there, the draw is similar to the hip draw—the gun is punched out into the firing position.

The draw from an ankle holster is different. If right-handed, the best way to wear an ankle holster is inside the left ankle. The best way to bring a gun into action from an ankle holster is to step back with the leg that doesn't hold the gun and kneel on that knee. Clear the pants cuff with your left hand. You need loose pant legs for the ankle holster, both to hide the outline of the gun and to get it into action. Draw the gun and shoot from the kneeling position. Kneeling makes you a smaller target, and you don't have to bend down from the waist, losing your balance, or center, as the martial artists say, and perhaps losing sight of your adversary.

With any of these draws, speed is fine, but accuracy is what counts. An illustration of what happens all too typically when that lesson is forgotten occurred on the west side of San Antonio a couple of days

*Ankle Draw : Shooter pulls up pants cuff with left hand and draws with right.*

before Christmas 1994. Four sheriff's deputies, equipped with a warrant for drugs, had to break down the front door of the house they had come to search. As they rushed in, a man in the living room raised a .22 caliber rifle and fired one shot at them. The deputies fired fifty-three rounds from their .40-caliber Glocks at the man, hitting him ten times. Only two of the hits were considered life threatening. They hit the man with only one shot in five at a distance that could not have been more than fifteen feet.

According to FBI statistics, the average number of rounds fired in gunfights involving police officers in the 1980s was three. However, in the 1990s, the average has quadrupled to about twelve rounds. Undoubtedly this coincides with the switch from revolvers to high-capacity semi-automatics.

As Thunder Ranch's Clint Smith puts it, "If you've got more, you'll shoot more."

## SIGHTS

Millett Sights, 7275 Murdy Circle, Huntington Beach, CA 92647; 714-842-5575; web site: http://www.millettsights.com

Novak's, Inc., 1206½ 30th Street, Parkersburg, WV 26101; 304-485-9295; web site: http://www.novaksights.com

## Chapter Eight

## *ADVANCED SHOOTING:*
## *BACK UP AND MOVE TO COVER*

The first time Leo Arredondo got into a gunfight, he was on his lunch break. He and his friend Raul "Bear" Garza were at De La Rosa Home and Auto Supply on Nogalitos Street in San Antonio when a red pickup pulled up in front of the auto-repair-shop bays. It was shortly after 3 o'clock in the afternoon. They knew there was likely to be trouble when they saw the driver, 17-year-old Valentino Garcia Jr. and his uncle, Ricky Garcia, 25, get out of the pickup.

Three of the five people in the garage that day had had problems with the Garcias. Eddie Mireles had been threatened. A couple of weeks before, Raul had been beaten with a pool cue by one member of the Garcia family, while another held a gun on him. Several months before that, Leo had gone to Raul's assistance when two of the Garcias attacked him. According to Leo, the Garcias had threatened to kill him. So he had bought a .380-caliber Davis semi-automatic.

"They had already been there harassing us, saying they were going to get us and stuff like that; they were going to kill everybody at the garage," Leo says.

The day of the shooting, April 30, 1992, Valentino and Ricky Garcia were looking for Mireles. They stood beside their pickup, waving handguns and taunting him to come out of the garage. When it became apparent that Mireles was not coming out, the Garcias got back into their truck as though to leave.

Then they apparently spotted Raul and got out again. Valentino started swearing at the stocky part-time mechanic. Raul said he didn't want any trouble and suggested they leave.

161

Ricky came around the front of the truck brandishing a .45 semi-automatic and yelled: "I've got something for you, too." He started walking toward Raul, shooting as he came. Raul ducked behind his large Snap-on toolbox where he kept a .38 Smith & Wesson revolver. He grabbed the gun and emptied it at Ricky Garcia. Ricky went down, hit in the left shoulder and right side of the abdomen.

Meanwhile Valentino had come around the pickup to help his uncle. Leo was taking cover behind a vehicle parked in one of the garage bays. He says Valentino fired one shot at him with a snub-nosed .38 revolver. Leo says he fired twice with his .380 Davis, using one hand, but concentrating on the sights, at a range of about fifteen yards. He saw Valentino fall, hit in the chest.

Ricky picked himself up and helped his nephew into the passenger side of the pickup. He got into the driver's side and drove off. Less than two blocks away, Ricky apparently lost consciousness and the truck hit a utility pole in the front yard of a house.

By the time police arrived, Valentino was dead and Ricky was in bad shape. The wounded man was rushed by ambulance to a nearby hospital. He recovered, but refused to tell police what had happened, except to say that it was Raul who had shot him. An autopsy revealed that Leo's bullet entered Valentino's chest high on the right side and had gone through his right lung, causing massive internal bleeding. He also had cocaine in his system, according to the medical examiner's report.

Raul and Leo fled the scene but later turned themselves in to police and gave statements. A case for murder and attempted murder against Raul and Leo was rejected by the District Attorney's office.

Assistant DA Carl Lobitz, in rejecting the case, wrote: "Eyewitness statements indicate that complainants [Ricky and Valentino] sought out defendants at the garage, provoked a confrontation, and fired at defendants first. Therefore, defendants were justified in employing deadly force in self-defense."

And that should have been the end of it. But blood feuds in Texas seldom die.

Four years later, on March 22, 1996, shortly before 10 p.m., Leo Arredondo was in the same garage on Nogalitos Street, helping a friend fix the brakes on a pickup. Again, a pickup, blue this time, pulled up in front of the loading bays, and two men got out. Again, they were both Garcias—San Henry Garcia, 34, and his older brother, Valentine or Valentino Sr., 40, come to avenge his dead son.

As they walked into the garage, Valentine pulled a short-barreled, pump-action shotgun from under his long, black overcoat.

According to witnesses, one of the Garcias demanded: "Where's that f---ing Leo."

Although he had never seen Valentine Sr., Leo knew they were Garcias and that they were there to kill him. He made a dash for the back of the shop where he had another Davis P-380 cached in a rack of tires. The Garcias opened fire with the shotgun and a .357 Magnum single-action Ruger revolver. Scooping up the Davis, Arredondo fired back.

When the smoke cleared, Valentine and Henry Garcia were lying on the garage floor, dead. Leo Arredondo had been hit in the legs by a shotgun blast and by a bullet that gouged his left thumb. He dragged himself toward the front doors before he collapsed.

This time, the shooting was very close and there was no time to take cover. Valentine was shot through the heart and Henry through the right eye with the bullet passing through the brain. That shot was fired from so close there was powder tattooing on Henry's face around the entrance wound.

According to the way the bodies, guns, and ejected cases were found, the shots were probably all fired from within ten feet or so. Police found five empty .380-caliber cases, indicating that Leo had fired all but one of the rounds in his Davis. Four empty .357 Magnum cases were found in the Ruger single action. Evidence investigators found one more round in the cylinder that had apparently misfired. It was loaded with only five. No empty cases from the 12-gauge shotgun were found at the scene, but as the shooting happened after dark, they might have been missed. Certainly Leo was hit in the legs by at least one shotgun blast.

In his statement to police, Leo said he had recently taken a peace officer's course and had qualified on the range.

What can we learn from these two gunfights?

First, you don't have to have a modified, compensated, laser-sighted, double-stacked, $3,000 gun shooting low-yield nuclear rounds to win in a shootout. Both times, Leo Arredondo used a .380-caliber Davis semi-automatic with a six-round magazine that retails for about $100. Richard Stengel, the firearms expert at the Bexar County Crime Laboratory, who examined the gun, said it had a single-action trigger pull of 10¾ pounds. Stengel's opinion of the Davis is not high.

"The safety sometimes will come off when you pull the trigger," he said. "If the trigger pull is not really heavy, then if you drop the gun it'll sometimes go off."

In a gunfight, who is shooting and how is more important than the cost and quality of the gun. In both shootouts, all the guns used by the other shooters were far superior in quality to Arredondo's Davis semi-autos. In both incidents, Leo says he used the sights, except when the last assailant was almost on top of him.

Comparing the two incidents is instructive. In the first fight, the ranges were longer and the winners took cover. Raul would probably have been hit had he not taken cover behind the Snap-on toolbox. Police found a .45-caliber spent bullet inside the toolbox. Leo shot Valentino Jr. using a vehicle for cover.

In the 1996 gunfight, no one took cover and the range was much shorter, maybe a dozen feet or less, and everyone was hit by gunfire. When cover is available, use it, and increase the range between you and your assailants if you can. More about these tactics later in this chapter.

There was a common factor in both of these gunfights that we can't take to the bank. All four attackers went down when shot. That is probably the exception rather than the rule, whether you are using a .380 or a .45, and it is something you should never count on.

# WHERE TO AIM

"If you don't take anything else out of this school with you, take the concept that when you shoot it's not going to work, and what will I do next?" says Clint Smith on the first day of a defensive handgun course at Thunder Ranch.

As previously discussed, just because you hit your assailant in a vital spot doesn't mean he's going to drop and quit the fight. He may still keep coming even after you've branded him with a brace of 230-grain slugs in the chest. Now what are you going to do?

Keep shooting until he goes down and is no longer able to do you damage. Cases have been documented where police officers have drawn their guns, fired twice, and reholstered their guns only to find that the bad guy is still coming on. The officers were trained in the double tap: draw and fire twice. They did under the stress of combat what they did in training. So when you practice, vary the number of shots you fire: sometimes one, sometimes six, and everything in between. Don't get hung up on the double tap.

If you can see all of your assailant, aim for his upper torso, the heart and lungs area. It is the largest vital area and sometimes one shot will put an attacker down. When you shoot at a target at usual gunfight ranges, you can see the holes in the paper. If you are concentrating on your front sight, you should not see the holes as they appear but only afterward. However, when you shoot at another human being, who may be wearing a jacket, a sweater, or a patterned shirt, you may not be able to see whether you are hitting him or not. You may not see any blood. This is one reason it is important to use the sights, except at the closest in-your-face ranges. You should know whether you are making hits by the sight picture when you press the trigger.

If you are making hits in the chest area and your attacker is still coming on, it is time to shift your point of aim. Many police officers today wear body armor, but so, too, do some criminals. Bullet-resistant vests have been stolen from stores catering to law-enforcement officers. Criminals have been arrested wearing body armor. The odds are against it, but your well-placed bullets could be getting absorbed by a Kevlar vest. If so, there are two other vulnerable areas to aim for: the head from the eyes up and the pelvis.

The head at eye level and above is the smallest target and the hardest to hit. The vital area is about three-inches high and five-inches wide. Why aim for the top of the head and not the whole head? A bullet through the cheek or jaw may spoil the punk's chances of an acting career, but, short of hitting the spinal column, there isn't much vital in the lower half of the face.

Imagine a man bobbing and weaving to make himself a more difficult target and coming at you with an Arkansas toothpick. Hitting him in that vital area is going to take a lot of discipline and skill. If your attacker is smart and shooting at you from behind cover, his head may be all the target he presents.

The third vital area is the pelvis. This is probably the best target on someone who is charging you. A good hit in the pelvis should stop your attacker's forward motion. The legs don't work too well from a shattered pelvis.

When hits in the upper torso don't seem to be having much effect, shoot for the head and pelvis, and keep shooting until he goes down.

# Backing Up

Most police officers who are killed by firearms are shot at a range of ten feet or less, according to FBI statistics. In the ten-year period from 1984 to 1993, 644 law-enforcement officers were shot and killed in the United States. Of those, 488 or 75 percent were shot by felons who were within ten feet of them. There are no comparable figures for civilians in gunfights, but it is reasonable to assume that the ten-foot zone of maximum danger applies to them as well.

"At this distance, he doesn't have to be good, he's only got to be lucky," says Clint Smith.

What can you do about it?

Maximize the distance to your attacker and minimize the target you present to him. This is what Thunder Ranch teaches very effectively in its Defensive Handgun courses.

Backing up during an armed confrontation is not an indication of cowardice. The graveyards are full of men who would not back up. It is common sense and good tactics for three reasons:

- It makes you harder to hit. You are moving, and with each backward step making yourself a smaller target.
- It gives your superior skill a better chance to triumph over his willingness to shoot. Luckily for the rest of us, most criminals are not good marksmen. There are exceptions. If you are a licensed gun carrier, your skill should exceed that of most would-be robbers, rapists, or murderers.
- Any witnesses to the confrontation will tell investigating police officers that you were retreating and trying to avoid a gunfight. This looks good to grand juries and prosecutors.

To back up, use a sort of crab-walk in which your legs are never crossed. This can be done to advantage up to about twenty yards. Beyond twenty yards, your chances of being hit by an assailant's bullet are greatly reduced.

Practice first with an empty gun on flat ground. The instructions are given for a right-handed shooter and should be reversed for a southpaw. Assume the Weaver or modified-Weaver stance. Your left foot should be half a pace ahead of your right, knees slightly bent, trunk of your body erect, gun in both hands, sights on the target. Lift your right leg and stretch it backward as far as you can. Put it down, toe first, then heel.

*Backing up: From your normal shooting position . . . (shown left). . . take a long step back with your right foot (for right-handed shooters) . . . (as shown at center)*

*. . . and bring your left foot back until you are again in your normal stance (as below right).*

Move your weight—or center, as the martial artists say—backward until most of your weight is on your right foot. Bring your left foot back half a pace until you are in your original stance. Grope backward again with your right toe and repeat the procedure. With practice, you can walk backward remarkably rapidly, keeping the sights nailed to the target and shooting all the while if necessary. Strive for smoothness, so your upper body is not bobbing up and down, but moves only to the rear. This makes it easier to keep the sights on the target. Get in the habit of shouting orders, such as "STOP" or "DROP THE GUN," in a loud, authoritative voice as you back up.

Another method of moving backwards or forwards is by using a gliding motion with your knees bent and your body balanced and leaning slightly into the gun. When advancing, this is more like a short, ordinary walking step, but with the body moving only horizontally. In a normal walk, the head tends to bob up and down with each step. Try to eliminate this vertical movement. It is easier to keep the sights on the target with this method, and it is faster than the crab-walk. It is particularly useful on a flat, unobstructed surface such as a parking lot, where there is nothing to trip over.

# Using Cover

There are two types of cover: cover from view, or concealment, and cover from fire. Anything that conceals you but won't stop a bullet is concealment. Examples are: bushes, some exterior house walls, sheetrock walls between the studs, most modern interior doors, settees or sofas, car doors, and bodywork.

"You are not safe behind a car door," advises Robert Butler, firearms instructor with U.S. Customs. "Most of them are just a thin piece of metal. Unless the bullet hits the window frame or some other obstruction, the bullet will go through them."

As I mentioned in the chapter on safety, I have seen many houses that have been hit during drive-by shootings. Rifle bullets, handgun bullets, and shotgun slugs went through the front walls of these houses, through all the interior walls, and often out through the back walls. In many cases, occupants were wounded or killed by bullets that had gone through at least one wall and often several. Firing a hollow-point bullet through sheetrock increases its penetration because the sheetrock will fill the hollow point and make it act like a round-nosed bullet. In other words, it will penetrate rather than expand. This is something to remember if you have to shoot someone in an apartment with neighbors just the other side of a sheetrock wall.

Cover from fire is anything bullets will not go through, such as thick tree trunks, concrete pillars, brick walls, or vehicle engine blocks. In seeking cover from fire, you must take into account what is being fired at you. Cover that will stop a pistol bullet may not protect you from an AK-47 or a rifled shotgun slug. But if there is cover available, take it.

Some people are reluctant to shoot through concealment cover to hit the man hiding behind it. Bill McLennan probably owes his life to a closed window. While circling a house looking for a felon, he passed a window. Later, when the man was captured, he told McLennan he was lucky to be alive because he would have shot him if the window had been open.

If you are in the open, you may be able to back up to cover, using the backward crab-walk described earlier. If the cover is to the side, you can get there by using a variation of the crab-walk.

To move to your right, take a step in that direction with your right foot. Move your left foot in the same direction until you are back in your normal shooting stance. Take another step with the right foot and repeat the process. All the time your gun should be in both hands, covering your attacker or shooting at him. With your knees bent and torso upright, you should be able to move quite rapidly sideways to cover. To move to the left, reverse the process, leading off with a sideways step to the left with the left foot.

When you reach cover, get as much of your body behind it as possible. Your hands and part of your head are all your assailant should be able to see. You can reduce the target area available to him by 90 percent under ideal circumstances. You can rest an arm or hand against hard cover, but don't let the gun touch it. The only thing that should protrude forward of the cover is the gun barrel. Don't stick your arms out beyond the wall or doorway.

You don't even have to be that close to cover to use it. For example, if you can keep a tree trunk between you and your attacker, you don't have to be pressed up against it. It is better to have the tree closer to you than to him, but it isn't essential.

Always use cover to reload if you can.

# OTHER SHOOTING POSITIONS

Most of your shooting will be done from a standing position, but you should also practice shooting from other positions. Kneeling is useful for shooting over or around cover such as a vehicle. It also reduces your size as a target if used out in the open. Most gunfights take place at short range, so it is faster and more versatile to extend both arms toward the target rather than take the time to rest one arm on your knee.

Lying prone is a very strong shooting position. You can rest your arms and hands on the ground to give you a very steady position for a long-range shot. Perhaps your adversary is armed with a rifle. Lying down also minimizes your exposure as a target. It is not for nothing that soldiers are trained to drop to the ground when they come under enemy fire. You can take advantage of low cover such as a tree stump or a curb while shooting from prone.

*Kneeling position for fast shooting.*

*Lying or prone position.*

*Students at Thunder Ranch practice shooting while lying on their backs (supine) and struggling to their feet.*

You should also practice shooting at a standing adversary while lying on your back and while getting to your feet. You may have tripped while backing up or you may have been knocked down by a fist or a bullet. You could be grappling with an attacker on the ground while his friend is trying to shoot you.

# Reloading

Reloading is like taking a pee. As my uncle used to say: "A wise man when he can and a fool when he must." There are two types of reload—the reload when the gun is empty and the tactical reload. They apply to both semi-automatics and revolvers, although the procedures are different.

Competition shooters plan the way they will shoot a stage in a practical match so they never run the gun dry. They reload, dropping live rounds and partly loaded magazines on the ground as they race to the next shooting box. This is fine for competition shooters who know ahead of time where all the targets are and who have no shortage of magazines or speedloaders.

However, in a gun fight, you will probably not count your rounds, and you will likely shoot your gun until the hammer clicks on an empty chamber or the slide locks back. You will probably have only one spare magazine or speed-loader—or two at most—and you won't know how many more rounds you will need. The bad guy might be down, but he may have friends you haven't spotted yet. You can't afford to drop live rounds.

There is a perception that shooting a gun until it is empty is bad luck or bad form. Not so.

"An empty gun is not bad luck," says Clint Smith. "It simply means you've been in a really good fight. What you need to do is get the gun loaded or you'll be having some bad luck."

# Empty Reload—Semi-Automatic

If you are armed with a semi-automatic, you should have one or two magazines in open-topped pouches on your left hip, if you are right-handed. Almost half the magazine should be exposed above the magazine pouch and belt.

When the slide locks open, remove your finger from the trigger and lay it along the outside of the trigger guard. Bend your right arm, moving the gun back toward you but keeping it at eye level.

At the same time, drop your left hand to the magazine on your belt. Grasp it between thumb and curled middle finger, with your forefinger pointing downward along the front edge of the magazine. Press the magazine release catch with your right thumb, dropping the magazine to the ground. You may have to shift your grip on the gun to reach the catch.

Draw the magazine with your left hand, letting the tip of your forefinger rest on the exposed bullet. As you move it toward the gun, turn your wrist over so the magazine is the right way up to enter the magazine well. Guide the magazine into the well with your forefinger, then use the heel of your hand to ram it home.

Put your left hand back on the gun. Drop the slide by

*Steps in the empty reload procedure for a semi-automatic:*
*1. Slide locks back.*

*2. Weak hand grasps full magazine.*

*3. Strong hand depresses magazine release, and magazine drops.*

depressing the slide stop with your left hand. If your slide is not locked back but the gun was still empty, rack the slide.

There are two ways to grasp the slide when racking it. You can hold it between your thumb and curled forefinger, with the thumb on the right of the slide. Pull the slide back as you would pull back a slingshot.

*4. Weak hand guides new magazine into magazine well.*

A better method is to grasp the slide overhand, with your curled forefinger on the right side of the slide and the thumb on the left side pointing to the rear. Pull the slide back sharply, and let it go as it reaches the end of its travel.

Finally, push the gun forward into the firing position, pick up your sight picture, and press the trigger, if necessary. When there is a lull in the action, you can retrieve your empty magazine.

*5. Seat magazine with heel of the weak hand.*

## TACTICAL RELOAD— SEMI-AUTOMATIC

Use a tactical reload to top up your gun during a break in the action. You may have

*6. Drop the slide with your weak thumb and resume firing position.*

disposed of one adversary but suspect he had company, or you may be behind cover.

Keeping the gun trained on the threat, move your finger off the trigger. Grab the new magazine with your left hand in the same way as for an empty reload. As you bring the new magazine up toward the gun, curl the forefinger down on the left side of the magazine so it is held between the fore and middle fingers. As your left hand reaches the bottom of the gun, depress the magazine release. Drop the old magazine into your left palm, gripping it between your thumb and forefinger. Insert the new magazine into the gun, and ram it home with the heel of your hand. Put the old magazine into a pocket on your left side, where you can reach it if you need more fire power. Put the left hand back on the gun, and resume firing if necessary.

# Empty Reload—Revolver

The way you carry your spare ammunition has a lot to do with the way you reload a revolver. The fastest way is to use a speedloader which holds all five or six rounds ready to be dropped into the cylinder at once. The problem with speedloaders is that they are bulky. This is fine for a uniformed patrolman who can wear them in the open on his Sam Brown belt. It is not so good for the plain clothes officer or civilian gun carrier. A speedloader is almost as difficult to conceal as the gun itself. Therefore, many civilians will either carry no spare rounds—not recommended—or will carry them loose in a pocket or in a flat pouch on the belt.

**WITH SPEEDLOADER:** Bring the gun back toward you a few inches, but keep it at or just below eye level. Keep the gun near eye level throughout the reloading process, so you can see any potential threat. Take your finger off the trigger and out of the trigger guard. Move your left hand forward under the gun. Use your fore- and middle-fingers to grasp the

*Tactical reload—
semi-automatic:
1. Draw a full magazine
from its pouch and curl
your forefinger down,
so the magazine is held
between your fore and
middle fingers as you
bring the magazine
up to the gun.*

*2. Depress the magazine
release with your strong
thumb, and drop the
partly-loaded magazine
into the palm of your
weak hand, grasping it
between thumb
and forefinger.*

*3. Insert the full magazine
and seat it with the palm
of the weak hand.*

cylinder on the right side and use your thumb on the left. Operate the cylinder latch with your right thumb: push it forward with a Smith & Wesson, pull it back with a Colt. Open the cylinder with the fingers and thumb of the left hand.

*Empty reload using a speedloader:*
*1. Operate the cylinder latch with the thumb of the strong hand.*

Take your right hand off the gun. Turn your left wrist a quarter turn to the right so the barrel is pointing vertically upward. Smack the ejector rod sharply downward with the heel of your right hand, knocking the empty cases out of the cylinder.

In some short-barreled revolvers, like Smith & Wesson's

*2. Open the cylinder with the weak hand.*

Chiefs Special and Centennial, the ejector rod is very short, and it may not punch the empties clear of the cylinder. You may have to pluck some of them out with your right hand.

When the cylinder is empty, turn your left hand back a quarter turn to the left and bend your wrist downward so the muzzle is pointing at the ground.

*3. Turn the gun muzzle upward. Hit the ejector rod sharply with the heel of the strong hand to eject empty cases.*

*4. Point the muzzle down. Grasp a full speedloader from pouch or pocket, and insert the rounds into the chambers.*

*5. Flick the speedloader out of the way, and close the cylinder.*

*6. Resume firing position.*

Grab your speedloader with your right hand with your fingers extending over the cartridges. Guide the bullets into the cylinder. Turn the knob on the back of the speedloader, releasing the rounds to drop into the cylinder. Flick the speedloader forward out of the way, then grasp the butt with your right hand. Close the cylinder with your left hand. Resume your two-handed grip and get the gun back into action.

There is another method of ejecting the spent cases, using the right hand. When you bring the gun back toward you, leave your finger inside the trigger guard. After opening the cylinder with both hands, take your left hand off the gun. Allow the gun to roll back in your right hand, using the trigger finger inside the trigger guard as a pivot. The barrel should now be vertical. Use the right thumb to press down on the ejector rod, punching out the empties.

Transfer the gun to the left hand, holding the cylinder open with thumb and two fingers as described earlier. The reload is completed as in the first method. I prefer the second method because it is the same technique I use for a partial or tactical reload. However, using your thumb to eject the cases is not quite as positive as giving the ejector rod a sharp tap with the heel of the left hand.

**WITHOUT SPEEDLOADER:** For most civilians, this is the more likely scenario. Spare rounds are likely to be kept loose in a left-side pocket or in a flat pouch on the left side of your belt. Galco makes a flat pouch which holds six rounds in pairs, which is ideal for this type of reload. True, it is slower than using a speedloader, but the rounds are held flat to the belt. Don't use a slide that keeps individual rounds in belt loops. Rounds kept this way for any length of time will grow green mold on the outside of the cases and are slow to get out of the loops. Use the second technique described earlier to eject the empties, keeping the gun in the strong hand.

Once the cylinder is empty, bring the gun down to waist level. Flip the gun forward at least one hundred fifty degrees, using the trigger finger through the trigger guard as a pivot. You are now gripping the gun in your right hand by its butt, with the muzzle pointed down at about a sixty-degree angle. Take your finger out of the trigger guard and lay it alongside the frame.

While you are ejecting the spent cases with your right hand, your left reaches for your spare rounds. Depending on how you carry them, take one, two, or more to the cylinder. Holding the gun by its butt in your shooting hand, push your thumb forward into the mouth of one of the chambers. You use your thumb to index the cylinder as you feed in the rounds using your thumb as a guide. Holding one or two rounds at a time, slide them down your right thumb into the chambers. With a Smith & Wesson or any revolver with a cylinder that turns anticlockwise when fired, use your thumb in the empty chambers to move the cylinder clockwise as you feed in the rounds. With a Colt which turns its cylinder clockwise when firing, use your thumb on top of the rounds you have just loaded to move the cylinder anticlockwise.

*Reloading revolver without speedloader:*

*1. After opening the cylinder, let the weapon rotate on the trigger finger until the muzzle is pointing up. Eject empties with the thumb of the strong hand.*

*2. Point the muzzle downward and put the tip of the strong hand thumb into one of the empty chambers. Slide a fresh round down that thumb into the adjacent chamber.*

Using the thumb to index the cylinder enables you to reload your revolver in total darkness or in daylight without looking down at it. The other advantage is that you can stop the reloading process at any point after loading the first round or two, close the cylinder, and the gun will fire. When you close the cylinder, make sure that the empty chamber your right thumb was holding is in the 12 o'clock position.

Most instructors teach students to reload single rounds with the right hand, holding the gun in the left hand as for loading with a speedloader. They say that under the stress of combat, your right hand will be able to manipulate the rounds into the chambers more easily than your left. Try both methods and pick the one you like best.

# T ACTICAL RELOAD—REVOLVER

There will be times when you have fired three or four shots from your revolver and you have time to reload, even though your gun is still partly loaded. Rather than fumble, trying to pull out the empty cases with your nails, dump empties and loaded rounds and start again. But don't dump them on the ground. Use the second method described earlier to empty the cylinder. Use your right thumb on the ejector rod, and cup your left hand under the cylinder to catch live rounds and empty cases. Put them into a pocket from which you can grab the live rounds later if you need them. Now reload as you would an empty revolver.

# I MMEDIATE ACTIONS OR IAs

Everyone who shoots a semi-automatic will, at some time or another, experience a malfunction or jam. You may be able to drop all your shots into the eyeball of a figure target in the blink of an eye at fifty yards, but until you can keep your gun running under adverse conditions, you are not an accomplished pistol fighter. Many handgun enthusiasts, the author included, have a long-running love affair with the Colt 1911 Government Model and its clones. In .45 ACP caliber, it is undoubtedly one of the finest fighting sidearms ever invented. However, it is temperamental, particularly after it has been accurized. In a recent class of twenty shooters at Thunder Ranch, about half were equipped with the 1911 type of semi-automatic, and all the malfunctions came from their end of the firing line. The following immediate actions, or IAs, as taught by Bill McLennan, will clear most malfunctions in a semi-automatic.

**FIRST IA—TWIST, TAP, RACK, READY:** If you press the trigger and your gun fails to fire, either the gun is empty—in which case the slide will be locked back on most semi-autos—or you have a malfunction. If your gun is empty, perform the empty reload described above. But perhaps your magazine is not seated, and the slide failed to pick up a round on its way forward; an empty case failed to eject and is stuck vertically, like a stovepipe, in the ejection port; or you had a dud round that failed to go off. Whatever, Twist, Tap, Rack, and Ready is your first immediate action.

Twist the gun to the side about sixty degrees so the ejection port is down. Tap the magazine to make sure it's seated properly. Grasp the slide overhand and jerk it briskly to the rear, racking it. As you let the slide go, it shunts forward, picking up a new round and feeding it into the chamber. You are now ready to resume firing if necessary.

*First Immediate Action:*

*1. Twist the weapon to the right so the ejection port is downward. Tap the bottom of the magazine with the heel of the weak hand to make sure it is seated properly.*

*2. Rack the slide and resume firing position.*

Some instructors teach a different technique to deal with a stovepipe case stuck in the ejection port. They teach students to knock the case out of the port with a wiping motion of the left hand. However, if the slide did not travel far enough to the rear to eject the empty case, it may not have traveled back far enough to pick up a new round. If this happens, you wipe away the stovepipe, and the slide slips forward onto an empty chamber. You will push the gun forward into the firing position and press the trigger—CLICK. Now you need to rack the slide. It is better to use Twist, Tap, Rack, and Ready to clear a stovepipe. The twist is specifically to let the stovepipe case fall clear of the gun. True, you may eject a live round, but you will be back in the action.

You can practice this at the range as follows: insert a loaded magazine in the gun; rack the slide to feed a round into the chamber; press the magazine-release button, and withdraw the magazine about an eighth of an inch. Take up a firing position and press the trigger. The gun will fire, but the slide will not pick up another round on its way forward. When you press the trigger again, the hammer will click on an empty chamber. Now twist the gun to the right, tap the magazine to seat it, rack the slide, push the gun forward into the firing position, and press the trigger.

**SECOND IA:** Sometimes the First IA won't work. For example, it won't clear a double feed. A double feed is when there is a live round or empty case still in the chamber, but the slide has picked up another round, which it is pushing up against the back of the one in the chamber, locking up the gun. When attempting to clear the gun with the First IA, you should be aware when you attempt to rack the slide that it is almost in the locked-back position and travels forward perhaps only a quarter of an inch.

Now you use the Second IA: Twist the gun to the right, adjusting the grip of your right hand so your right thumb can reach the slide stop. Grasp the slide and pull it to the rear. Lock it back with the slide stop. Withdraw the magazine. Put it in your pocket if you have another loaded magazine available. A damaged magazine can

*A malfunction where the slide sticks three-quarters of the way back like this is probably caused by a double feed.*

be the cause of the malfunction, so it is better to replace it with a fresh magazine if you have one. If not, tuck the magazine between the ring and little fingers of your right hand. Rack the slide three times to make sure you have removed the round or empty case in the chamber or anything else that caused the gun to lock up. Insert

*Second Immediate Action:*
*1. Lock the slide back, take out the magazine, hold it between the ring and little fingers of the strong hand, and rack the slide three or four times.*

*2. (at top) Replace the magazine.*
*3. (center) Rack the slide.*
*4. (at left) Resume firing position.*

a new magazine or the one you have been holding in your gun hand. Rack the slide to load a round and you are ready to fire.

You can practice the Second IA as follows: Lock the slide to the rear with the gun empty. Point the muzzle at the ground, barrel vertical. Drop a live or dummy round into the chamber. Keeping the muzzle pointing downward, insert a fresh magazine. Ease the slide gently forward, so the top round in the magazine pushes up against the back of the round in the chamber.

Bring the gun up into the firing position and press the trigger. Nothing happens. Bring the gun back toward you at belt level. Twist the gun to the right side, ejection port downward. Lock the slide back. Remove the magazine and put it in your pocket or tuck it between your ring and little fingers. Rack the slide several times. Reload and fire at the target. If you are practicing with a partner, you can take turns setting up malfunctions for each other.

**THIRD IA:** If the slide is seized and will not move, grasp it in an overhand grip with the thumb pointing to the rear. Release your grip on the weapon with the right hand, and with your right palm strike the butt of the gun several times, trying to push it forward. You'll usually be able to free a seized slide this way. Rack the slide and get the gun running again. The slide can seize due to defective ammunition, like extruded primers, deformed cases, etc. If the Third IA doesn't cure a seized slide, you can rest the ejection port or rear sight against some object like the edge of a table, and try the palm strike from there.

*Third Immediate Action: Hold the weapon by the slide in the weak hand, and strike the butt high up under the hammer with the palm of the strong hand.*

# Hip SHOOTING

Having emphasized in the last chapter the importance of using the sights at any range beyond arm's length, there are other schools of thought about self-defense shooting that you should be aware of.

Some experts can do amazing things shooting from waist level without using the sights. This is commonly referred to as hip shooting, though the gun is usually held forward of the hip. Former Border Patrolman Bill Jordan could shoot aspirin tablets off the fender of a car without hitting the car. Ed McGivern was also a pretty fair hand at hip shooting, hitting a one-inch bull's-eye most of the time at fifteen feet. Bill McLennan practiced hip or point shooting in his earlier days and got quite good at it. He used a .22 caliber K-frame Smith & Wesson, similar in size and feel to his .357 Magnum service revolver.

"I could afford .22 ammunition, and at fifteen feet or so I could get match boxes drawing and shooting from the hip. But I was on the range and shot three hundred and four hundred rounds a day for months on end, and I got real good at it. I no longer have that skill because I haven't stayed at it. Within months it had diminished, and within a few years it was gone. I can hone it back probably quicker than a person can learn it, but it doesn't stay with you."

So unless you can afford the time and money to shoot more rounds than McDonald's has hamburgers, stick with the advice of Wyatt Earp and Frank Hamer: get that gun up to eye level whenever you shoot at something beyond arm's reach.

# Point SHOOTING

In the 1920s and 30s, the Chinese city of Shanghai was a violent place. Gunfights between the British-led police force and local criminals exceeded six hundred over a 12 ½-year period with the police winning most of them. The credit goes to

Captains W. E. "Dan" Fairbairn and E. A. "Bill" Sykes, who developed a close-range shooting system that gave the police more edge than a two-handed sword. During World War II, Fairbairn and Sykes taught their skills to British commandos and secret agents. Their system was introduced into the United States by Colonel Rex Applegate, who taught it to agents of the Office of Strategic Services, forerunner of the CIA.

Unlike the "New Technique," as taught by Jeff Cooper, Clint Smith, Chuck Taylor, and others, the shooter using the Fairbairn-Sykes-Applegate technique, also known as the "point shooting" method, ignores the sights and shoots one-handed. The shooter adopts a crouch, shoulders square with the target, gun in one hand. He or she keeps the gun on the center line of the body and raises it with a straight arm to eye level. The shooter squeezes off a shot, or several, focusing on the target without using the sights. In their book, *Shooting to Live*, Fairbairn and Sykes recommend teaching this method at ranges of six feet and twelve feet.

Some teachers and advocates of the New Technique and of the point shooting method tend to become polarized and think their technique is the only correct one. In fact, the two methods are closer to each other than some of their advocates acknowledge. We can learn from both.

Teachers of the New Technique advocate shooting with both hands on the gun and using the sights under most circumstances. Point shooters use one hand and ignore the sights. However, New Technique shooters also practice firing with one hand in case the other is holding onto something or is disabled, and point shooters use both hands and the sights at longer ranges.

For close-in work, teachers of the New Technique recommend shooting from a "retention draw" position. In this technique the gun is held as in Step 2 of the draw described in the previous chapter (page 152–156). Shots are fired with the gun well below eye level, one-handed, with the forearm against the side. The other hand can be used to push away an attacker. This position is remarkably similar to the "quarter- or close-hip position" as illustrated in the book by Fairbairn and Sykes. They recommend practicing this position at a range of three feet.

*Retention-draw firing position.*

Other teachers with excellent qualifications vary in the amount of emphasis they place on using the sights at ranges from arm's length to seven yards.

Jim Cirillo, a former member of the New York City Police stakeout squad and a seasoned gunfighter, teaches his students to find the sights "subliminally," as he calls it. He says his students shoot better with the sights taped over, using the silhouette of the gun to aim.

Massad Ayoob, one of the best defensive handgun trainers in the nation, has made a scientific study of contemporary gunfights. In his book, *StressFire*, he recommends looking over the top of the gun, but getting the front sight onto the target. He suggests that trained police officers miss with three out of four shots fired in gunfights because they allow their focus to be drawn to the target instead of remaining on the sights. However, when it is too dark to see the sights, Ayoob recommends an isosceles point.

Brian Enos, one of the top practical competition shooters, talks of looking through the sights at the target, rather than focusing on them, for fast shooting at close range.

As mentioned earlier, Jerry Lane of Heckler & Koch says that for most of the last decade police officers have principally been taught the Weaver stance. The shooter stands at an angle to the target, with the support arm bent sharply at the elbow, almost as though holding a rifle, and with the head canted to one side to line up the sights.

"It is totally opposite of what we will do during periods of extreme stress," Lane says. "What we will do is, we'll step forward, square to the target, and both arms will go out in front of us. We'll bend slightly at the knees, lean forward, and look at the target."

This applies at ranges up to twenty feet, where most gunfights take place, Lane says. Beyond twenty feet, the trained person feels less threatened, will slow down, and will use the sights.

Even officers who have been trained only in the Weaver stance will adopt a different position under life-threatening conditions at close range.

"They get in a shooting, they square to the target, use the isosceles shooting position, and it's like 78 percent of the time," Lane says.

Bruce Siddle of PPCT Management Systems teaches the law-enforcement and special-warfare communities how to condition people for combat stress. He says that under extreme stress the eyes dilate and you cannot physically focus on the front sight.

In his book, *Sharpening the Warrior's Edge*, Siddle states that the body's reaction to extreme stress results in changes to the visual system. Your ability to focus your eyes on anything close, such as sights or instruments, deteriorates, and you have difficulty in visual tracking. You also lose peripheral vision.

"You lose near vision, so you can't see your front sight," Siddle says.

Your focus will be on the threat. If you have had "Watch the front sight" drilled into you in training, but suddenly you are faced with a real-life threat, and you can't see the front sight clearly, you will be disconcerted. You may even panic.

However, Cirillo, in his book, *Guns, Bullets, and Gunfights*, states that during his first shootout as a member of the New York City Police stakeout squad he was able to see his sights as clearly as if he were on a target range. Different people will react differently at different times.

Robert Butler, U.S. Customs firearms instructor, says that at really close range you can just point and shoot. "You need to go to the range; teach yourself how to hold that weapon and proper trigger control. Your arms are pointed straight out, you've got a proper grip, and that weapon will be pointed pretty well at the center of the target."

These differences in technique by different experts should not confuse the student. It's just a matter of choosing the right technique for the shooter and conditions. At ranges of four to eight feet, it is not difficult to hit the torso area of a figure target without using the sights. With practice you can extend this easily to twelve or fifteen feet. You should practice this because most gunfights happen in poor light when you can't see the sights anyway. Practice shooting in twilight and semi-darkness.

At arm's-length range, up to about four feet, practice shooting one handed with the forearm pressed against your ribs, where it is difficult for an attacker to grab your gun. This is Fairbairn's "quarter- or close-hip" position, while at Thunder Ranch it is referred to as the retention-draw position.

If you are attacked at arm's length, you will draw and fire your first couple of shots as soon as the gun comes out of the holster, from the retention position. As you back up, you move into a two-handed point without aligning the sights, and eventually you concentrate on the front sight for fast-aimed fire. The distance at which you change from one position to the next depends upon your preference, skill level, and the circumstances—that is, can you see the sights or is it too dark? Personally, I change from the retention position to the two-handed point at about four feet and from the point to aimed fire using the sights, or at least the front sight, at about twelve feet.

However, if you are backing up while shooting and your attacker is bobbing and weaving, you will need to align the sights to keep making hits even at close range. Try out these pointing techniques and see which ones are best for you, but most of your practice shooting should be done by aligning the sights and focusing on the front sight. Taking a flash sight picture not only improves your accuracy but teaches your body a muscle memory that is part of the two-handed, eye-level pointing technique. If in doubt, focus on the front sight.

## Chapter Nine

# WINNING A GUNFIGHT: MIND-SET AND TACTICS

Gunsmith Greg Ferris had just started working on a customer's .45 semi-automatic in the workshop part of his San Antonio store when he heard the front-door buzzer sounding. Out of habit or paranoia—he had been held up before—he poked his head around the doorway into the counter area.

What he saw was not a customer. Three stocky Hispanic teenagers in street-gang garb were charging across the display area, heading straight for him. The youth in the lead was grasping a small, chrome-plated semi-automatic which was pointed at him.

Ferris ducked back behind cover, his hand reaching for the custom .38 Super semi-automatic that was ready for action in a wall mount attached to the side of his work bench.

"Get your ass back out here, motherf----r," one of the attackers yelled.

"I did lean back around the corner, weapon now in my right hand unsupported, bringing it up to eye level with the muzzle trained to the front display area, while I remained hugging as tight to the corner as I could so as to keep the solid wall between us," Ferris said.

As he looked over his sights, he saw another robber crashing through the swing door at the end of the counter. He was wielding a 12-gauge, pump shotgun, and it was pointed at Ferris's face.

"At this point," Ferris said, "everything went into super slow motion."

He didn't realize until afterward that the robber with the shotgun fired the first shot. People who heard the sequence of shots said they heard a big bang first. The load of bird shot whipped past Ferris's right shoulder, missing him by less than a foot, and smashed into the gun safe behind him, blasting a six-inch circle on the black-painted steel.

Ferris began firing at the youth with the shotgun.

"I don't recall seeing the sights, but I can remember visually noting my weapon was recoiling with each shot."

While shooting, Ferris yelled for his assistant, Mike Falcon, to get the Remington shotgun that was kept loaded with buckshot and slugs for such emergencies.

The youth with the pump shotgun dived to the right, onto the floor by the display counter. Ferris yelled at him to drop the shotgun, not realizing he had hit the robber in the chest.

"He was lying on his right side, looking straight at me, and was attempting to work the action of the shotgun," Ferris said.

Aware the robber was trying to reload and fire at him again, the gunsmith fired another shot at him. This action convinced the robber to quit the fight. He then rolled onto his back and released his hold on the shotgun.

As Ferris looked up, he saw the other two robbers crowded around the front door. The one with the chrome-plated semiautomatic was turning in a crouch toward Ferris with his arm extended. Afraid the robber was going to shoot him, the gunsmith again opened fire.

"I fired until color and motion were no longer present in the doorway," Ferris said.

The two thugs he was shooting at ran out of the store and were picked up by a fourth, who was the driver of the getaway car. Ferris returned his attention to the downed robber behind the counter.

He heard a noise near the front door and turned his gun toward it. It was his assistant Mike Falcon coming through a door from another room holding a shotgun.

"We both swung our weapons almost to bear on each other and then, as if we hit our muzzles on an invisible barrier, stopped together upon recognition of each other and swung the muzzles away," Ferris said.

He told Falcon that the other two had escaped onto the street. His assistant ran out in time to fire two quick shots at the fleeing car.

Meanwhile, Ferris's wife, Melinda, came into the display area armed with a .38 Special Derringer she had taken from a briefcase in the office.

The robber on the floor started whining: "Don't kill me, don't kill me; think of my family."

Ferris told him to shut up.

When police and paramedics arrived, the robber on the floor was rushed by ambulance to a nearby hospital with a single bullet wound to the chest. He died about two hours later. He was identified as a 17-year-old gang member.

An 18-year-old, suspected of being the robber with the chromed semi-automatic, was dropped off at another hospital with three gunshot wounds. He survived and was charged in the attack.

While I have called these gang members robbers out of convenience, it is doubtful that mere robbery was all they had in mind. Police intelligence later determined that they were on a mission to increase the reputation of their gang and, had Ferris not been armed and ready to shoot, he, his assistant, and his wife may well have been murdered.

What can we learn from this incident?

First, Ferris was prepared. He had been robbed four years previously. He and his customers had been forced to lie on the floor while two robbers looted his store. It was only through their inattentiveness that Ferris managed to get to a shotgun and opened fire, wounding and paralyzing one robber and capturing the other. He was determined never to be caught off guard again, so he took precautions. He placed several guns at strategic places in the store, so he would never be far from one of them. Hence the shotgun was readily available to his assistant, and the .38 Super that saved his life was within arm's reach while he was at his work bench.

While both of Ferris's gunfights have happened in his gun store, yours may occur somewhere else—in your home, in your car, or on the street. Carjacking, a term unheard of a decade ago, is now a household word. In fact, the getaway car used in Ferris's shootout with the gang members had been taken from a woman at gunpoint shortly before they attacked the gun store.

Carjacking—or vehicle-jacking—was on James Turner's mind early on the morning of February 17, 1997. It would cost him a lot of blood.

Jim Eichelberg runs a trapline of vending machines in northwest Houston. He services these machines early in the morning before the traffic gets too heavy. He often has a few thousand dollars on him from the vending machines, so he has a Texas concealed-handgun license and usually carried a gun. The gun is a snub-nosed Smith & Wesson Model 37 five-shot revolver which weighs 13.5 ounces. In it he carried MagSafe rounds in .38 caliber. These rounds kick less than regular ammunition in the light gun and the bullets are designed to fragment on contact, so they won't go through three apartment walls and hit a little old lady two rooms away. Eichelberg has been shooting most of his life. He practices with his father-in-law at least once a week, he says.

That morning, he left his home about 5 a.m. when it was still dark and started his route. About 5:45 a.m., the 49-year-old Eichelberg was driving his 1985 Ford van east on Milwee towards the Northwest Freeway. Just before he reached the stop sign at the freeway service road, he passed a man walking in the direction he was driving.

Eichelberg pulled up at the stop sign and waited for the traffic to clear on the service road. As he waited, he looked in his rearview mirror, but he couldn't see the man he had just passed. Wondering why the man had disappeared, Eichelberg looked at the rearview mirror on the passenger side. He saw the man running along the passenger side of the van. The man was holding a revolver in his right hand.

"You could see that gun. It was almost like there was a spotlight on it because the street light down the street was reflecting off that gun," Eichelberg said. "I got a real good look at that gun."

Eichelberg had no doubt that the man was going to try to rob him or hijack his van. His gun was on the floor of the vehicle under his jacket and a mass of paperwork. He groped desperately for the gun. By the time he found it, the man was yelling at him through the passenger door window.

"He had his face against the window. His nose was almost touching it, and he had the gun next to his head," Eichelberg said.

The man was later identified as James Turner, 32, a skinny black parolee who was dressed all in black. Turner was shouting at Eichelberg and pointing the revolver at him through the window. However, with the noise of the traffic on the service road and the windows being closed, Eichelberg couldn't hear what he was saying.

"I didn't figure he was there to sell me newspapers."

Eichelberg brought his gun up and fired one shot at Turner.

The window shattered and Turner's face disappeared. Eichelberg thought he had hit him but he wasn't sure. He was deaf and half-blinded by the explosion of his gun inside the van. He was aware he was not in a good position if the man came back so he jumped out of the van. He started running towards the back of the van, still holding his revolver. Eichelberg was hoping to put some distance between himself and his would-be attacker.

Turner apparently had the same idea. He started running back the way he had come. The two men met at the back of the van.

"Bam! He fired at me. I wasn't hearing too good, but I heard a three-fifty-seven being shot at me," Eichelberg said.

He stopped and fired at the moment when Turner was stationary.

"It was just like the concealed-carry class. There's the silhouette target for half a second."

He estimated the range at eight or ten feet. He said he couldn't see the sights because it was still dark. Turner started to run away. He jumped across a ditch on the shoulder of the road then stopped, turned, and fired again at Eichelberg from about twenty feet.

"There's that silhouette target again for half a second. Bang! I fired one off, right then, right quick," he recalled. "I didn't know if I had got him or not."

They exchanged more shots as Turner ran towards the corner of a fence in an overgrown lot.

"He got right to where the fence made a corner and that's the last time he shot at me," Eichelberg said. "This last time he took aim at me, but he was just too far away. And I let fly one right there."

He and his father-in-law later measured the range at fifty-one feet. Turner disappeared into the darkness. After a few moments, Eichelberg returned to his van and drove to a nearby service station where he used a pay phone to call police. He told them someone had tried to hijack his van, that he had exchanged shots with the man, and that he was a concealed-handgun license holder.

After a few minutes, two police cars arrived, but they didn't seem too interested in picking Eichelberg up. The officers asked him where he had last seen the would-be hijacker then drove off and began to search the area. Eichelberg waited patiently at the gas station until another police car pulled up and the officer told him to get in.

"I jumped in the front seat and he said: 'You got him,'" Eichelberg recalled.

The officer drove him to a convenience store about a block from where Eichelberg had last seen him. Turner had apparently collapsed from loss of blood in front of the store.

The police officers immediately recognized Turner as someone they had arrested more than once in the past. Turner whined that somebody had shot him but denied that he had shot anyone or that he had had a gun. Police asked Eichelberg whether he was sure Turner had a gun.

"I know he had a gun. I know a muzzle flash when I see one, and it was pointed at me, by God. There's a gun," Eichelberg told them.

The police searched Turner's back trail and found the gun wrapped in Turner's jacket some distance from where he collapsed. They showed Eichelberg the gun, a Smith & Wesson .357-caliber revolver with a four-inch barrel. It had five empty cases in the cylinder and one live round.

Both men had fired five shots. Turner had missed with every shot; Eichelberg had scored with all his.

"I made six wounds with five shots," he said.

The first shot hit Turner in the chest and would probably have killed him if Eichelberg had been shooting regular hollow points or ball ammunition.

"The police told me that I put one right over his heart, and they said there was a pattern of about two inches, so it was glass and shrapnel. The bullet had exploded when it hit that window."

With his next four shots, Eichelberg had hit Turner twice in the buttocks and once in the thigh, and one bullet went through his hand into his groin.

Later when Eichelberg was giving detectives a statement at the homicide office, the doctor at Ben Taub Hospital who treated Turner phoned up.

"He asked me what I had shot this guy with. He was full of holes," Eichelberg said.

Apparently the bullets had exploded on contact leaving shrapnel wounds. Despite having been hit by five bullets, Turner was stitched up and sent to jail the following day.

Eichelberg was not the only person who called police from Milwee and Northwest Freeway. They received a 911-call from Jim Barber, a man who had been filling his car at a nearby gas station. It became apparent that before he had accosted Eichelberg, Turner had tried to carjack Barber's vehicle. He had stuck his gun in Barber's chest and demanded his wallet and keys. However, Turner had been unable to find the right key to start the car and had fled on foot. The keys were later found in Turner's pocket at the hospital. Some crack cocaine was also found on him, and police believe he was high when he attempted to rob Barber and Eichelberg.

Afterwards, a detective from the burglary division called Eichelberg on the phone. "He was mad. He said: 'Why the hell didn't you carry something bigger?' I explained to the guy it's not my responsibility to do anything but defend myself."

As a result of this incident, Turner was sentenced to fifty years in prison as a habitual criminal. And Jim Eichelberg is now carrying a Charter Arms Bulldog five-shot .44 Special with hollow points.

# Mind-set

The first lesson about gunfight survival is the Boy Scout motto: "Be Prepared." And that means a lot more than just having a gun within reach and knowing how to use it. To win a gunfight, you need to be more than able to shoot your attacker: you must be willing. When I took the course to become a Texas concealed-handgun instructor, the section on the use of deadly force was taught to us by Commander Albert Rodriguez of the Texas Department of Public Safety Training Academy. The first thing he asked us was: "Are you mentally prepared to take a life?"

If you do not believe you can kill another human being, you have no business carrying a gun. It is true that, in most of the encounters between crooks and honest citizens,

production of the gun is enough to deter a criminal attack—
but only if the criminal believes you will shoot. You would have
to be a very good poker player to bluff a street-wise crook into
believing you will shoot, if you have serious doubts about it.
Unless you are mentally and morally able to drop the hammer on another human being, carrying a gun is not for you.
Most law-abiding citizens have a natural reluctance to pulling
the trigger, and this is a good trait.

As mentioned in an earlier chapter, Jeff Cooper origi-
nated the color-code system to progressively overcome that reluctance in time for law-abiding citizens to effectively protect
themselves. Old-time Western gunfighters used to say that the
winner of a gunfight was usually the man who first realized he
was in a shooting situation. Realizing as quickly as possible that
you are in a shooting situation is critical, and Cooper's color
code helps you do this.

Imagine for a moment that you have just finished
work in a downtown office building, and it's dark. You ride
down in the elevator still thinking about the budget for your
department that you have been working on. You are still
going over the details of that budget in your mind as you
mumble, "Good night," to the security guard at his desk by
the doors.

As you step out onto the street, you are wondering if you
allocated enough money for paperclips. You turn automatically to your left and start walking toward your car in the parking lot three blocks away, as you have done every work day for
the last three years. Your head is bent, and your eyes stare unsee-
ingly at the sidewalk a few feet in front of you. You fail to notice
the youth across the street, acting as a spotter. As you reach
the corner of the building, you are estimating the toilet
paper requirements of your department.

This is Condition White. You are oblivious to your surroundings. As Clint Smith would put it: you are food, about
to be eaten.

As you turn the corner, you almost bump into two youths with their caps on backward. You are surprised; they are not. One of them has a black handgun pointed at your midriff.

"Gimme your wallet, motherf----r!" rasps the one with the gun.

What do you do? You are caught completely off guard. Moving from that state to survival mode takes longer than you have. You may be robbed, and you may be shot and killed.

Let us change the scenario. As you leave the building, you are alert. You scan the street up and down, looking for potential threats. You know it's late, and this is not the best part of downtown after dark. You are in Condition Yellow. You notice the spotter standing on the corner on the other side of the street, drawing on a cigarette. There seems to be no reason for him to be there at this time of night. But he might be waiting for a friend. You think he's seen you, but when you look at him, he's looking elsewhere. You feel that he's a threat, and as you walk toward the corner you're trying to figure out what he's going to do. You cast glances all around you to make sure he has no pals with him. You have identified a possible threat. You are in Condition Orange.

As you reach the corner, you take it wide in case there is someone waiting. Out of the corner of your eye, you see the spotter making a movement that could be a signal. You think about turning around and walking back to the building, but it's too late. You are on them. But you are not surprised. You know this is a shooting situation when you see the youth with the gun. You are in Condition Red.

"Gimme your wallet, motherf----r."

"Okay, okay. Don't shoot."

You reach back, but it's your gun you reach for, not your wallet. You are about six feet from the youth with the gun. He is the most obvious threat. There is no hesitation. As your gun reaches eye level, you fire. Several times. You couldn't miss, he's so close. You are backing up, still shooting, as you have been taught. You are going to use the corner of the building as cover. Suddenly, your right leg gives way, and you are on the ground, on your back. You must have been hit. Your attacker is still shooting at you. He's leaning toward you. You must keep fighting. Your sights are on his chest. You fire again, and again. He goes down. His buddy is running down the street. Your slide is locked back. You reload, still lying on the ground. You are trying to see the spotter. You see him running away. The guy who shot you is lying on the ground, not moving. You've been hit, but you have survived.

The color code ratchets up your readiness and willingness to shoot. Another approach that may help you to pull the trigger on another human being is to dehumanize him. Think of your assailant as a target, rather than a person possibly with a wife, a mother, children. When we go to war with another nation, we try to dehumanize our enemy. We talked of "Gooks" and "Japs" in an attempt to make killing them easier. It may help you to pull the trigger if you look on your attackers as "trash" or "peckerwoods" or "scumbags."

The politically-correct crowd may have a field day over such advice, but who cares, if it helps keep you alive? Jeff Cooper recommends turning fear into anger or righteous indignation. How dare this man take my belongings at gunpoint? What gives this man the right to point a gun at me?

Shoot for the man, not for his weapon. Pick a spot on the "target" that you want to hit. It may be a belt buckle or a shirt button. This also helps you avoid allowing your mind to be captured by his weapon. People who analyze police gunfights have noticed that a disproportionate number of rounds fired hit the weapon being fired by the other combatant. This is not the result of a misguided attempt to shoot the gun out of his hand, a la Hopalong Cassidy. It is the result of the officer's attention being so concentrated on his opponent's weapon that he hits it.

The scenario above illustrates some other principles of winning a gunfight. The robber has a gun. This makes him all powerful in his own mind. He is not expecting you to fight. You reinforce this belief when you appear to accede to his demands, saying: "Okay, okay. Don't shoot."

There is nothing fair about a gunfight. Take every advantage you can. Lie and cheat. If you can misdirect him while you draw and shoot, so much the better. If he is holding a gun on you, give him no warning—draw and shoot. It may appear that he just wants to rob you, but you can't take the chance. Maybe he wants to take you on a tour of automated teller machines as he loots your bank accounts. And maybe he'll kill you for fun along the way, as happened to San Antonio contractor Joe Ince. Never, ever let a crook take your gun. Despite the whining of the gun-control activists and the propaganda of some government agencies, people who fight crime at gunpoint are less likely to be killed or injured or to lose their property than those who offer no resistance.

Winning a gunfight requires an attitude. Different experts have referred to it in different ways. Former U.S. Border Patrolman Bill Jordan named his book about gunfighting *No Second Place Winner*. Jordan's book title underlines the reality that, unlike in a shooting competition, "there is no second place winner in a gunfight." You cannot afford to be in second place in a gunfight. You have to win, or you will probably die.

It is the attitude displayed by Texas Ranger Captain Bill McDonald when he said, "No man in the wrong can stand up against a fellow that's right and keeps on a-coming." Once the fight starts, you must keep on a-coming, figuratively at least. Good tactics dictate that you may be backing up or moving sideways to cover, but figuratively you're still "a-coming," and you're still shooting.

Personal defense expert Jeff Cooper urges aggressiveness and ruthlessness in responding to a deadly attack. I would add determination.

Repeat to yourself: "I WILL FIGHT AND KEEP FIGHTING UNTIL THE THREAT GOES AWAY." It takes three thousand repetitions before a physical action becomes so ingrained that it becomes a reaction—an act performed without thought. Make a poster of those words and hang it on the wall where you conduct your dry-firing practice.

Brainwash yourself: "I WILL FIGHT AND KEEP FIGHTING UNTIL THE THREAT GOES AWAY." It is what the winner of every gunfight, from Wild Bill Hickok to Leo Arredondo, has done.

You cannot let pain or fear stop you from continuing to fight. In a close-range gunfight, you may well be hit. Leo Arredondo, the auto mechanic on the south side of San Antonio, is a good example of a man who kept fighting after he was wounded. He was hit by a shotgun blast in the legs and went down, but he kept on fighting until both his attackers lay dead. You must keep on fighting whether you are still standing or lying on the ground.

This attitude toward self defense was articulated for a nation by Prime Minister Winston Churchill in the dark days of 1940 when Britain faced the threat of invasion from Germany. He told the British people, "We shall defend our island, whatever the cost may be; we shall fight on the beaches, we shall fight on the landing grounds, we shall fight in the fields and in the streets, we shall fight in the hills; we shall never surrender."

While the British people had months and years to defend their island, you will probably have only seconds to defend your life. However, the principle is the same.

As well as impregnating this attitude in your psyche, you can include it in your training. In martial arts we are taught never to stop a throw or move without completing it. Even if you have made a mistake, do not hesitate, but continue it through to the end. In the same way, when you are training for self defense, never allow a malfunction or an empty gun to stop you from hitting the target or completing the stage of fire.

Another lesson repeated frequently in the literature of Western gunfighters is that the man who wins in a gunfight is the one who takes the time to shoot accurately.

In his book, *They Called Him Wild Bill*, Joseph Rosa quotes Hickok's advice to a Colonel North in the 1860s: "Whenever you get into a row be sure and not shoot too quick. Take time. I've known many a feller slip up for shootin' in a hurry."

Luther North claimed his brother Frank regularly used to beat Hickok at target shooting. Wild Bill once told him, "Frank, you can beat the hell out of me shootin' at pieces of paper, but I can beat you when it comes to hittin' men."

In his biography of Wyatt Earp, Stuart Lake quotes the lawman as dispensing similar advice and recounting several incidents to illustrate his point. Earp apparently witnessed a gunfight in Deadwood, South Dakota, in which a man with the flamboyant name of Turkey Creek Jack Johnson took on two partners. The partners and Johnson closed on each other, conveniently right outside the cemetery, at a range of fifty yards. According to Earp, the two partners opened up with two guns each as Johnson walked toward them, gun in hand but not firing a shot. At about thirty yards, Johnson fired two carefully-aimed shots and killed both men. Earp said the partners fired sixteen shots between them at Johnson, causing him two or three minor flesh wounds.

Most civilians are not going to be trading shots with adversaries at thirty yards. They are more likely to be shooting at twenty feet, the range cited by Earp in a gunfight between Cockeyed Frank Loving and Levi Richardson in Dodge City's Long Branch Saloon. Richardson was a noted pistol shot who had won several gunfights, until he took up gun fanning, according to Earp. Loving was about twenty years old and was a fair shot, who until then had never fired a gun at another human being. When they quarreled in the Long Branch, Richardson left to get his gun from his hotel room. When he returned, he shouted to Loving that he was going to kill him.

Loving picked up his gun and stood up. Richardson started shooting, fanning his single action at a distance of twenty feet, according to Earp.

"While Levi was pumping lead at him, young Loving raised his gun as cool as you please and fired three shots," Lake quotes Earp as saying. All Loving's shots hit Richardson, killing him. One of Richardson's shots grazed Loving's hand.

It is natural, when your life is in imminent danger, to try to get your gun into action as quickly as possible and to shoot as fast as you can, sights be damned. This urge must be suppressed. Trained police officers have missed their attackers at ranges of six feet because they panicked.

"Wyatt Earp talked a lot about how you have to stand there and look death in the face, control your fear, and don't worry about this person shooting at you," says Bill McLennan. "I would say you ought to be moving and using cover, but you've still got to use those sights and control the fear."

Bill Jordan recommends convincing yourself that the other guy is going to screw up and that all you have to do is stay cool and make that first shot a hit. He quotes Texas Ranger Captain John Hughes: "If you get in a gunfight, don't let yourself feel rushed. Take your time, fast."

## ADRENALINE AND SURVIVAL

The early morning of August 1, 1991, was a warm summer night with a partly cloudy sky, like many that had preceded it. But for San Antonio Police Officer Shayne Katzfey, it would be like no other. It was the night he shot and killed a man.

"The average person who's never been involved in a shooting cannot fathom the mental stress and the physical stress that you undergo right during the event and immediately afterward," Katzfey says. "It's nothing like anything I have gone through before, and I pray to God it never happens to me again."

Katzfey, then 25, was on routine patrol on the northwest side of the city. He had been a police officer for nearly three years. Shortly after 4:30 a.m., he and another officer were dispatched to an apartment complex for a report of two suspicious men, possibly trying to break into a vehicle. The resident who had phoned police told the officers he could see a man hiding in one of the enclosed yards behind the ground-floor apartments. The officers edged their way along the outside of the six-foot-high wooden fence that enclosed the yards, looking for the men. Katzfey was in front, holding his flashlight in one hand and his .357 Magnum service revolver in the other. All of a sudden, a man burst out of a gate in the fence right in front of Katzfey, his hands in front of him, apparently grabbing for the officer's gun. Reacting to his training, Katzfey fired, hitting the man once in the chest.

When you believe your life is at risk, your body takes measures automatically to ensure your survival. These changes affect different people in different ways and can be very disconcerting if you are not expecting them. Not everyone will experience all the symptoms, and different people will feel them to different degrees. Katzfey was quite unprepared for what happened in his body and for the aftermath.

Under stress the body dumps massive amounts of adrenaline into your system and with it a hormone called ACTH (adrenocorticotropic hormone), which sends messages to the brain, putting it into survival mode. The immediate effect prepares you to fight or flee.

Jean Souza, a counselor who works with police officers and their families in San Antonio, has studied the effects of adrenaline and ACTH on law-enforcement officers, fire fighters, and paramedics. She teaches at the San Antonio Police Academy, consults nationwide, and is writing a book on the subject.

Souza says ACTH focuses attention to the lower brain, where the automatic survival functions are controlled. It restricts messages from the cortex, where reasoning and decision-making take place.

"In a survival situation, an officer or fire fighter has to be able to leap tall buildings in a single bound, without the cortex supplying him with too many details about how many floors are in the building or that he never was very good at the long jump," Souza says.

While she was talking about police officers and fire fighters, this also applies to anyone in a survival situation like a gunfight. In this condition, the brain sends blood to the big muscles of the arms and legs. This is the condition that gives the ninety-pound woman the strength to lift a car off her child or husband. The fight or flight response has not changed since caveman days, when people fought with their bare hands or with clubs and rocks. Extra strength was needed, and often is still needed, to fight, run, and leap. So the lower brain directs blood to the arms and legs. Katzfey says he experienced this rush of blood to the big muscles.

"You can run like the dickens, and you're strong like you've never been before," he says.

Unfortunately, this redirection of the blood and oxygen starves the extremities. In particular, fingers get cold, numb, and clumsy. Our bodies have not yet adapted to the possibility that fighting may involve a delicate trigger squeeze. We can lose the fine motor skills necessary for trigger pressing, reloading, or clearing a malfunction.

The body also tries to eliminate anything superfluous to survival. This is why some people mess themselves in a crisis, while others vomit. After the shooting, Katzfey went behind a dumpster and threw up.

"It was very embarrassing, because you don't do that at major crime scenes," he says. "It's not because you can't handle the thought or stresses you are under; it's because your body is reacting in a survival mode to make you be able to continue to fight, should it be necessary."

Katzfey also experienced tunnel vision in which the eyes focus on the assailant or even just the gun. This is why the gun or the hand holding it are often hit by bullets during a gunfight.

"I could tell you everything just outside the shoulders and from about the waist up on the person who attacked me," Katzfey says, more than five years after the shooting. "I still have a picture in my mind of just what that looked like."

Souza says tunnel vision is "a physical lock-on to the threat." It is the body's way of focusing all your attention on dealing with the immediate threat to the exclusion of anything else. It is a problem because you are focused on the target when, at anything further than halitosis range, you should be looking at the sights. You are also oblivious to any other threat, and criminals often travel in packs. Katzfey says the other officer a few paces behind him was his protection against tunnel vision.

"Had I been alone, I would've had no protection, and thank God there was no secondary threat that presented itself right that moment, because, frankly, I would have been defenseless against it," he says.

Since the shooting, Katzfey has trained himself to overcome tunnel vision. You can break the lock-on effect by moving your head or looking deliberately away from the threat. You won't do this unless you incorporate it into your training. Every time you fire at a target, look from side to side after you shoot until it becomes a habit.

Katzfey also experienced auditory exclusion, what he calls "tunnel hearing." Immediately after the shooting, he tried to use his radio to call for an ambulance. When you press the transmission switch on the radio, it emits a distinctive tone, and then you talk. Katzfey couldn't hear the tone while he was frantically calling for paramedics. In fact the radio was working perfectly, but he was aghast when he later heard a tape recording of his transmission played on a local television station. "Tunnel hearing" filters out anything that is not vital to survival, Katzfey says.

"There were witnesses at the shooting that said they heard people talking afterward, and I don't remember any talking afterward except me trying to get my radio to work," he says.

Loud noises such as gun shots do not seem as loud. Normally a .45 or .357 Magnum fired indoors without ear protection would make the shooter wince at the noise. Not so when you are in survival mode. The noise is filtered, and often a shooter will be unaware of how many shots she or he has fired.

In his second gunfight, Greg Ferris thought he had fired more shots at the shotgun-toting gangbanger than he did. Others have found themselves pressing the trigger again and again on an empty gun because they are not aware they have emptied it. Some instructors will tell you to always count your shots as you fire them. This may be practical in a competition, but not in a gunfight. The first indication you will likely have that you need to reload in a gunfight is when you are pulling the trigger on an empty cylinder or when you find the slide locked back on a semi-automatic.

Massad Ayoob, a nationally-known expert in personal defense, warns of the disconcerting effect of tachypsychia. This is a medical term for what Ferris experienced in his second fight—the slow motion effect experienced by many people during crisis situations. Katzfey's shooting incident was over in the blink of an eye, and he says he didn't experience this phenomenon. It is caused by the brain using its full power to gather and process data under the compelling effect of a life or death situation. If you haven't yet experienced this effect in an emergency, it can be disconcerting. It is the same slow motion experienced in dreams where you feel as though you are moving in molasses. Although you are in fact moving very rapidly, you can be panicked by this distortion of time, because you seem to be moving in slow motion.

Bruce Siddle of PPCT Management Systems believes that these body changes are linked to heart rate. His research shows that fine and complex motor skills deteriorate between 115 and 145 heart beats per minute. However, Jerry Lane of Heckler & Koch says there is more to these body changes than just an increase in heart rate.

"Probably most of all the adrenaline and the threat have to be there for the heart rate and the blood pressure and everything else to start really going up," Lane says.

He has raised his heart rate to 165 beats a minute on a treadmill, but there was no threat and he experienced none of the other symptoms of extreme stress.

"This was a test I did," Lane says. "I went over and picked up a pen and just started writing. I was writing just fine, because none of these other things were present."

You need to be aware of all these possible changes that can affect your ability to coolly deliver aimed shots during a fire fight. They can also affect your memory of what happened. If you tell an investigator that you fired only one shot, when in fact you fired several, your credibility will be destroyed with anyone who does not make allowance for these body changes. This is why it is best not to give police any statement of what you think happened until you have talked to your lawyer.

While these changes are affecting your body, making it more difficult to land your shots on the target, remember that the same thing is almost certainly happening to your adversary.

# TACTICS

According to military doctrine, to attack a defended position you need to outnumber the defenders by at least two to one and preferably three or four to one. The annals of war are riddled with incidents where a small number of defenders kept a much larger army of attackers at bay for long periods.

In U.S. history, the most celebrated such fight is the battle for the Alamo in the spring of 1836. At the former Catholic mission, about one hundred eighty frontiersmen with their long rifles kept several thousand crack Mexican troops at bay. For almost two weeks, this ragtag group of individualists, led by William Barret Travis and accompanied by the legendary Jim Bowie and David Crockett, defied the might of Mexico's army and changed history. Before the last shot was fired on March 6 and the last of the defenders shot, hacked, and bayoneted to death, hundreds of Mexican soldiers had breathed their last. The most reliable sources put the butcher's bill for the Mexican army under General Santa Anna at between six hundred and sixteen hundred killed.

Twenty-seven years later and seven hundred miles further south, about sixty soldiers of the French Foreign Legion were caught in the open by a well-armed Mexican cavalry force of eight hundred under a Colonel Milan. The legionnaires under Captain Jean Danjou fought their way to an abandoned farm-house in the hamlet of Camerone. By the time they reached the farmhouse, the legionnaires were down to forty-six and the Mexicans were joined by reinforcements of twelve hundred infantrymen. For nine hours, a dwindling force of legionnaires beat back attacks by two thousand Mexican soldiers. When the defenders were down to five, the last standing officer, a Second Lieutenant Maudet, ordered bayonets fixed and led a final charge into the Mexican infantry.

Colonel Milan, impressed by the valor of the defenders, stopped the fight and allowed the surviving three to keep their rifles. Mexican casualties were estimated at about three hundred. The Battle of Camerone, fought on April 30, 1863, is celebrated each year by the French Foreign Legion as its proudest memory.

Not all such battles have ended with the massacre of the defenders, however. In 1879, King Cetewayo's Zulus were giving the British Army a bad time in South Africa. On January 22, a force of twenty thousand Zulus annihilated about seventeen hundred British soldiers camped at Isandhlwana. On the same day a few miles away at Rorke's Drift, 137 of their colleagues were attacked at a farm and mission station that was serving as a hospital and supply base. The defenders included thirty-six sick and wounded from the hospital and eighty-four soldiers of the 24th Regiment of Foot. They were led by Lieutenant John Chard of the Royal Engineers and Lieutenant Gonville Bromhead of the 24th, two undistinguished officers in their early thirties.

Given a few hours warning of the nearby massacre at Isandhlwana, the troops built fortifications of mealie bags and biscuit boxes to join the hospital and the storehouse. About forty-five hundred Zulus attacked in the late afternoon. Attack followed attack with dead Zulus piling up around the makeshift fort until about 4 o'clock the following morning, when the attackers had had enough. About eighty of the defenders were still standing, while fifteen were dead, two dying, and the rest wounded.

They had fired twenty thousand rounds of ammunition. Eleven Victoria Crosses were awarded to the defenders, more than for any other single action. The Victoria Cross is the British equivalent of the U.S. Congressional Medal of Honor.

In each of these three actions, defenders, skilled in the use of their weapons, used cover to maximum advantage against assailants who had to push their attacks over open ground. Self defense against individuals is just war on a small scale. The same principles apply. The use of cover applies therefore to individuals as it does to armies. Take cover, whether it's in your bedroom or behind a tree, and let him or them bring the attack to you.

If you hear someone breaking into your house, the smartest course of action is to barricade yourself in your bedroom and call 9-1-1. A cellular phone is particularly useful for this as its wires cannot be cut by intruders. However, there are situations when you will go in harm's way.

You are in the Luby's Cafeteria in Killeen with your family. You have eaten your lunch and are having a cup of coffee while you question your kids about how they are doing in school. You had a couple of fill-ups of ice tea earlier, and your bladder reminds you that you need to go. You are in the restroom when there is a tremendous crash. There are screams and the sound of gunfire: a steady rhythm—bang, bang, bang. Wisdom dictates that you stay in the bathroom and not put yourself in harm's way, but your loved ones are there. Nothing is going to stop you from going in.

Consider another scenario. You are asleep at home in your bed with your partner. You are awakened by the sound of breaking glass. You can hear other strange noises. You get out of bed and grab your gun from the chair with your discarded clothes on it. You pull on your jeans. Suddenly you hear a scream and a high-pitched voice filled with terror shouting: "Daddy, daddy," or "Mommy, mommy." You should stay put and dial 9-1-1 on the cellular phone, but those are your kids down the hall.

In both situations, you are going to go. It may not be the best decision for your own survival, but you will never forgive yourself if you don't go. The question asked by Thunder Ranch director Clint Smith, is: "Are you gonna' go smart or are you gonna' go dumb?"

There are various procedures you can follow that may give you the edge to win a gunfight. They are called tactics. We have discussed some tactics already, such as maximizing the range by backing up to allow your superior weapons skill to prevail and minimizing your exposure to your assailant by use of cover. Tactics vary from maneuvering to keep the sun in your opponent's eyes to procedures to follow when coming to the aid of a family member or close friend.

It was more the latter that Clint Smith was referring to when he said: "The more that you know about tactics, the less you'll want to use them."

Here are some suggestions if you really feel you have to clear a house or other building. Now you must become the hunter. Move slowly and as silently as you can. Be aware that every step you take gives you a new field of view and field of fire. Those fields, while opening in front of you, are also closing behind you. Watch behind you for someone following you, and look up for someone hiding above you.

Keep your gun between you and the threat. Keep as far as you can from where the threat could be. This means that, if you

*Using cover, an instructor approaches an open door in Thunder Ranch's "Terminator," a range designed for practicing building-clearing tactics.*

are moving down a hallway and there is a doorway to your left, hug the right-hand wall of the hallway. This prevents your sticking your gun ahead of your field of view where someone on the other side of a corner can grab it. Don't peek around corners or from cover.

If you poke your head out for a quick glance and then move back behind cover, you have given your position away, and your opponent will just wait with his gun trained on the spot where you disappeared. When you look out from cover and you see someone who shouldn't be there, keep him covered and challenge him. Engage if he makes a clearly threatening move. Always look around cover, if possible, not over it. Reload behind cover and try not to run your gun dry before you reload.

Doorways and hallways are particularly dangerous because they restrict your movement. When you approach a closed door, look for the hinge pins. If you can see them, the door opens toward you. Don't stand in front of the door when you open it. Remember most doors and interior walls are not bullet-proof. You can use this to your advantage, but so can those threatening you.

When searching for the threat, watch for shadows and movement. A quick movement will attract the eye faster than anything else. As you move, look for potential areas of cover you can use if attacked. Look for things out of place. A chair knocked over or a television set near the door are indications that someone has been there and may be waiting in ambush for you.

Look for reflections in windows, mirrors, glass panels in doors, or pictures. Adele Morris, the wife of a retired pawnbroker in San Antonio, was tied up with duct tape by a pair of robbers who told her not to look around. She was amazed to see reflected in the glass doors of her fireplace the dial of her safe, passing behind her as the robbers wheeled it out on a dolly.

Avoid being silhouetted against a window, a light-colored wall, or the sky, and beware of being backlit by standing in the doorway of a lighted room, if your assailant may be in the darkened hallway. Watch for toes or shoes under cars and drapes.

If you are trying to locate a potential attacker in the darkness, try throwing something to draw his fire: pocket change, your hat. When you shoot, move away from your muzzle flash before you receive an incoming burst of fire. Use a flashlight sparingly unless you are up against only one opponent, in which case you can blind him with it. In a dangerous situation, the fastest draw is to have the gun in your hand.

Above all, be safe. Remember your safety rules, particularly the ones about knowing what your bullet will hit and keeping your finger off the trigger until you are ready to shoot. You may mean only to keep him covered, but under the stress of a potentially life-threatening confrontation, your finger may ride that trigger too heavily. There are no excuses for shooting someone by mistake. Keep your finger off the trigger while you have someone covered. Shoot only at a genuine threat. Don't make a mistake and shoot a foreign student who doesn't speak good English or a drunk who wandered into your house by mistake. Even if you are cleared by a jury, you'll feel like hell, and your hard-earned money will be making some lawyer's payments on his Lexus or Jaguar.

As mentioned earlier in this chapter, individual self defense is just war on a small scale, and surprise is one of the principles of war. Perhaps the best tactic of all is: do the unexpected. When a man in his early twenties tried to rob a convenience store in Universal City on a late summer evening, the clerks thwarted him by not taking him seriously.

The man walked into the Diamond Shamrock gas station and convenience store on Pat Booker Road in the San Antonio suburb shortly before 10 p.m. He went to the back of the store and put a brown paper bag over his head. The would-be robber approached the counter where clerk Randy Larson, 45, was serving customers. He did not show a weapon, but kept his right hand behind his back inside his pants as though he had a gun.

"I don't want to scare anybody, but I need all the money in the cash drawer," the man said. "This is for real."

"Are you the unknown comic, or a robber?" asked Larson, referring to "the unknown comic" from the television program, "The Gong Show," in which one of the actors always wore a paper bag over his head.

The robber repeated his demand in a serious tone, so Larson turned to the other clerk, Claude Campos, 28, who was beside the coffee machine, and told him to call the police as they were being robbed. Larson turned back to the robber and told him he couldn't open the cash register. Meanwhile a ten-year-old boy came up to the counter to buy a piece of gum. He handed over the money, and Larson opened the cash register to accept it.

"You all are playing with me," said the frustrated robber and walked out. He was last seen walking rapidly across the road toward an apartment complex with the bag still on his head.

In this case, Larson realized that the robber was quite inexperienced and surprised him by not obeying his orders. In more serious cases, you will almost certainly surprise an assailant by launching an instant counter attack. You are rolling the dice by making such a response: you may be killed. But the last thing a robber or rapist expects when he points a gun at you is for you to pull a gun and fight back. This is where surprise works for you.

As Jeff Cooper, the grand old man of defensive pistolcraft, puts it: "May he never choose you—but if he does, surprise him."

# Chapter Ten

## DEADLY FORCE:
## WHEN TO USE IT AND WHAT HAPPENS WHEN YOU DO

Joe Archer (not his real name) was lying on the couch in his suburban home one night about 11:30 watching television when he heard what he thought were two gun shots.

"The dog was barking like crazy, so I knew somebody was out there," Archer said.

His first thought was that his pickup or boat was being broken into, as they were both parked in the driveway. He ran outside, dressed only in his shorts.

Looking down the slope to his left, he saw a young man on his neighbor's front lawn with what appeared to be a bag in his hand and a young woman at the intersection perhaps twenty-five yards away.

"What are you doing?" Archer called out.

"It's none of your f---ing business. Go back inside," the youth yelled back.

"Do you live in this neighborhood?" Archer asked.

The youth said he was having a fight with his girlfriend and again swore at Archer.

"Well, don't you come on my Goddamn property," Archer barked.

He turned and started walking back toward his front door.

"That's when he started coming up the hill onto my property," Archer recalled.

The youth appeared very agitated, Archer told police later. "The man was too boisterous and too aggressive to be normal. I felt that he was under the influence of drugs or alcohol," Archer said in his statement.

At this time, Archer was 57 years old. He had spent thirty years in the U.S. Army, including two tours in Vietnam, retiring as a command sergeant major. After retiring from the military, he had become a school district police officer in a nearby jurisdiction.

Archer went back into his house to get his gun and possibly arrest the youth for trespassing.

"I expected to get my gun and he'd be out in the front yard and say, 'Come on out,' or something like that. I'm going to surprise him and say, 'Look, I'm a police officer, you're under arrest, you get down on the ground.' That's all I was going to do," Archer said. "Call the [city] police and that would be the end of it."

The bedroom door in Archer's house is about six feet from the front door. Archer ducked into the bedroom where his wife was sleeping and retrieved his service revolver from under the bed.

When Archer came out of the bedroom, cocking the .357 Magnum as he turned toward the front door, the youth filled the doorway, an arm's length away.

Instinctively, Archer fired. The youth tumbled backward out of the door, shot through the brain. His blood spattered the wallpaper in the hallway.

Archer is still not sure what happened. It happened too fast. Was it the trained reaction of a former jungle fighter? Perhaps. In his statement, Archer said, "When he began to come through my door I felt threatened, and I was defending myself. It was not my intention to shoot: it just happened."

Archer likens his reaction to that of a baseball pitcher when a ball is coming straight for his head.

"Whether you do that by instinct or whether it's a planned process and you kinda turn your head to catch the ball, I don't know. All I know is I came out and cocked that pistol and had a vision in my mind of him being in the front yard and, as it was, he was right there in front of my face, coming in my house, and I shot."

Initially, it appeared that Archer would be exonerated, even though the man had not been armed. The "shots" Archer had heard earlier were the noises made by the youth hitting a wall with his bag in his rage at his girlfriend. Archer and his wife were questioned and gave statements, but he was not arrested.

However, when the District Attorney's office got the case, Archer found he was in a heap of trouble. The assistant DA said she could prove the man was outside the house when Archer shot him. Retired Texas Ranger Al Cuellar, who is familiar with the case, disputes this. He says the blood spatters on the wall paper near the door show that the youth was shot while inside the front door.

The assistant DA also said the gun was touching the youth's face when he was shot.

"His [Archer's] biggest problem was that it was a contact wound," she said.

Archer is adamant that the gun was three or four feet from the youth's face when he fired.

Archer got a lawyer who took the case for expenses but no fee. To Archer, it appeared obvious that the lawyer didn't want to take the case to trial. He pressured Archer to plead guilty to involuntary manslaughter. Archer tried to get another lawyer, but the man wanted $15,000 to go to trial. Archer said he never found out whether he was indicted or no-billed by the grand jury. Court records show he waived indictment and pleaded no contest. Archer said he was told if he didn't strike a plea bargain, he would be charged with murder. Under this threat, Archer pleaded guilty to involuntary manslaughter and received ten years probation.

"It's a sad story," says Cuellar. "He paid lawyers, his insurance went up, he lost his ability to own a gun in the future, he lost his job, and he was right—but he's alive."

Three years after the shooting, and after having threatened to kill Archer, the dead man's brother was released from a mental institution in another state.

Archer's case shows that for the law-abiding citizen who takes up arms, events have a way of getting out of hand. Archer had no intention of shooting the man. He just wanted to get control of the situation. But he was surprised into shooting when the scenario he was expecting changed abruptly. Once the legal system grinds into gear, the average person has no control of the outcome.

Archer realized these things almost immediately. When his wife asked him what had happened, he replied, "I think I just ruined my life."

"You start shooting, even if you're right, it's very difficult—and this guy's right," says Cuellar.

Investigators, prosecutors, and even your own defense lawyer all have their own agendas. The prosecutor is going to be pressured by the relatives of the person you shot to charge you with murder. They may go to the news media with their side of the story, which will increase the pressure on the DA's office. The DA is susceptible to such pressures, particularly before an election. Archer feels that his case suffered from bad timing. The police officers accused of beating Rodney King were acquitted about the same time as Archer's shooting, and Los Angeles was aflame with riots. A local television news report even linked Archer's shooting with the Los Angeles riots, Archer says.

There are pressures on defense lawyers also that work against a defendant. Any lawyer who takes a case pro bono, for no fee, is going to want to dispose of it as quickly as possible, so he can continue earning a living from clients who pay. The lawyer also has to work within the system. He has to deal with your prosecutor and judge when your case is but a distant memory. Of course, these factors may make no difference, but you can never be sure. In the legal system, as in other areas of life, you tend to get what you pay for. Anybody who trusts the legal system to dispense justice is as foolish as the person who believes that the police will protect him or her from crime.

For an investigator who just arrives on the scene of a shooting, you are the suspect, particularly if the other guy isn't alive to be questioned. This is true, as in Archer's case, even if the shooter is another police officer. The investigator's job is to get as much information as possible from the suspect—you—before you have had time to think of the consequences of being totally honest.

The investigator will take advantage of your urge to get it off your chest—to justify what you did. He may sympathize with you, saying that anyone would have done what you did. But he will write the statement, and all the time he will be trying to fit you into one of several little boxes with labels like MURDER, MANSLAUGHTER, or JUSTIFIABLE HOMICIDE. He knows each of the elements the prosecutor would need to prove to put you into each of the boxes, and you don't. He will subtly try to discourage you from calling your lawyer, because he knows that a lawyer will shut you up.

Archer said he didn't have his reading glasses when asked to read and sign the statement, so they gave him a magnifying glass. It wasn't the same as being able to read it properly. He also complained that the detective did not put everything he said into the statement, and he had to request that something he had said be added.

Many years ago, when I was a teenager in England, I was involved in a motorcycle accident. I was riding to work in heavy fog when another motorcycle appeared suddenly out of the mist. We collided at an intersection. Neither of us was hurt badly, although the other guy's motorbike was a wreck. When the policeman was filling in the accident report, he said: "The cause of the accident was the fog, right?"

I had been brought up to believe that an accident was always somebody's fault, and I had obviously been going too fast for the conditions. The policeman posed the question three times before I got the message. He was trying to assist me by putting the blame on the conditions. He knew what the right answers were to keep me out of trouble, and I didn't.

One of the legal requirements for the use of deadly force is that you be in fear of losing your life or of being seriously injured. This was not spelled out in Archer's statement, and Cuellar says that was one of the things that went against him when the case reached the District Attorney's office. You cannot rely on a helpful detective prompting you with: "You were in fear of your life, weren't you?" or some such leading question.

Archer said that before he testified in front of the grand jury, his lawyer prompted him to say that he was "scared to death." He ignored the advice. He explained it this way: "What is the first thing you have to do to go into a combat zone? You've got to overcome your fear. And that's taught on billboards, on posters, on every infantry training base that there is in the military. You overcome your fear. And you do that by building confidence in your ability to use these weapons, to be better at your skill than them."

For thirty years he had been a combat soldier, and "overcome your fear" had been part of his creed. He wasn't about to admit that he was afraid to anyone.

Bill McLennan, former chief firearms instructor for the San Antonio Police Department, advises politely declining to make any statement before getting a lawyer on the scene.

"I'd tell the police when they show up that I really don't want to make any statement until I've had an opportunity to talk to my lawyer," McLennan says.

Most police officers, who know how the system works, will give you the same advice. Talk to your lawyer before you give the police a statement.

McLennan recommends talking over your self-defense tactics with your lawyer before you get involved in any shootings. Memorize his home and office phone numbers so you can call him from jail if necessary. Call your lawyer when you call the police—immediately after a shooting.

"Tell the police there's been a shooting and nothing more," McLennan says. "Tell your lawyer exactly what happened and follow his advice to the letter."

When Gordon Hale shot Kenny Tavai in self defense on Mockingbird Lane in Dallas, police arrested him. He gave them a detailed statement explaining what had happened, then they booked him for murder. He went to jail and had his mugshot and fingerprints taken, just like a common criminal. He appeared in front of a magistrate who set his bond at $25,000. He had to pay a bondsman $2,500, or 10 percent, to post his bond so he could get out of jail. That $2,500 is the bondsman's fee and is non-returnable.

The legal bill came to more than $9,000. Most of that went to Hale's lawyer, Vincent Perini, but about $2,000 went for expert testimony from a pathologist. In total, it cost Hale almost $12,000 to prove his innocence. A month after the shooting, a grand jury no-billed Gordon Hale.

"That's what you get for being right," Hale's father says. "M'boy, my wife, everybody in the family hates that something happened like this, that the man's dead. We regret it, we sympathize with his family, but I'm glad my son's alive."

Joe Archer was able to find a lawyer to handle his case without charging him a fee, probably because he was a police officer, but he feels he was not well represented. Gordon Hale's defense cost $12,000, and his lawyer, Vincent Perini, did an excellent job. The reality is that if you shoot someone in self defense and you are justified, you may well be arrested, and your case will go before a grand jury. You will need a lawyer and you may need some expert witnesses. Even if you are exonerated by a grand jury, you may be sued by your assailant or his family. Then you will need a civil lawyer and more money.

The jurisdiction where the shooting happens may have a lot to do with how you are treated. Geographically, the South and West are much more accepting of guns and shooting than are the Midwest and Northeast. You are also much more likely to find a sympathetic jury for a self-defense shooting in a rural community than you are in a big city.

Racism can also work against you. Bernhard Goetz became something of a hero to many New Yorkers when he shot four black youths on a subway train in December 1984. He said they were trying to rob him. He was acquitted of attempted murder by a mostly white jury in a subsequent trial, though he was convicted of illegally possessing a gun. In April 1996, a civil jury of four blacks and two Hispanics awarded Darrell Cabey, who was paralyzed by one of Goetz's bullets, $43 million in damages. Cabey's lawyer fought successfully to have the trial moved to the Bronx, where a jury would be composed of minorities.

Politics may also play a part in your treatment. If you shoot the mayor's criminally-inclined son, you will almost certainly be arrested, no matter how justified you were.

The attitude of the police chief or district attorney toward the concealed-carry law may also affect your treatment. Dallas Police Chief Ben Click lobbied against allowing citizens to carry concealed handguns before the bill was passed. When it became obvious the bill was going to pass, Click ceased speaking out against it, says his spokesman Sergeant Jim Chandler.

"At that time he was no longer in any type of opposition to the bill, although his position remained: more guns on the street is not the answer to crime. That has been his position all along and continues to be his position," Chandler said.

Gordon Hale's father believes his son was arrested because of Click's opposition to the law.

"I think Ben Click was against it, and he had probably instructed his officers, 'if you catch someone, let's make an example,'" Hale's father says.

Chandler denies this. "That is totally incorrect. There was no instruction like that given. The case was handled the way it was because the detectives strongly felt . . . like the use of deadly force in that case was more than was legally justified. And it didn't matter that that man could legally carry that gun," Chandler says.

It seems extremely unlikely that the police chief of a major city would give such instructions to his officers. However, knowing how a police chief feels about the law may have some influence on the officers' actions when deciding whether to arrest a self-defense shooter or to let him remain free pending a grand jury verdict.

His lawyer believes Hale had two strikes against him from the start: the shooting occurred as a result of a minor traffic dispute; and the man he shot was unarmed—that is, he had no weapon.

The people who were against the concealed-carry law had argued that every minor traffic accident would lead to a shooting, and here was an opportunity to crow that they had been right all along.

"It pushed all the buttons," says lawyer Perini.

Typical was the reaction of the *Dallas Morning News*, which attacked Hale's actions and misstated the law regarding the use of deadly force.

"The big problem we had early on in the case was that the spin the police and the *Dallas Morning News* put on this was that it was just somebody attacking with his bare fists and how dare he wield his gun under those circumstances. That's what outraged me," Perini says.

The *Dallas Morning News* said that deadly force can only be used when a person "feels he is in imminent danger of being killed."

This is not true. In Texas and most other states, you can use deadly force to protect yourself from serious bodily injury. You don't have to sit there and be beaten up, because fists can inflict serious bodily injury.

"Movies and television trivialize the danger from fists," Perini says. "You can be very seriously injured by fists, and the movies make it look like you can be just pounded and pounded and pounded and then dust yourself off and go about your business. Most people who receive really good licks to the face have something to show for it. You lose teeth, you get a broken jaw, you crush your cheek bones, and you injure your eyes."

As a result of the beating Kenny Tavai inflicted on him, Gordon Hale has suffered some blurred vision and needs to wear glasses to do his work—something he never did before.

"In a Texas criminal case, that would qualify as serious bodily injury. Now the law doesn't require that you suffer serious bodily injury before you're entitled to shoot: you're entitled to shoot to prevent it. What he was really doing was he shot to prevent further bodily injury," Perini says.

While the Dallas police and the local media assumed that Hale used excessive force, probably because his attacker was not armed, a grand jury decided that what Hale did was reasonable under the circumstances. Hale resorted to his gun once Tavai grabbed his shirt and started pounding his head and face. He was trapped in his pickup which was stuck in traffic. Hale had two options: allow himself to be beaten senseless or even killed by the younger, stronger man, or use his gun. Could he have used the gun to threaten Tavai into backing off? Unlikely, and he ran the risk of Tavai taking the gun away from him and shooting him with it. Could Hale have avoided the attack by being less confrontational during his argument with Tavai? It is possible, but a man can hardly be faulted for insisting on calling the police.

Get a copy of the laws affecting the use of deadly force in your state and become thoroughly familiar with them. In many of the states that have recently passed concealed-carry legislation, you are required to learn about those laws as part of a mandatory training program. State laws vary on this. In some states, you are required to retreat to the extent of leaving your house before using deadly force, if this is possible. In many states you have a right to protect your property by using deadly force under some circumstances. Most instructors caution against this even if it's legal. Ask yourself: is it worth killing somebody over a television set?

My advice is to use deadly force only to protect yourself, a loved one, or a very close friend from the imminent threat of serious bodily injury or death.

Don't get involved in third-party disputes. If you see a shabbily-dressed man with long hair running from a bank with a gun in his hand, he might be a bank robber, but he might also be an undercover cop chasing a bank robber. Get a good description of him, note his direction of flight, and call police. Avoid domestic disputes. If you come across a man beating a woman, you are in a tricky situation. If you interfere, both of them may turn on you. He may accuse you of threatening him, particularly if you pull a gun on him. And when it comes to court, she'll almost certainly back him up. He's the only husband she has, and who'll feed the children if he goes to jail and can't work? On the other hand, if you ignore it and he kills or maims her, you'll feel bad.

If you are forced to shoot in self defense, don't make any threats or statements that you wouldn't want a jury to hear later. There may be witnesses that you can't see, but who can hear you. And, as the officers involved in the beating of Rodney King found out, there are a lot of video cameras out there.

"I'm gonna blow yore ass away, scumbag," or "Go ahead, make my day, punk," are not the sort of statements that make it look as though you were doing everything you could to avoid taking another person's life. Leave the heavy dialogue to Clint Eastwood or Bruce Willis. "Stop!" "Drop that gun, now!" or "Don't do it!" are much more acceptable to a grand jury.

After the shooting stops and he's lying on the ground leaking blood out of the holes you put in him, don't go up to him. He may still be dangerous. Stay behind cover or out of range and call first for an ambulance. Tell the dispatcher that there has been a shooting and that someone is hurt, and give the location. Don't tell them that you've shot anyone, just that someone has been shot. Then call the police and tell them the same thing. Remember that telephone calls to police and emergency medical services are recorded. Next call your lawyer. You should have his or her phone number memorized. If the guy you have shot runs off, let him go. It's not your job to chase him down and capture him. Your job is to survive.

When the police arrive, unless you are holding your attacker at gunpoint, put the gun away. If they drive up to the scene of a shooting, they don't know who the good guys are. Tell them that you are a licensed gun carrier and show them the permit. If it was a clearly justified shooting, tell them that you were attacked and fired in self defense, advises retired detective McLennan.

"I would be polite. I wouldn't be hard ass about it, but I would tell the police that I really don't want to make any statement until I've had an opportunity to talk to my lawyer," McLennan says.

This is advice that Pete Kanakidis could have used.

Kanakidis was a quietly successful and law-abiding businessman who owned River Oaks Automotive Center in an upscale Houston neighborhood. He and his fiancee often worked late at his auto-repair shop and felt they would both benefit from being able to carry handguns legally. They took the training in the fall of 1995 and in due course received their licenses.

Late in the afternoon of May 30, 1996, Kanakidis heard Hispanic music blaring from the radio of a Suburban even before it turned into his auto-repair shop. When three men got out of the vehicle and advanced towards him yelling and cursing, he knew he was in trouble.

Two of the men who got out of the Suburban were brothers who used to work for Kanakidis at his business. The third man was their friend, Alejandro Cruz Arroyo, 26. The brothers were angry because Kanakidis had earlier threatened to call the police in a dispute over some tools and money.

Kanakidis, then 27, left the customer he was talking to and walked over to the three men hoping to calm them down. But the brothers were in no mood to be placated. They kept cursing and threatening him. One of the brothers was poking him in the chest while the other had his hands balled into fists. Kanakidis was aware that Arroyo had slipped behind him, apparently to cut off his retreat.

"I was trying to defuse the situation but it was getting worse," Kanakidis said.

While he was arguing with the men, he saw his younger brother near the office. He yelled at him to call the police and stay in the office. As Kanakidis tried to walk away from the two brothers they launched into him with their fists, he said. He was knocked to the ground and beaten by the two brothers. He said he was not sure if Arroyo took part in the initial attack.

"I don't know if it was just two of them or three of them, but I knew I was in big trouble."

Kanakidis managed to get away from his attackers, but they chased him and caught him. One of them broke his nose with an uppercut to the face. They bent him over a tire rack and beat him while one tried to choke him. Again, he broke loose and ran to his truck where he kept a .45 Colt semi-automatic. He grabbed the gun and pointed it up in the air so his assailants could see it. He didn't point it at them, he said. They backed off and walked across the street, though they did not seem particularly intimidated by the gun. Hoping that the confrontation was over, Kanakidis put the gun back in his truck then ran to the office.

"I'm constantly running back and forth, I'm hyperventilating, I can't breath out of my nose, I'm bleeding, and I'm telling them: 'Call the police, call the police.'"

He ran outside to see the three men coming back across the street. He ran to his truck, pulled out his gun, waved it in the air again, and yelled at the men to leave. Again, the men retreated across the street and Kanakidis put the gun back. He ran back to the office to find out why it was taking the police so long to arrive. When he emerged, he saw Arroyo back on his property, walking between the tire rack and a small white car. When Arroyo spotted Kanakidis, he changed direction and got into the Suburban.

The repair-shop owner hastened over to his pickup to get his gun, but changed his mind, thinking that perhaps Arroyo was going to drive off peacefully. Kanakidis walked out to the street hoping to see the police arriving. He saw no patrol cars or flashing lights so he walked back into the shop's parking lot. Arroyo was eyeing him in the rear-view mirror of the Suburban and appeared to be fumbling between the seats.

"I'm thinking to myself, this guy's going for a gun. That's when I really, really got scared," Kanakidis said.

He ran back to his truck and grabbed his Colt. Kanakidis felt he had to get Arroyo to leave before he or one of his customers got shot. He came up behind the Suburban, yelling all the time that he had called the police and for Arroyo to leave. He made eye contact with Arroyo in the rear-view mirror. He heard Arroyo gun the engine then he heard the thunk as the driver slammed the vehicle into reverse.

"I didn't take it that he was trying to leave. I took it that he was trying to run me over," Kanakidis recalled.

He ran back a few steps, then stopped. When he turned around he found the driver's door of the Suburban right beside him. He continued to yell at Arroyo to leave but the driver started to open the door as if to get out. Kanakidis slammed the door. Arroyo tried to grab him or punch him through the window. Arroyo made a sudden movement downwards with his right arm.

"I couldn't see his right hand from where I was standing. I felt that he was pulling a gun out," Kanakidis said. "I felt that my life was in danger."

Kanakidis instinctively raised his gun and fired.

The round-nosed jacketed bullet hit Arroyo in the mouth. It was a fatal wound.

Arroyo had no gun but police did find a sawed-off baseball bat under the front seat.

Shortly afterwards, the paramedics arrived and cleaned up Kanakidis' face. Then the first police officer showed up. The auto-shop owner was understandably upset and blamed the police for not arriving in time to prevent the shooting. He said the officer ambled casually over to him with his hands in his pockets and asked what was going on.

Kanakidis jumped to his feet and angrily retorted: "What do you mean, what's going on? Look around. None of this would have happened if you guys would've showed up earlier."

It was a mistake.

The officer became angry and shouted questions aggressively at Kanakidis.

"I was scared. He was yelling at me," the repair-shop owner said. "I didn't feel it was beneficial to me to say anything at the time because of the way he was acting. I didn't feel he was on my side."

Kanakidis declined to answer any further questions. He was taken to a local hospital and treated for injuries he suffered during the beating. When he was released from the hospital, police charged him with murder.

Kanakidis hired Mike Hinton, a prominent defense lawyer and former prosecutor, to defend him. Hinton says his client was charged with murder because the antagonistic attitude of the first police officer spilled over to the other investigators.

"It never should have happened this way. He never should have been charged," Hinton says.

Kanakidis had tried repeatedly to stop the confrontation from escalating, just as he had been taught in the training course for his concealed-handgun license, his lawyer says.

Several months later, he was indicted by a grand jury. Hinton would not let Kanakidis testify before the grand jury, he says, because the prosecutor would not let him see the offense report outlining the allegations against his client.

More than a year later, in August 1997, the case went to trial. Hinton said that he and the District Attorney agreed that Kanakidis's concealed-handgun license was irrelevant to the case, as the shooting took place on his own property.

Assistant District Attorney Sally Ring, who prosecuted the case, said there was no evidence that Arroyo had been one of Kanakidis's assailants.

"There was no evidence that the deceased ever laid a hand on Mr. Kanakidis," she said.

Ring said it appeared that when Arroyo backed up in the Suburban he was trying to get away rather than back over the auto-shop owner.

"I think he [Kanakidis] should have been convicted of murder, and I wouldn't have prosecuted the case if I didn't feel that way," she said. "If I thought it was genuinely self defense, it would not have been prosecuted."

A jury of seven men and five women deliberated about four hours before finding Kanakidis not guilty.

"Thank God the jury system worked and he was acquitted," Hinton says.

But the ordeal cost Kanakidis dearly—financially and emotionally. Before the incident, he had been planning to get married. He had to postpone the wedding until after the trial. His legal bills exceeded $75,000 and he had to pass ownership of his business over to his future father-in-law. And then there was the act of taking a life.

"It's something I think about a lot. It's not a good feeling to know that you've killed a man. It's something I have to live with for the rest of my life."

After the shooting, Kanakidis was so distraught he didn't even want to own a gun and decided not to renew his concealed-handgun license, but he has since changed his mind.

"That gun actually saved me. I think I am going to keep my license," he said.

The case of Pete Kanakidis illustrates how expensive it can be, even if you are justified in pulling the trigger. If the shooting is not a really clear-cut case of self defense, you can face more legal fees in a civil case.

The police will certainly take your gun as evidence and they may handcuff you and take you to jail, as they did with Gordon Hale and Kanakidis. The auto-shop owner spent nearly twenty-four hours in a jail cell with thirty other prisoners, he said.

When firearms instructor Greg Ferris is teaching a class for concealed-carry licensing in Texas, he keeps a plaque at the front of the classroom which reads: "I WAS IN FEAR OF LOSING MY LIFE OR BEING SERIOUSLY INJURED."

In that single sentence is the justification for using deadly force. And the threat doesn't have to be real. It is your perception of the situation that counts. If someone is threatening you with an empty gun or with a realistic replica of a gun and you shoot them, you are justified, if you believed at the time you fired that your life was in danger.

# RESIDUAL ADRENALINE AND PSYCHOLOGICAL AFTER-EFFECTS

When Police Officer Shayne Katzfey fired the shot that killed the man who was diving for his gun, he was shooting in self defense. The dead man had powder burns on the inside of his forearms which corroborated Katzfey's statement that the man's hands were reaching for the officer's revolver when he fired.

However the officer who wrote the first report classified the incident not as a self-defense shooting but as an accidental shooting. The man who was killed was not a thief or burglar but a resident in his own backyard when he came out of the gate and went for Katzfey's gun. The initial report on the shooting is a public document and was given to the news media. At a subsequent news conference, police officials said Katzfey was in shock and they were relying mostly on what his partner told them about the incident. But the other officer was behind Katzfey and couldn't see the man lunge for the gun. The police officials told the media that the shooting appeared accidental and referred to the dead man as "totally innocent."

The impression that the shooting was an accident was never publicly corrected. Consequently the media reported and reinforced the impression that Katzfey had screwed up.

"Everybody in the city is reading and hearing and watching and seeing that I made a mistake," he says. For months afterward, Katzfey was racked with self-doubt. He didn't find vindication until three years later, when a federal jury exonerated him by rejecting a claim for damages by the dead man's relatives.

Massad Ayoob of Lethal Force Institute has made part of his living for many years studying and reporting on gunfights. He includes education about post-shooting trauma as part of many of his self-defense courses. He says post-shooting trauma is caused at least in part by the way society views and deals with people who have killed others. Some people appear to believe that it's wrong to survive by killing another person. Mostly, these are people who have never had their lives threatened by an armed criminal. There is a lot of truth to the old saying that the difference between a liberal and a conservative is one mugging.

Clint Smith of Thunder Ranch says one thing he can never predict for students is what form the threat will take. Most police officers and probably civilians who carry guns fanta-size at some time or other about winning a gunfight. Invariably the person indulging in the fantasy imagines that the antag-onist is an armed adult with a criminal record who probably shoots first.

When the man you have just killed was unarmed, the clearly-justified fantasy goes out the window and self-doubt creeps in. To some extent, how clearly justified your shooting appeared to be to you and, just as importantly, to others will affect how you react to it.

"If you are surrounded by positive information, positive feedback from your shooting; if it's cut and dried, you didn't have a choice, there was no two ways about it, and everybody on God's green earth understands that, then you are not as likely to have as many of those lingering effects," Katzfey says.

Immediately after Katzfey's shooting, his thoughts swung wildly between being thankful that the man didn't get his gun to oh-my-God-I've-just-killed-another-human-being.

"It's like standing in the surf and the waves of emotion are just washing over you, and you don't know how to feel, and you can't control them," he says.

This emotional surf ride owes much to the adrenaline that was triggered by the need to survive. Katzfey was overdosing on adrenaline and its accompanying hormone ACTH that was still surging through his system. When you are taken to the police station to make a statement about what happened, you will probably be offered coffee or perhaps a cola. The last thing your body needs at such a time is caffeine on top of ACTH, warns Katzfey. What you need is lots of water, followed by hard exercise such as running, bicycling, or beating the stress out of your system on a punching bag in the gym, he says.

Aikido instructor David Ham was astonished at his behav-ior as he coped with the after effects of adrenaline. He says he was calm and felt no fear during the incident when he gave a thumbs up sign to the teenage gangbanger who had the drop on him with a sawed-off shotgun.

After the youths drove off, Ham made a detour to the police station to report the incident. Consequently, he arrived home later than anticipated. His wife, Lisa, chided him for being late and told him one of his aikido students had phoned to ask where "the heck" he was.

"I blew up, and I blew up like I've never blown up before in my life," Ham says. "I said something to the tune of: 'Well, blank him, and I really don't want to hear this right now.'

"She was stunned to say the least, by the intensity of the response, much less the language that was involved, so she tried to figure what the problem was.

"She said: 'Gosh, you seem to be…'

"I said, 'Just don't talk to me right now. I don't want to talk to you. I don't want to hear about it. I'm telling you right now, this is not the time. Don't you blankety-blank talk to me.'

"Her mouth dropped open, and I kept coming. I walked down the stairs into the living room, got in her face, and said: 'I'm telling you right now, don't blankety-blank talk to blankety-blank me.'"

He turned around and walked out of the room. Ham went to the bathroom and noticed his hands were shaking. He ran around the block and got himself under control. He returned to the house, apologized, and told Lisa what had happened.

"She immediately understood. She said, 'I thought you were having a mental breakdown,'" Ham recalls.

He says his outburst was totally out of character. Unknown to him at the time, he was dealing with the after-effects of the adrenaline rush caused by his brush with death.

Counseling psychologist Jean Souza says it can take months or even years for adrenaline and ACTH to dissipate out of your system. Meanwhile, you will experience symptoms such as irritability, restlessness, and uneasiness. You may have trouble getting to sleep and experience body jerking, teeth grinding, and nightmares when you do. You may have bouts of self-doubt, depression, crying, and headaches. These symptoms can lead to over dependence on alcohol or prescription drugs or to digestive problems, and can even result in marriage breakup and job changes.

Katzfey coped with the after-effect of his shooting incident by learning all he could about post-shooting trauma. He and Souza helped form San Antonio's Police Officer Support Team, a group of officers who have been involved in shooting incidents and who help other officers through the aftermath. Unfortunately, there are no such groups for civilians.

It wasn't until he went on a training course in Palm Springs about six months after the shooting that he realized other people suffered from the same problems. A doctor explained in layman's terms what Katzfey had been going through.

"I've never talked to this man, I don't know who he is, but the guy's inside my head. Because everything he's talking about I know about, because I've been going through it. I couldn't imagine that somebody could have that detailed an amount of knowledge about just how I had been feeling," Katzfey says.

Fortunately there are things you can do to help counteract the ACTH in your system. Souza recommends percussive exercise for at least twenty minutes a day. This includes running, fast walking, punching bag, weight lifting, racquet ball, and martial arts. Moving the major muscles produces endorphins which counteract the effects of ACTH.

She also suggests taking psyllium, a water-soluble natural fiber that absorbs and carries cholesterol and ACTH out of the system. Psyllium can be bought over the counter in health food stores and pharmacies in brand names such as Metamucil, Fiberall, Konsyl-D, and Serutan.

"It is not a laxative designed for the elderly, and it is not even remotely related to Geritol," Souza says.

She recommends a maintenance dose of three to six grams of psyllium a day, depending upon the stressfulness of your job. Up to nine grams a day is appropriate after a shooting or similar high-stress incident. Coupled with psyllium, you need to drink between two and four quarts of water a day, Souza says. Alcohol, coffee, and sodas are no substitute for water, as they dehydrate the system and so require more water to counteract.

While the last thing you want to do is shoot someone, if you have to, knowing what to expect afterward will help you weather it. As Clint Smith says, "If you pull a pistol out and shoot, your trouble just begins, it doesn't end."

# Chapter Eleven

## *PRACTICE: YOUR LIFE DEPENDS ON IT*

Ted Bonnet stood with his hands on the cash register. Suddenly he whipped out a battered .45 1911 Government Model semi-automatic and ripped off two shots at each of the two figures on the other side of the counter.

Without a pause, he sprinted for the doorway of the store, reloading as he ran. He fired two quick shots at the figure hiding behind a car, parked beside the gas pumps about thirty yards away, and a couple more shots at two heads, showing above the pumps.

Bonnet carefully squeezed off two shots, hitting another figure behind the car, almost obscured by the hostage he was holding . . . .

No, this was not a gas-station holdup, though it was set up to simulate one. It was "Walt's Garage," a stage of fire in the fifteenth annual U.S. Practical Shooting Association's (USPSA) National Pistol Championships.

Bonnet, a pilot from San Antonio, won the Limited Gun category.

USPSA is the national body of the International Practical Shooting Confederation, generally known by its initials, IPSC, and pronounced "ipsick." This type of competition, whether at a local or national level, provides excellent practice at shooting fast and accurately under pressure. Several of the top self-defense instructors, such as Jeff Cooper, Ray Chapman, and Massad Ayoob, have been IPSC shooters.

When Cooper and others created IPSC in 1976, the intention was to provide competition that would enhance self-defense skills. In the subsequent couple of decades, IPSC has become an international sport with professional competitors who have developed a minor arms race around winning. In the early days, competitors used fairly standard .45-caliber Colt 1911 Government Models with a few minor modifications. Now, the top competitors shoot optical-sighted, compensated race guns with double-column magazines. They cost several thousand dollars and are about as concealable as backhoes. In reaction to the expense and impracticality of these guns, a Limited Class has been established in which competitors use standard pistols with only a few modifications allowed.

While IPSC competition is good practice in many ways, its stages are nothing like the sort of gun battle a civilian gun carrier is likely to encounter. For safety reasons, IPSC shooters run sideways or forward from one shooting box to the next. They don't shoot while backing up. They tend to reload while sprinting from one firing position to the next, dropping partially filled magazines along the way. They are running against the clock. Most of the shooting is done at ranges between ten and fifty yards. Real-life gunfights most often occur between three and twenty feet. Competition shooters may run through thirty rounds at more than a dozen targets, a highly unlikely occurrence in a real shootout. Even in Limited Class, high-capacity semi-automatics are most frequently used, and the gun is not concealed but worn in full view. IPSC shooters do not use cover as much as they should, and inevitably the shooting is done during bright daylight, not in the dark or half-light of reality. Before an IPSC stage of fire, you get a walk-through in which you examine the course of fire and plan your attack—your route, where you will reload, and how many shots you will need to fire at each shooting box. There are no walk-throughs in a real gunfight, although you should try to plan how you will handle a situation before the shooting starts.

Having said all that, however, IPSC shooting is fun and it teaches accuracy and confidence. Most IPSC stages are scored by dividing the score on the targets by the time it took you to complete the stage. This cranks up the pressure and encourages you to shoot as fast as you can make hits.

IPSC stages have become more complicated over the years as competitors and their equipment have become better and more sophisticated. However, one of the old standards by which to measure your performance is the El Presidente. You start with your back to three IPSC figure targets, spaced about a target's width apart, with your hands up, that is, with your wrists above your shoulders. At the start signal, you turn, draw your gun, and fire two shots at each target, reload, and fire two more shots at each target. An expert such as Ted Bonnet or Rob Leatham can complete the drill in less than five seconds with center-chest hits. The exercise is usually done at ten yards, but can be done at any distance—twelve, seven, or five yards. If your gun is concealed and you do a tactical reload it will take longer, and if you use a revolver it will take a lot longer. Always strive for center hits, no matter what the range or whether the target is torso, head, or pelvis. Keep a record of your scores and compete against yourself.

Another popular exercise is the "Bill Drill." Face a single target, draw and fire six shots, or five if your are using a five-shot revolver, trying to keep your hits in the A zone of an IPSC target. This exercise can be shot at any range from five feet to fifty yards, but you should concentrate on the closer ranges. It teaches you to handle recoil and bring your sights back onto the target after each shot. Again, record your scores and times so you can compare your ability from month to month.

NRA Action Pistol shooting is another competitive "practical" shooting style. Unlike IPSC stages, Action Pistol strings have specific time limits. Whereas no two IPSC stages will be the same, Action Pistol uses a limited number of stages that are always the same. Stages include moving targets, banks of steel plates, and shooting from behind barricades.

While both IPSC and NRA Action Pistol provide training in shooting accurately under stress, the best of the practical shooting sports for honing real-life skills is a relative new comer. The International Defensive Pistol Association (IDPA) was created by Bill Wilson, Ken Hackathorn, and several others with extensive experience in practical shooting. They believed IPSC had deviated too far from its initial concept of providing defensive-shooting practice under the stress of competition.

IDPA rules were written to make sure the guns and gear used were the type that would normally be carried by concealed-handgun license holders. Competitors are divided into four divisions according to the type of gun used. They cover practical handguns from out-of-the-box revolvers and semi-automatics to slightly improved semi-autos. Compensators and optical sights and not allowed. Magazines are limited to ten rounds and holsters have to be practical. Shooting and reloading must be done behind cover where possible and partly empty magazines may not be discarded. Any practical shooting competition, or gunfight for that matter, is a compromise between speed and accuracy. IDPA competition places more emphasis on accuracy. IPSC is more speed oriented.

Another way of improving reflexes and defensive handgun skills is with video training. I have tried two versions put out by Advanced Interactive Systems. One system uses real handguns that have been modified slightly to fire plastic bullets from compressed air cartridges and can be erected in any indoor training setting. The other requires an indoor range that allows students or customers to use their own guns with full loads.

Both systems project scenarios onto a screen about eight by ten feet, and the shooter must react to what is happening. In the live-fire system, the screen is made of self-healing latex. AIS has various programs for law-enforcement and civilian training on discs. Each program has about ten different scenarios, and each scenario has three or four options within it. The civilian version I tried was specifically oriented to the concealed-handgun license holder. The scenarios had titles like "Carjacking," "Home Burglary at Night," "Robbery at Gas Station." In one option of Carjacking, the bad guy is armed with a gun, in another, a knife. The shooter first has to decide if and when to shoot and then make sure he hits the bad guy and no one else. The scenarios are realistic and it is surprising how quickly a bad situation can develop. This type of training is both fun and educational.

I had the opportunity of watching the U.S. Customs at a quarterly weapon training session. The handgun training was split into two parts. First, there was a shoot-and-move course, designed by Special Agent Robert Butler, where agents ran from one piece of cover to another engaging figure targets or steel plates at each stop. Butler, who was the range officer, ran along with each shooter giving advice and yelling at him to go faster. The shouting was designed to fluster the shooter and to add to the stress. Butler urged the agents to shoot and reload while behind cover. This was good. In IPSC or NRA Action Pistol, lip service is paid to using cover, but this was more like real life.

The second part of the course consisted of firing strings of shots, most from a standing position, in specific time periods at various distances up to twenty-five yards. While the first shoot-and-move stage was more interesting and realistic, the second, almost sedentary, course was the one that counted. Several agents fired tight groups by taking the full time limit for each string rather than by firing as fast as they could make good hits. This is not as realistic for self-defense practice as it could be. However, any practice is better than none.

"I really can't stress enough on training," Butler says. "Shooting at different types of targets—not always the same standard target—blue or grey or black or whatever target you pick. But I would encourage them to seek cover. That is not on the [U.S. Customs] training program. If you're in a situation, move to cover first. If you're in a situation where you can't, then shoot it out and hope he misses and you don't."

*Concealed-handgun license applicant shooting the required course in Texas. It is advisable to shoot your state's qualification course at least once a year and record your scores.*

Whether or not you choose to take part in any of the so-called practical or combat shooting disciplines, you should also practice self-defense shooting with the gun you normally carry, be it a Glock Model 22 or a Smith & Wesson Centennial, in the way you normally carry it. Don't do your self-defense practice with a fifteen-shot Para-Ordnance .45 from an unconcealed hip holster if you normally carry a Walther PPK/S in a shoulder holster. You need to practice the things you don't do when you're competition shooting and what you're not good at, like shooting one-handed.

Fire at ranges from three to twenty feet. Shoot while backing up and while moving sideways to cover. Shoot while lying on your back, as though you had tripped when backing up or had been shot and had fallen. Shoot while scrambling to get up and back up further. Practice tactical and empty reloads, as well as immediate actions to clear malfunctions. Draw from concealed and practice shooting in your regular clothes, be they a business suit or jeans and a lumberjack shirt. You may find your jacket is too tight around the armpits as you thrust your arms forward into a shooting stance. Practice shooting with one hand, left and right. If you can arrange moving and bobbing targets, so much the better.

Imagine every possible situation you may be in and try to adapt your practice to it. For example, if you can get a vehicle onto your range, practice what you would do if someone tried to hijack the vehicle. Also shoot using the car as cover, preferably the engine block. Your practice should be limited only by your imagination, safe practice, and the rules of the range you are using.

Butler recommends that a civilian gun carrier should practice at least once a month for the first year and a minimum of once a quarter after that.

"I would stay with one gun, because in a stress situation you'll know how to use it," he says.

Shooting a lot of different guns and wearing them in different places may confuse you in a tight situation. "Beware the man with one gun" is an old and true saying.

Keep a record of your practice sessions—how many rounds you fired, at what range, and how well you performed. If your state has a mandatory course of fire required to obtain a concealed-carry license, it might be a good idea to shoot that course four times a year and record your scores. If you get into a shooting scrape, you may be questioned about your ability with a gun, and you will have an advantage if you can document your training. You also ought to keep a list of all the books that you have read, like this one and others in the bibliography, so you can testify: "I was taught to keep shooting until my attacker was no longer a threat, your honor. I learned that in this book, and that magazine article, and this course at that shooting school."

In addition to targets and target stands, shooting glasses, and ear protection, a timer is a useful piece of gear for practice. A timer gives you a starting signal in the form of a "beep," then records the sound of each subsequent shot fired. It enables you to record how long it took after the beep for you to fire the first shot and the time between shots, as well as the timing for the whole string. Timers vary in sophistication and price from about $100 to more than $200. I have found a PACT Club Timer, one of the least expensive, to work reliably over several years. Competition Electronics, Inc., also makes a line of timers.

# DRY FIRING

Dry firing is shooting with an empty gun to develop correct shooting habits and skill. It is usually done at home between sessions at the range. You should have a particular place to perform dry firing, preferably against a bulletproof wall. Fix up some kind of aiming marks. They could be small figure targets cut from cardboard or photographs taken from magazines. Don't use pictures of political figures, such as Teddy Kennedy or Bill Clinton, whatever you think of them, because it sends the wrong message to anyone who might see them. For example, if you are forced to shoot a burglar or robber in self defense in your home, you will be playing host to a lot of police officers. Some of them may not like the idea of civilians carrying guns to protect themselves and may be looking for anything to cast you in a bad light. The last thing you want is for any of them to testify to your grand jury that: "Yes sir, he had pictures of the president on a wall along with other targets." Remember that your private space may one day be seen by investigators who may have a lot to do with how you are treated by the legal system. For the same reason, avoid incendiary bumper stickers on your car or elsewhere—the kind that say "Protected by Smith & Wesson" or "No One Ever Raped a .44 Magnum."

When you start your dry firing session, unload your gun and leave all ammunition in another room. Practice snapping the empty gun at the targets as though they were real and the gun loaded. Dry firing is better if you are using a double-action revolver or semi-automatic because you can "fire" more than one shot at a time. Dry fire is not just snapping the gun to learn trigger control and sight alignment. It's practicing drawing and reholstering without looking at the gun; it's practicing tactical reloads and empty reloads. It's all of it.

When you have finished your dry-firing session, leave the place where you practice, and reload your gun. Then put the gun away or holster it and leave it alone. Of the three rounds I have fired by accident in my life, one was when I had been practicing the draw and dry firing with a .45-caliber Smith & Wesson revolver. I finished dry firing and reloaded the gun. Then without thinking I did one more draw and . . . Bang! The 260-grain Keith bullet made a neat hole in the window pane and embedded itself in a creek bank outside. That happened in the late 1960s, but I remember it as clearly today as if it had happened last week. Casual dry firing at the television, or whatever else presents itself as you wander around the house, is an invitation to disaster. How are you going to explain to your husband or wife that hole in the photo of your mother-in-law?

# TRAINING SCHOOLS AND COURSES

The best way to get a good grounding in using a handgun for self defense is to take a course from an expert. Some of these courses are taught at static training schools like Thunder Ranch in Texas and Gunsite in Arizona. Others are taught by instructors, like John Farnum of Defense Training International and Chuck Taylor of the American Small Arms Academy, who will travel anywhere in the country to put on a course for a minimum number of students. A selection of some of the best-known schools and courses follows. It is by no means complete. There are many other excellent schools and instructors located around the country. Before putting up money for any school or course, it is well to check it out with previous customers and other experts. The best known schools are not inexpensive. They will charge up to $1,000 for a five-day course, and that does not include ammunition. Most schools require evidence that a student has no criminal record. In addition to defensive handgun instruction, most of the schools also teach other weapons such as shotgun and rifle and some give instruction in unarmed defense.

**AMERICAN SMALL ARMS ACADEMY**, P.O. Box 12111, Prescott, AZ 86304; 520-778-5623. Chuck Taylor, director.

Taylor is well known to those interested in firearms as the author hundreds of articles on weapons, tactics, and wound ballistics, as well as four books, including *The Complete Book of Combat Handgunning*. He earned the title of Four Weapons Combat Master in 1981 and has trained special-operations units and law-enforcement officers in the U.S. and abroad. Taylor was operations manager for Jeff Cooper at Gunsite at one time. More recently, he was director of instruction at Front Sight Firearms Training Institute in California. In addition to his writing, Taylor teaches courses at ranges and shooting schools around the country.

**CHAPMAN ACADEMY OF PRACTICAL SHOOTING,** 3450 Academy Road, Hallsville, MO 65255; 573-696-5544. Ray Chapman, president; John Skaggs, director.

Chapman has been involved in practical pistol training and competition since the 1950s, when he, Jeff Cooper, and three others used to compete at Big Bear, California. Chapman won the first World Practical Pistol championship in 1975, as well as more than 250 other practical-shooting competitions. He established the Chapman Academy in 1979. While Chapman is still president of the school, he is no longer involved in the day-to-day running of it. He does still teach some courses. The school offers three-day weekend courses in addition to its five-day introductory and advanced defensive pistol courses.

**DEFENSE TRAINING INTERNATIONAL, INC.,** P.O. Box 917, LaPorte, CO 80535; 970-482-2520. John Farnam, president.

Farnam has a military and law-enforcement background. He has been holding classes around the country from Florida to California, New Hampshire to Washington for more than twenty years. In June 1996, he received the Tactical Advocate of the Year award from the National Tactical Association.

DTI offers two-day, weekend courses on defensive use of a handgun. Curriculum includes threat evaluation, lethal-threat management, low-light shooting, holding suspects at gunpoint, and performing under stress.

**FIREARMS ACADEMY OF SEATTLE, INC.,** P.O. Box 400, Onalaska, WA 98570; 360-978-6100; web site: http://landru.i-link.net/fasinc/FAS.htm. Marty Hayes, director; Gila Hayes, staff instructor.

The Firearms Academy of Seattle is owned and operated by the husband-and-wife team of Marty and Gila Hayes. Both have solid backgrounds in firearms training. In addition to running his own show, Marty Hayes is a staff instructor for Lethal Force Institute and an adjunct instructor for Defense Training International. He is also a police officer and firearms instructor for his department. Gila Hayes is one of the few nationally known women instructors in self defense. She has learned from some of the best instructors in the country, including Massad Ayoob, Clint Smith, Chuck Taylor, Jim Cirillo, and Louis Awerbuck. She is field editor for *Women & Guns* and writes for other gun magazines.

The school occupies forty acres and includes six tactical ranges. Training courses go from the basic Civilian Firearms Responsibility Course to the advanced Dynamic Handgun Skills. Most of the courses last eighteen hours over two days.

**GUNSITE ACADEMY, INC.,** 2900 West Gunsite Road, Paulden, AZ 86334; 520-636-4565; web site: http://www. gunsite.net. Owen Buz Mills, owner.

Gunsite is the original home of the American Pistol Institute which was founded by Jeff Cooper in 1977. Cooper sold the operation in 1992 to Richard Jee, who operated it until 1999 when it was bought by Mills. Cooper himself has retired from regular teaching. The school is located on a thousand acres of rolling juniper hills north of Prescott and contains ten pistol ranges. It offers several defensive handgun courses for students of different levels of expertise. Gunsite also provides some of its classes at other locations around the country.

**LETHAL FORCE INSTITUTE**, P.O. Box 122, Concord, NH 03301; 603-224-6814; web site http://www.ayoob.com. Massad Ayoob, director.

Ayoob is a world-renowned firearms and self-defense journalist, author, and trainer. A most popular series of articles has been his "Ayoob Files" in *American Handgunner* magazine. In each edition, he relates and analyzes a shooting incident for the lessons it teaches. In addition to writing and teaching, Ayoob has appeared in numerous trials as an expert witness on self defense. He founded LFI in 1981.

LFI offers many courses in armed and unarmed self defense to civilians as well as law-enforcement officers. LFI-I: Judicious Use of Deadly Force is a forty-hour course that teaches students home- and street-defense tactics, psychological preparation for violent encounters, and justifying your actions in court, as well as combat shooting. An LFI-I course is also available for women only. LFI courses are taught at the home range in New Hampshire and at other ranges around the country and even abroad.

**PEREGRINE CORPORATION**, P.O. Box 170, Bowers, PA 19511; 610-682-7147; email: pergrin@talon.net. Emanuel Kapelsohn, director.

Kapelsohn is certified as a firearms instructor by the FBI, NRA, and Heckler & Koch. He was a staff instructor for Jeff Cooper at Gunsite. He is a vice president of the International Association of Law Enforcement Firearms Instructors and a charter member of the American Society of Law Enforcement Trainers. He has trained and certified firearms instructors and armorers for major police departments nationwide. He is a prolific writer in the firearms field, a practicing trial lawyer, and an expert witness in court cases involving firearms and the use of force.

Kapelsohn teaches the use of handguns and other weapons for self defense to qualified civilians as well as law-enforcement personnel. His courses range from basic to advanced, are taught on location, and are geared to the specific needs of his clients.

**THE SMITH & WESSON ACADEMY**, 2100 Roosevelt Avenue, Springfield, MA 01104; 413-781-8300, ext. 265 or 255; web site http://www.smith-wesson.com/academy/index.html. Bert DuVernay, director.

The academy was founded in 1969 to train law-enforcement officers. It was opened to civilians in 1994 with a wide range of programs covering basic firearms' safety through advanced training. A $2.7-million expansion project was completed in 1997. The academy provides several half-day and one-day basic handgun courses. Two three-day courses are offered for beginners up to intermediate skill level: Dynamics of Personal Protection and Concealed Carry Handgun. Dynamics covers handgun defense at home, business, or on the street, while Concealed Carry concentrates more on defense away from the home. One or other of these courses is required before taking more advanced courses. Some courses are held for women only.

**THUNDER RANCH, INC.**, HCR 1, Box 53, Mountain Home, TX 78058; 830-640-3138; web site: http://www.thunderranchinc.com. Clint Smith, director.

Smith is a Marine Corps veteran with two infantry tours in Vietnam and a former police officer involved in firearms training and SWAT operations. He served as Jeff Cooper's operations officer at the American Pistol Institute. He founded International Training Consultants, Inc., a mobile firearms training program, which led to the development of Thunder Ranch in the Texas Hill Country.

Thunder Ranch offers three levels of Defensive Handgun courses. The courses take five days, except that a three-day version of Defensive Handgun I is also available. In addition Thunder Ranch offers a five-day Home & Vehicle Defense course. The Defensive Handgun I includes some classroom instruction but most of the time is spent on the range learning to shoot from the ground, while backing up and from cover. Students also get a session in the Terminator, a maze of rooms and passages with lurking targets.

*Instructor checking a line of shooters at Thunder Ranch.*

**YAVAPAI FIREARMS ACADEMY, LTD.**, P.O. Box 27290, Prescott Valley, AZ 86312; 520-772-8262; Louis Awerbuck, director.

Awerbuck worked for Jeff Cooper as chief rangemaster at Gunsite until 1987. He has more than twenty-five years' experience in small-arms instruction to the military, police, and civilians. He is the author of two books, *The Defensive Shotgun* and *Hit or Myth,* and has contributed articles to *SWAT* and *Soldier of Fortune* magazines. He also served in the South African Defense Force.

Yavapai does not have a home range, but Awerbuck will travel to anywhere in the country to teach classes of ten to twelve students. He offers three-day Tactical Handgun courses which encompass gunhandling, marksmanship, and tactics. Yavapai offers other courses such as Home Defense Tactics.

In addition to the nationally-known shooting schools and courses, good local instructors can provide lessons to individuals and small groups. Your local police department or shooting club may be able to put you in touch with such instructors.

Much good information about firearms and self-defense tactics can be gleaned from magazines such as *American Handgunner, Combat Handguns,* and *Handguns* as well as gun magazines of more general interest such as *American Guardian, American Rifleman, Guns, Guns & Ammo, Gun World, Shooting Times,* and *Women & Guns.*

# HANDLOADING

If you practice as much as you should, you will need to reload—not just the gun but the ammunition. With the price of store-bought practice ammo at between twenty and thirty cents a round, you need to do something to keep the cost of your range sessions down or your household budget will take on overtones of the federal deficit. Handloading can cut the cost of your practice ammo down to between three and ten cents a round, depending on caliber and whether you buy your bullets or make them. A two-hundred-round practice session with handloads should cost less than $20. This compares favorably to $40 or more for the same session with store-bought ammunition.

While Hornady, Lee, Lyman, RCBS, and other companies make good progressive reloaders, practical handgun competitors overwhelmingly favor the presses made by Dillon Precision. For example, in the 1995 U.S. Practical Shooting Association's Open National championship, all the top ten competitors used Dillon Reloaders. This is not the exception, it's the rule and has been for a number of years. For the beginning handloader, Dillon's Square Deal B is the least expensive press at about $230. According to the Dillon catalogue, the most popular and versatile of their presses is the RL 550B, which sells for about $300. I have made many thousands of rounds of ammunition of various calibers with my 550, and it has never given me any trouble. They are robust and reliable.

You will also need a powder scale to set and check the powder charges thrown by the reloading press. Any of the manufacturers of good handloading equipment make balance scales and electronic scales.

*Dillon 550B handloading press on a Strong Mount.*

I have used a Redding balance scale for several decades and found it quite adequate.

Cases get dirty from burning powder each time you fire them, so a case cleaner and polisher is almost essential. Most case cleaners work on a vibration principle, but a few rotate. Both types use a cleaning medium made of ground corn cobs or crushed walnut shells to which some polishing liquid can be added. Dillon makes a case/media separator, but I have used a colander and a plastic bucket for years.

There are many other handloading tools and gadgets, but these are the basics. Casting, sizing, and lubricating your own bullets will save you more money in the long run, but lead and jacketed bullets can be bought for a reasonable price, and buying them means you spend more time shooting than reloading. When you get into handloading, you will need at least one good reference manual. Manufacturers of handloading tools, such as Lyman and Hornady, publish excellent handloading manuals, while powder manufacturers like Accurate and Hodgdon provide guides to the uses of their products.

A round of ammunition is composed of the case or casing, powder charge, primer, and bullet. The most expensive component is the case but, unlike the other parts, the case can be used repeatedly. Always use store-bought ammunition in your gun when you are carrying it for self defense. Shooting handloads in self defense just gives the lawyer for the shootee an opportunity to make you out as some gun-crazed weirdo who was just waiting to try out your cop-killing ammunition on his poor unsuspecting client. Besides, modern manufactured ammunition is as good as it gets for self defense. Some reputable brands are mentioned in Chapter 4. You should cycle your street ammunition through your gun and replace it perhaps once a year, although it should work effectively for many years.

You have several choices in acquiring cases for reloading your practice ammo. You can buy the ammunition complete, shoot it, and then reload the empties; you can buy unprimed or primed cases in bulk; or you can scrounge empties at your local range. Don't buy the aluminum cased ammunition, because it cannot be reloaded. Powder and primers have to be bought either from your local store, at gun shows, or by mail order. You can cast your own bullets or you can buy them ready made. Lead bullets are cheaper, but tend to lead up your barrel; jacketed bullets are more expensive, don't lead your barrel, and if completely jacketed are safer. There are no minute particles of lead exhaled from your gun into the air for you to inhale.

# Care and Cleaning

With modern smokeless powders and non-corrosive primers, you don't have to clean your pistol or revolver after every trip to the range. However you may want to do it just to keep your clothes clean. If you are in the habit of tucking a five-shot revolver into your waistband, like U.S. Customs Special Agent Robert Butler does, you don't want a lot of burnt powder and oil stains on your shirt or blouse.

Butler recommends a dry cleaning method, particularly for a revolver. You need a bronze brush on the end of a cleaning rod. First, unload the gun. Push the brush through and pull it back through each chamber of the revolver's cylinder. Then clean the barrel in the same way, but make sure the end of the brush does not hit the firing pin hole. You can then use a mop or swab to wipe the powder and lead residue loosened by the bronze brush. Using another bronze brush, shaped like a toothbrush, clean all the places where there is a build-up of residue—the face of the cylinder, around the rear end of the barrel, under the star of the extractor. Wipe the loosened residue off with a rag or possibly an old toothbrush and your gun is clean. You can put a drop of oil in the action and around the yoke or crane every once in a while, and your revolver should keep firing as long as you have ammunition for it.

Break Free CLP is the best lubricating oil I have found. Never use WD 40 or any penetrating oil because it will migrate into your ammunition and affect the powder or priming compound, causing misfires. WD 40 will air harden and freeze your action as effectively as squirting Super Glue into it.

The procedure for wet cleaning is much the same, but you use a solvent like Hoppe's No. 9 on your bronze brushes, then wipe out the bore and chambers with cloth patches. Wipe off the other parts with a rag, as in dry cleaning. Some people clean their guns by dropping the fouled parts into a container of a powerful industrial solvent such as Du Pont's Prep-Sol. Keep the sights, if they have inserts or are colored, and the stocks out of this stuff.

You can follow a similar procedure in cleaning a semi-automatic. Most semi-autos should be disassembled for cleaning. Unload the gun first. Remove the slide and barrel from the frame. Wet- or dry-clean the parts, then put them back together. Clean around the lips of your magazines. When you have finished cleaning, be sure to lubricate the slide rails, around the outside end of the barrel, the locking lugs, and where the hammer and sear engage. Rack the slide a few times and wipe off the excess oil. Don't over-oil your gun or you will be wearing the oil as well as the gun.

## TIMERS
Competition Electronics, Inc., 3469 Precision Drive, Rockford, IL 61109; 815-874-8001; web site: http://www.competitionelectronics.com

PACT, Inc., P.O. Box 535025, Grand Prairie, TX 75053; 972-641-0049.

## HANDLOADING EQUIPMENT
Dillon Precision Products, Inc., 8009 East Dillon's Way, Scottsdale, AZ 85260; 800-762-3845; web site: http://www.dillonprecision.com

Hornady Manufacturing Co., P.O. Box 1848, Grand Island, NE 68802; 800-338-3220; web site: http://www.hornady.com

Lee Precision, Inc., 4275 Highway U, Hartford, WI 53027; 414-673-3075; web site: http://www.leeprecision.com

Lyman Products Corp., 475 Smith Street, Middletown, CT 06457; 800-225-9626; web site: http://www.lymanproducts.com

RCBS, Division of Blount, Inc., 605 Oro Dam Boulevard, Oroville, CA 95965; 800-533-5000.

## PRACTICAL SHOOTING ORGANIZATIONS

Action Pistol, National Rifle Association, 11250 Waples Mill Road, Fairfax, VA 22030; 800-672-3888; web site: http://www.nra.org

International Defensive Pistol Association, P.O. Box 639, Berryville, AR 72616; 870-545-3886; web site: http://idpa.com

U.S. Practical Shooting Association (affiliated with the International Practical Shooting Confederation), P.O. Box 811, Sedro Woolley, WA 98284; 360-855-2245; web site: http://www.uspsa.com

## VIDEO TRAINING

Advanced Interactive Systems, 565 Andover Park West, Suite 201, Tukwila, WA 98188; 800-441-4487; web site: http://www.ais-sim.com

## Chapter Twelve

## STATE CONCEALED-HANDGUN CARRY LAWS

As of this writing—fall 1999—more than two-and-a-half million people in thirty states have licenses to carry concealed handguns. In total, thirty-one states have what the NRA describes as "right-to-carry-concealed" laws regarding handguns. One of them, Vermont, requires no license or permit for anyone legally entitled to possess a handgun to carry it in the open or concealed. Twenty-five of the thirty states that issue licenses to anyone who qualifies keep statewide tallies of how many licenses are currently valid. Those states account for more than 2.4 million license holders. In these states, licenses have been issued to an average of 2 percent of the states' residents. Extrapolating to the other five states that keep no statewide figures, an estimated 2.7 million people in thirty states have licenses, with more being added daily. This is an increase of about three hundred thousand license holders or 12.5 percent in the last two-and-a-half years. I completed a similar survey for the first edition of this book in the spring of 1997. At that time, I estimated 2.4 million civilians had concealed-handgun licenses in the thirty "right-to-carry-concealed" states that issue licenses.

The 2.7 million or so license holders comprise only a small fraction of the seventeen million U.S. residents that criminology professor Gary Kleck estimates carry guns for self defense outside their own homes. The Florida State University professor has conducted several surveys on self-defense. In his book, *Targeting Guns: Firearms and Their Control,* Kleck estimates 8.8 percent of the population carries guns for protection on the person or in a vehicle. This is more than four times the average 2 percent that hold concealed-carry licenses in right-to-carry states. Of the people surveyed, 3.7 percent, or nationally an estimated seven million, carried on the person. The survey of about eighteen hundred people was conducted in 1993 and included states where concealed carry by civilians is illegal. Kleck concludes that issuing concealed-carry licenses does not necessarily increase the number of guns on the street by 2 percent, but in many cases just makes legal what people have been doing illegally all along.

"The big unknown is you really don't know how much carrying increases. You just know how many permit holders there are," Kleck said.

The increase in licenses or permits has mostly been in states where right-to-carry laws are relatively new. For example, in Kentucky concealed-handgun legislation went into effect October 1, 1996. In January 1997, 8,300 licenses had been issued. By September 1999, Kentucky had 52,191 licenses in circulation. Other states where concealed-weapons licenses sold like lottery tickets in approximately the same time period were: Alaska, from 5,783 to 10,567 licenses; Arkansas, from 10,800 to 23,500; Louisiana, from 800 to 11,860; North Carolina, from 21,659 to 41,063; Oklahoma, from 15,070 to 30,406; South Carolina, from 1,920 to 22,055; Texas, from 117,395 to 198,010; Utah, from 14,300 to 26,835; and Wyoming, from 3,330 to 5,714.

Another trend that has accelerated in the late 1990s is that more states are honoring licenses or permits from other states. Idaho, Indiana, Kentucky, and Michigan will honor any valid concealed-handgun license issued in any state. Wyoming will honor any license issued by another state agency and Montana, as of the fall of 1999, will recognize licenses from thirty-four other states. Many states, such as Georgia and Oklahoma, are choosier about which licenses to honor and negotiate specific reciprocity agreements. Others, like Connecticut and Nevada, honor no licenses but their own. A few states, such as Maine and New Hampshire, will issue licenses to people who live in other states.

Most of the states that have passed concealed-carry laws in the late 1980s and 1990s, such as Florida and Texas, stipulate that anybody who meets certain criteria, such as being 21 years old, sane, and having no criminal record, SHALL be issued a license. Some states, such as Alabama, give varying degrees of discretion to issuing authorities, but most law-abiding adult residents can get a license.

Florida is generally accepted to have taken the lead in passing the new wave of what have become known as "shall-issue" laws that has swept the country. Some states have had a tradition of allowing their law-abiding citizens to carry handguns for self-defense. For example, since 1961 Washington State has had a non-discretionary concealed-carry law, which stipulates that sheriffs and police chiefs "shall issue" concealed-carry licenses providing applicants qualify. However, Florida is generally accepted as starting the trend when it passed its non-discretionary statute in 1987. Other states followed. Some states, like Arizona and Kentucky, previously had an open-carry law but no provision for civilians to carry handguns concealed. Others, like Montana, had regulated the wearing of arms for decades, but permits were issued at the discretion of authorities. Yet others, such as Texas, had no previous provision for civilians to wear handguns in public at all.

The blood bath predicted by the gun-control advocates has not come to pass. Quite the contrary, licensed handgun carriers seem to be particularly law abiding. In his analysis of Texas arrest records, engineer Bill Sturdevant found that Texans 21 years and older were eight times more likely to be arrested for a violent crime than were license holders.

In states with shall-issue laws, not everyone gets a permit. The proportion of residents who go to the trouble of acquiring concealed-carry licenses varies by state. In many states with relatively new shall-issue laws, such as Arkansas and Louisiana, less than 1 percent of the population is licensed. The highest rate is almost 6 percent in South Dakota.

As Gary Kleck notes, many people undoubtedly carry guns illegally as they have always done. These people include not just habitual criminals, but otherwise law-abiding citizens, many of them women, who for a variety of reasons do not wish to go through the licensing process. Some feel that by applying for a concealed-carry license, they are admitting to the government that they own firearms. Should the government decide to confiscate weapons, as has happened in Britain, Australia and California, they will be first to be visited by police. They believe registration, of people or weapons, is the first step to confiscation. Others believe the Second Amendment in the Bill of Rights gives them the right to keep and bear arms already and that they don't need any government approval or license to carry firearms.

Cost is probably a more important factor in who gets licensed to carry concealed handguns. The charge for licenses varies by state, from South Dakota where the fee is $10 for four years to Texas where a four-year license costs $140. In addition, the cost is higher when the price of a mandatory training course is thrown in. In Texas, the mandatory training course seems to vary between $50 and $200. Judging by the South Dakota and Texas experiences, it is likely that the costs of expensive license and training programs are deterrents to carrying legally. If a husband and wife have to spend more than $500 for licenses and training programs, only the wealthy and the dedicated are going to afford it.

Suzanna Gratia Hupp, whose parents were murdered in the Killeen shooting in 1991, says the Texas concealed-handgun law is a big step in the right direction. However, she criticizes it for its cost. She says the inner city poor—mostly blacks and Hispanics—who live in the highest crime areas can't afford licenses. They are the ones who need them the most.

"I think our permitting system is discriminatory at best and racist at worst," Hupp says. "At the very least, we should get rid of the fees."

Hupp, who is a representative in the Texas Legislature, likens the cost of the license to the poll tax. For the first half of the 20th Century, Texans had to pay a poll tax for registering to vote. This effectively kept most blacks and Hispanics from voting.

"They are taxing me to be able to exercise a right, and I think that is fundamentally wrong," she says.

There is also less interest in concealed-handgun licenses where it is already legal to carry a loaded gun in your car or pickup. For example, in Louisiana a vehicle is regarded as an extension of a person's home. Many people who get licenses do not intend to wear or carry guns. They just want to carry them in their vehicles for emergencies. This is confirmed in Gary Kleck's survey of all gun carriers, legal and illegal. He found more than half carried only in their vehicles. Most of these people will see little advantage in getting a license in Louisiana. In neighboring Texas, it has never been legal to carry a loaded gun in your vehicle (unless you qualify as a "traveller"). Consequently, one Texan out of a hundred has a license, compared with one person in four hundred in Louisiana.

Texas keeps a breakdown of license holders by age, race, and gender. As of October 1, 1999, the number of license holders by age increased steadily from 237 aged 21 to 6,698 aged 52. From 53 onward, the numbers decline fairly steadily until at age 96, one person held a license. More than three-quarters— 79 percent—of license holders were age 40 or older. About one-half were in their 40s or 50s. By gender, only about 20 percent were women. By race, the majority—92 percent—was listed as white. For some reason in a state with a large Hispanic population, there is no Hispanic category. They are apparently lumped in with whites. So in Texas, the profile of a typical concealed-handgun license holder is a white or Hispanic man, aged 40 through 70—not your high-crime age group.

*A group of applicants for Texas concealed-handgun licenses going through the qualification course.*

In Florida, 84 percent of license holders are over the age of 35, but only 14 percent of those with licenses are women. Florida does not provide a breakdown by race.

Even among those who are licensed to carry, most do not pack their guns all the time. In hot climates, guns are harder to hide in skimpy clothing. Unless you are used to carrying a gun, it may make you feel awkward and embarrassed, so many people will end up keeping the gun at home or in the car.

The nineteen states that prevent most law-abiding citizens from carrying handguns for protection include those that contain our largest cities with the highest violent crime rates— New York, Chicago, and Los Angeles. They fall into two categories: those that prohibit civilians carrying guns at all and those where permits are issued at the discretion of the authorities.

Discretionary states are: California, Colorado, Delaware, Hawaii, Iowa, Maryland, Massachusetts, Michigan, Minnesota, New Jersey, New York, and Rhode Island. In these states, residents usually have to show a "need"—which apparently does not include self-protection—or they have to be politically well connected. Sometimes, those public figures who have acquired carry permits have been strong advocates of gun control or prohibition. The former publisher of the *New York Times*, Arthur Ochs Sulzberger, whose paper exhibits a strong anti-gun stance, is one. U.S. Senator Diane Feinstein of California, who has consistently supported gun-control legislation, is another.

In some discretionary states, such as California, New York, and Colorado, there is little consistency. Permits may be relatively easy to get in some counties or cities and impossible to get in others. It depends on the attitude of the local authorities. However, it appears they are much harder to acquire in the large cities. It is almost impossible for an ordinary citizen to get a concealed-handgun permit in Los Angeles, New York City, or Denver—cities where residents need them most.

States with an outright ban on civilians carrying concealed handguns are Illinois, Kansas, Missouri, Nebraska, New Mexico, Ohio, and Wisconsin.

In states with relatively new shall-issue laws, a shaking down period follows passage of the statute. For example, in Texas and many other states, employers and all private-property owners have the right to ban firearms from their premises. This affects customers and employees.

"If you can tell somebody they can't eat at your diner because they have no shoes or no shirt, then you have the right to tell them they can't come in there with a concealed weapon," says former Texas Senator Jerry Patterson, one of the authors of the Texas concealed-handgun law. "It may be a stupid policy, but private-property owners have the right to make that policy."

Before the concealed-handgun law took effect, a boom occurred in the sign-making business in Texas. Restaurants, video stores, shopping malls, city governments, and public transportation bodies rushed to erect signs prohibiting licensed gun carriers from packing protection on their premises. Most of these signs have disappeared. As customers complained, managers realized the signs were bad for business and that the concealed-carry law was not a threat to public safety.

Businesses and employers prohibiting guns on their premises are not a major problem for Texas customers. The business has to be correctly signed to have legal standing and very few are. If the business is correctly signed, you have two legal options: you can leave your gun in your car, or you can take your business elsewhere.

If, however, you are an employee, things are different. Many employers—particularly in large businesses—prohibit their workers from carrying firearms. If you are caught transgressing the ban, you can be fired. This is no help to the nurse or store clerk who works late and has to cross a darkened parking lot to get to her car. Former Senator Patterson and Texas Representative Ron Wilson acknowledge this is a problem that was not solved by the legislation.

The Texas law includes a long list of places—such as racetracks, theme parks, and bars—where carrying a handgun is specifically prohibited by the statute. While Patterson supports the right of a property or business owner to ban guns from his premises, he says the only other places where guns should not be carried legally are public schools, bars, and sporting events where alcohol is sold. Both legislators say the number of prohibited locations needs to be pared down.

Some public transit corporations have tried to prevent permit holders from traveling armed on public buses. Patterson says any rules made by a transit company are just that: rules. They have no force of law. The transit companies cannot charge people with trespass because you can only trespass on real property, not vehicles.

"When the bad guys are aware of the rule that bus riders are unarmed, what are the bad guys going to do?" Patterson asks.

"They're going to go to bus stops and start bumping off bus riders. So what we have created is a target area. Transit authorities have created a killing field for criminals."

Patterson and Wilson feel the Texas law is a good start but should be modified to shake the bugs out of it. The Texas concealed handgun law was passed in 1995 and modified by the Legislature in 1997. Some banned locations such as hospitals and racetracks were required to post signs; private property signs were required to have specific wording; driveways and parking lots were excluded from otherwise banned locations; and alterations were made in mental health requirements for license holders. Patterson said the changes were mostly improvements.

"It's better than it was when first passed. I still think there are some improvements to be made," he said.

This shakedown period is occurring in most states with relatively new shall-issue laws. Florida has amended its law more than once. The law there now requires that license applicants pass a shooting test.

David Kopel, research director of the Independence Institute and co-author of the research paper, "Shall Issue: The New Wave of Concealed Handgun Permit Laws," predicts more states will pass these laws followed by a national concealed-handgun-carry system.

"I think it's going to continue to spread until it's the law in around forty states. At which point, I think the pressure to nationalize the issue will become overwhelming," Kopel says.

Despite some recent setbacks, he foresees shall-issue laws passing in Kansas, Colorado, New Mexico, Nebraska, and Missouri in the next few years.

When the Brady Act passed Congress, mandating background checks and waiting periods for handgun purchasers, twenty-two states already had similar laws. Legislators in those states could vote for the bill knowing that it would not affect their constituents. This will work to the advantage of gun carriers when legislation for a national concealed-carry system reaches Congress, Kopel says. A majority of legislators will be able to vote for the bill knowing that it won't affect their states because they already have concealed-carry laws.

The states classified by the NRA as "right-to-carry-concealed" are listed along with some details of their laws and numbers of license holders. Since the last edition of this book, many states have developed web sites that contain concealed-carry laws and procedures. Where possible, I have included web-site addresses. Another change I made was to leave out details of licenses that have been suspended and revoked. What I wanted to show was the number of licenses suspended or revoked for criminal activity. However, these numbers were not readily available for many states, and there was little consistency in what the figures that were available represented. Some states included in their revoked licenses statistics people who moved out of state or died; other states didn't.

## NOTES:

• Almost all jurisdictions require a person with a concealed-carry license to carry it when packing the handgun and to produce it when requested by a law-enforcement officer.

• A felony is generally defined as a crime for which a person can be sentenced to more than one year in prison. A misdemeanor is a crime for which a sentence of up to a year can be given.

• Most states will not issue carry licenses to persons who have been judged guilty of the juvenile equivalent of a felony.

• Most state laws include an appeal process if a license is denied or revoked.

• Federal law prohibits the carrying of firearms in federal facilities with the exception of some military bases, where the rules are at the discretion of the base commander.

• State population figures used to calculate the percentage of a state's population with licenses are estimates by the U.S.

Bureau of the Census updated to July 1, 1998.

• While I have generally used the word "license," many states refer to their concealed-carry document as a "permit."

## WARNING:

The following information was derived principally from the government departments that issue or administer the licenses. It was current at time of writing, but has been condensed and abbreviated. The information presented here is only a general guide. Any person who wishes to carry a concealed handgun should read and understand federal law relating to ownership and possession of handguns and the state laws affecting concealed-carry licenses, as well as the circumstances in which someone is justified in using deadly or lethal force.

*As of January 2000, the NRA classified thirty-one "right-to-carry" states (shown in black) in which law-abiding residents are allowed to carry handguns.*

## CONCEALED-CARRY LICENSES BY STATE

| STATE | POPULATION (x 1,000) | LICENSES Fall 1999 | % OF POPULATION |
|---|---|---|---|
| Alabama | 4,352 | N/A | N/A |
| Alaska | 614 | 10,567 | 1.72 |
| Arizona | 4,669 | 59,500 | 1.27 |
| Arkansas | 2,538 | 23,500 | 0.92 |
| Connecticut | 3,274 | 140,000 | 4.27 |
| Florida | 14,916 | 238,609 | 1.60 |
| Georgia | 7,642 | N/A | N/A |
| Idaho | 1,229 | 30,892 | 2.51 |
| Indiana | 5,899 | 295,428 | 5.01 |
| Kentucky | 3,936 | 52,191 | 1.33 |
| Louisiana | 4,369 | 11,860 | 0.27 |
| Maine | 1,244 | N/A | N/A |
| Mississippi | 2,752 | 17,000 | 0.62 |
| Montana | 880 | 7,328 | 0.83 |
| Nevada | 1,747 | 12,720* | 0.73 |
| New Hampshire | 1,185 | N/A | N/A |
| North Carolina | 7,546 | 41,063 | 0.54 |
| North Dakota | 638 | 5,284 | 0.82 |
| Oklahoma | 3,347 | 30,406 | 0.91 |
| Oregon | 3,282 | 96,540 | 2.94 |
| Pennsylvania | 12,001 | 636,232 | 5.30 |
| South Carolina | 3,836 | 22,055 | 0.57 |
| South Dakota | 738 | 43,783 | 5.93 |
| Tennessee | 5,431 | 81,112 | 1.49 |
| Texas | 19,760 | 198,010 | 1.00 |
| Utah | 2,100 | 26,835 | 1.28 |
| Virginia | 6,791 | 91,900 | 1.35 |
| Washington | 5,689 | 234.274 | 4.12 |
| West Virginia | 1,811 | N/A | N/A |
| Wyoming | 481 | 5,714 | 1.19 |
| Total | 134,697 | 2,412,803 | |

**State populations:**
25 states that have total license numbers: **118,463,000**
30 states that have right-to-carry: **134,697,000**
5 states without total license numbers but with right-to-carry: **16,234,000**
(Population estimates for states as of July 1,1998 from Census PIO.)
**CCW licenses:**
In 25 states that keep totals: **2,412,803**
**License holders as a percentage of population:**
In 25 states that keep totals: **2.04 percent.**
Extrapolating for 30 states at 2.04 percent of population: **2.7 million licenses.**
* Estimate based on number of applications in the state and the rejection rate in Las Vegas.

## CONCEALED-CARRY RECIPROCITY BY STATE—TABLE 1

| STATE | OTHER STATE LICENSES HONORED |
|---|---|
| Alabama | None |
| Alaska | Revising list, only Texas at present |
| Arizona | Arkansas, Kentucky, Texas, Utah |
| Arkansas | Arizona, Florida, Kentucky, Oklahoma, South Carolina, Tennessee, Texas, Utah |
| Connecticut | None |
| Florida | Arkansas, Georgia, Idaho, Indiana, Kentucky, Louisiana, Michigan, Mississippi, Montana, New Hampshire, North Dakota, Tennessee, Wyoming |
| Georgia | Florida, Idaho, Indiana, Kentucky, Michigan, Montana, New Hampshire, Tennessee. |
| Idaho | All licenses |
| Indiana | All licenses |
| Kentucky | All licenses |
| Louisiana | Florida, Kentucky, Tennessee, Texas |
| Maine | None |
| Michigan | All licenses |
| Mississippi | Florida, Kentucky, Tennessee, Wyoming |
| Montana | Alaska, Arizona, Arkansas, California, Colorado, Connecticut, Florida, Georgia, Idaho, Indiana, Iowa, Kentucky, Louisiana, Maryland, Massachusetts, Michigan, Minnesota, Mississippi, Nevada, New Jersey, New York, North Carolina, North Dakota, Oklahoma, Oregon, Pennsylvania, South Carolina, Tennessee, Texas, Utah, Virginia, Washington, West Virginia, Wyoming |
| Nevada | None |
| New Hampshire | Florida, Georgia |
| North Carolina | None |
| North Dakota | Florida, New Hampshire, Wyoming |
| Oklahoma | Arkansas, Texas, Utah, Wyoming |
| Oregon | None |
| Pennsylvania | None |
| South Carolina | Arkansas, Tennessee, Utah, Wyoming |
| South Dakota | None |
| Tennessee | Arkansas, Florida, Georgia, Kentucky, Louisiana, Mississippi, South Carolina, Virginia |
| Texas | Arizona, Arkansas, Louisiana, Oklahoma |
| Utah | Alaska, Arizona, Arkansas, Hawaii, Louisiana, Nevada, North Carolina, Oklahoma, South Carolina, Tennessee, Texas |
| Vermont | No license required |
| Virginia | Tennessee |
| Washington | None |
| West Virginia | Kentucky |
| Wyoming | Alaska, Arizona, Arkansas, Connecticut, Delaware, Florida, Kentucky, Louisiana, Maryland, Mississippi, New Jersey, North Dakota, Oklahoma, Rhode Island, South Carolina, Tennessee, Texas, Utah |

## CONCEALED-CARRY RECIPROCITY BY STATE—TABLE 2

| STATE | OTHER STATES WHERE LICENSE IS HONORED |
|---|---|
| Alabama | Idaho, Indiana, Kentucky, Michigan |
| Alaska | Idaho, Indiana, Kentucky, Michigan, Montana, Utah, Wyoming |
| Arizona | Arkansas, Idaho, Indiana, Kentucky, Michigan, Montana, Texas, Utah, Wyoming |
| Arkansas | Arizona, Florida, Idaho, Indiana, Kentucky, Michigan, Montana, Oklahoma, Pennsylvania (in vehicle only), South Carolina, Tennessee, Texas, Utah, Wyoming |
| California | Idaho, Indiana, Kentucky, Michigan, Montana |
| Colorado | Idaho, Indiana, Kentucky, Michigan, Montana |
| Connecticut | Idaho, Indiana, Kentucky, Michigan, Montana, Wyoming |
| Delaware | Idaho, Indiana, Kentucky, Michigan |
| Florida | Arkansas, Georgia, Idaho, Indiana, Kentucky, Louisiana, Michigan, Mississippi, Montana, New Hampshire, North Dakota, Tennessee, Wyoming |
| Georgia | Florida, Idaho, Indiana, Kentucky, Michigan, Montana, New Hampshire, Tennessee |
| Hawaii | Idaho, Indiana, Kentucky, Michigan, Utah |
| Idaho | Florida, Georgia, Indiana, Kentucky, Michigan, Montana |
| Indiana | Florida. Georgia, Idaho, Kentucky, Michigan, Montana |
| Iowa | Idaho, Indiana, Kentucky, Michigan, Montana |
| Kentucky | Arizona, Arkansas, Florida, Georgia, Idaho, Indiana, Louisiana, Michigan, Mississippi, Montana, Tennessee, West Virginia, Wyoming |
| Louisiana | Florida, Idaho, Indiana, Kentucky, Michigan, Montana, Tennessee, Texas, Utah, Wyoming |
| Maine | Idaho, Indiana, Kentucky, Michigan, Wyoming (if state issued) |
| Maryland | Idaho, Indiana, Kentucky, Michigan, Montana, Wyoming |
| Massachusetts | Idaho, Indiana, Kentucky, Michigan, Montana |
| Michigan | Idaho, Indiana, Kentucky, Montana |
| Minnesota | Idaho, Indiana, Kentucky, Michigan, Montana |
| Mississippi | Florida, Idaho, Indiana, Kentucky, Michigan, Montana, Tennessee, Wyoming |
| Montana | Florida, Georgia, Idaho, Indiana, Kentucky, Michigan |
| Nevada | Idaho, Indiana, Kentucky, Michigan, Montana, Utah |
| New Hampshire | Florida, Georgia, Idaho, Indiana, Kentucky, Michigan, North Dakota |
| New Jersey | Idaho, Indiana, Kentucky, Michigan, Montana, Wyoming |
| New York | Idaho, Indiana, Kentucky, Michigan, Montana |
| North Carolina | Idaho, Indiana, Kentucky, Michigan, Montana, Utah |
| North Dakota | Florida, Idaho, Indiana, Kentucky, Michigan, Montana, Wyoming |
| Oklahoma | Arkansas, Idaho, Indiana, Kentucky, Michigan, Montana, Texas, Utah, Wyoming |
| Oregon | Idaho, Indiana, Kentucky, Michigan, Montana |
| Pennsylvania | Idaho, Indiana, Kentucky, Michigan, Montana |
| Rhode Island | Idaho, Indiana, Kentucky, Michigan, Wyoming |
| South Carolina | Arkansas, Idaho, Indiana, Kentucky, Michigan, Montana, Tennessee, Utah, Wyoming |
| South Dakota | Idaho, Indiana, Kentucky, Michigan |
| Tennessee | Arkansas, Florida, Georgia, Idaho, Indiana, Kentucky, Louisiana, Michigan, Mississippi, Montana, South Carolina, Utah, Virginia, Wyoming |
| Texas | Arizona, Arkansas, Idaho, Indiana, Kentucky, Louisiana, Michigan, Montana, Oklahoma, Utah, Wyoming |
| Utah | Arizona, Arkansas, Idaho, Indiana, Kentucky, Michigan, Montana, Oklahoma, South Carolina, Wyoming |
| Virginia | Idaho, Indiana, Kentucky, Michigan, Montana |
| Washington | Idaho, Indiana, Kentucky, Michigan, Montana |
| West Virginia | Idaho, Indiana, Kentucky, Michigan, Montana |
| Wyoming | Florida, Idaho, Indiana, Kentucky, Michigan, Mississippi, Montana, North Dakota, Oklahoma, South Carolina |

## FEDERAL LAW

Federal law prohibits the following people from possessing firearms, which means they cannot legally acquire state concealed-handgun licenses.
- Anyone who has been convicted of a felony.
- A fugitive from justice.
- Anyone judged by a court to be mentally defective or who has been committed to a mental institution.
- An illegal alien.
- A former U.S. citizen who has renounced his/her citizenship.
- Anyone who has been dishonorably discharged from the military.
- Anyone currently subject to a court order to prevent domestic violence or harassment.
- Anyone who has been convicted of a misdemeanor crime of domestic violence.

For further information about federal firearms laws, contact your local office of the federal Bureau of Alcohol, Tobacco and Firearms.

## ALABAMA

Concealed-carry law took effect: Alabama has regulated firearms since the 1800s and the law has been revised many times. The last major revision was in 1975.

Administered by: The sheriff of each county.

License cost and duration: Cost varies between $7.50 and $30 depending on the county and is good for one year.

Apply to: Sheriff of the county in which applicant resides. Non-residents planning to travel through Alabama may get up-to-date information from the Alabama Department of Public Safety, Public Information/ Education Unit, P.O. Box 1511, Montgomery, AL 36102-1511. Telephone: 334-242-4445. Web site: http://www.dps.state.al.us.

Applicant qualifications: Qualified or unlimited licenses to carry handgun concealed or in a vehicle issued by the county sheriff, who has discretion to determine if the applicant is a suitable person; pass background check; 19 years or older; not convicted of committing or attempting to commit a crime of violence; not a drug addict or habitual drunkard; not of unsound mind.

Training course: Not required.

Places license holders may not carry: Public demonstrations; school property.

Reciprocity: Alabama does not recognize concealed-carry licenses from other states. Alabama licenses are honored by the following states: Idaho, Indiana, Kentucky, and Michigan.

Licenses currently in use: No statewide figures available.

## ALASKA

Concealed-carry law took effect: January 1, 1995.

Administered by: Alaska Department of Public Safety.

License cost and duration: $99 for five years; renewal $25.

Apply to: Alaska Concealed Handgun Permit Program, 5700 East Tudor Road, Anchorage, AK 99507. Telephone: 907-269-0392. Web site: http://www.dps.state.ak.us/achp/

Applicant qualifications: Twenty-one years or older; eligible under state and federal law to own or possess a handgun; resident of state for at least 90 days; not convicted in the last six years of two or more Class A misdemeanors; not ordered by a court in the last three years to complete an alcohol or substance abuse program.

Training course: Twelve hours instruction in law relating to firearms, use of deadly force, safe and responsible use of a handgun, self defense; plus competency test for each action and maximum caliber licensee wishes to carry.

Places license holders may not carry: Schools, school grounds or school buses; anywhere alcohol is sold for consumption on premises except restaurants where the person carrying the firearm does not consume alcohol; licensed child-care facilities or assisted living homes for the elderly or mentally or physically disabled; court-houses, courtrooms, or offices of the Alaska Court System; within domestic violence or sexual assault shelters that receive state funding; in private residences without permission; federal facilities; the secure areas of airports; within certain National Park areas; buildings or facilities that are posted to prohibit carrying concealed handguns.

Reciprocity: Alaska has no reciprocity agreement with other states. However, it may honor licenses from some other states for visitors who have not been in Alaska for more than 120 days, provided the other state's concealed-handgun program is as stringent as that of Alaska. As of October 1999, the state was revising its list of approved states as a result of recent changes in the Alaska law. Other states that recognize Alaska licenses: Idaho, Indiana, Kentucky, Michigan, Montana, Utah, and Wyoming. For latest information, call, write, or check web site.

Licenses currently in use: 10,567 as of August 31, 1999.

License holders as a percentage of state population: 1.72.

## ARIZONA

Concealed-carry law took effect: July 18, 1994.

Administered by: Arizona Department of Public Safety.

License cost and duration: $50 for four years; renewals $50.

Apply to: Concealed Weapon Permit Unit, Arizona Department of Public Safety, P.O. Box 6488, Phoenix, AZ 85005-6488. Telephone 800-256-6280. Web site: http://www.dps.state.az.us/ccw

Applicant qualifications: U.S citizen; legal resident of the state for at least six months; 21 years or older; pass criminal-record check; not under indictment or convicted of a felony; not convicted of a misdemeanor of domestic violence; not under a court order; not a fugitive from justice; not a user of or addicted to a controlled substance; not dishonorably discharged from the military; never renounced U.S. citizenship; not mentally ill, found mentally incompetent, or committed to mental institution; completed training course.

Training course: Sixteen hours of instruction; law relating to firearms; use of deadly force; safety; weapon care and maintenance; shooting techniques; mental conditioning; judgmental shooting; written test and 10-round range test.

Places license holders may not carry: Places that sell alcohol for on premises consumption including restaurants but not hotel rooms; polling places on election day; grounds of correctional facilities; school grounds; nuclear generating stations; federal facilities; buildings including businesses and government buildings where signs are posted prohibiting weapons; private property without consent of the owner.

Reciprocity: Arizona recognizes licenses from Arkansas, Kentucky, Texas, and Utah. Arizona licenses are honored by Arkansas, Idaho, Indiana, Kentucky, Michigan, Montana, Texas, Utah, and Wyoming. For latest information, call, write, or check web site.

Licenses currently in use: 59,500 as of August 1999.

License holders as a percentage of state population: 1.27.

## ARKANSAS

Concealed-carry law took effect: July 28, 1995.

Administered by: Arkansas State Police.

License cost and duration: $139 for four years; renewals $50.

Apply to: Arkansas State Police, Regulatory Services, P.O. Box 5901, Little Rock, AR 72215. Telephone 501-618-8600. Web site: http://www.state.ar.us./asp/asp.html Click on Concealed Handgun License Information.

Applicant qualifications: Resident of the state for at least one year; 21 years or older; pass criminal-record check, no felony convictions; no mental or physical infirmity that would preclude safe handgun handling; not threatened or attempted suicide; not a chronic abuser of alcohol or drugs; not a fugitive from justice; not judged mentally incompetent or committed to a mental institution; signed oath of allegiance to United States and Arkansas constitutions; passed training course. Violent misdemeanor conviction in past five years may be grounds for denial of license. Two types of license are issued. With a restricted license, the holder may not carry a semi-automatic handgun. Any type of legal handgun may be carried with an unrestricted license.

Training course: Five hours minimum; handguns and ammunition; fundamentals; self-defense and the law; a range test.

Places license holders may not carry: Law enforcement or prison facilities; government buildings, offices, or meeting places; polling places; courthouses or courtrooms; public parks; athletic events; establishments where alcohol is sold for consumption on premises; schools or colleges; airport terminals; churches or other places of worship; posted businesses; private homes without permission; while participating in parades or demonstrations.

Reciprocity: Arkansas recognizes concealed-carry licenses from Arizona, Florida, Kentucky, Oklahoma, South Carolina, Tennessee, Texas, and Utah. Arkansas licenses are honored by Arizona, Florida, Idaho, Indiana, Kentucky, Michigan, Montana, Oklahoma, Pennsylvania (in vehicles only), South Carolina, Tennessee, Texas,

Utah, and Wyoming. For latest information, call, write, or check web site.

Licenses currently in use: about 23,500 to August 1999.

License holders as a percentage of state population: 0.92.

## CONNECTICUT

Concealed-carry law took effect: sometime prior to 1977; changes in the law in 1994 made some license holders ineligible and their licenses were revoked.

Administered by: Connecticut State Police.

License cost and duration: $35 for five years; renewals $35.

Apply to: Connecticut State Police, Special Licensing and Firearms Division, 1111 Country Club Road, P.O. Box 2794, Middletown, CT 06457. Telephone: 860-685-8294. Web site: http://www.state.ct.us/dps/special.htm. License application forms can be picked up at any police station. An applicant for a state permit must first obtain a local permit through local police department, or first selectman; once a state permit is issued, there is no requirement to keep the local permit up to date.

Applicant qualifications: First requirement is a locally issued permit. An applicant should also: be 21 years or older; a legal resident of the U.S.; pass a criminal-record check; have no felony convictions or outstanding charges; no convictions or outstanding charges for 11 misdemeanors, mostly involving violence or the threat of violence; not have been discharged in preceding 20 years after having been found not guilty of a crime by reason of mental disease or defect; not been confined in previous 12 months by court order for mental illness; not subject to a restraining or protective order as a result of use, attempted use or threatened use of physical force against another person. There should be no evidence that the applicant is an "unsuitable person" or that he/she intends to use a handgun unlawfully.

Training course: An approved course on safety and use of handguns taught a certified government or private instructor.

Places license holders may not carry: Places where "mature judgment" dictates that no handguns should be carried, such as bars or other places where alcohol is being consumed; in stressful situations such as arguments; after consuming alcohol or illegal drugs; in buildings housing the general assembly or any of its committees, or the offices of any of its members, officers, or employees; residential or commercial buildings whose owners prohibit handguns.

Reciprocity: Connecticut does not honor out-of-state concealed-carry licenses; however the state will issue licenses to residents of other states. Connecticut licenses are honored by Idaho, Indiana, Kentucky, Michigan, Montana, and Wyoming.

Licenses currently in use: about 140,000 as of August 1999.

License holders as a percentage of state population: 4.27.

## FLORIDA

Concealed-carry law took effect: October 1, 1987.

Administered by: Florida Department of State.

License cost and duration: $117 for five years.

Apply to: Florida Department of State, Division of Licensing, P.O. Box 6687, Tallahassee, FL 32314-6687. Telephone 850-488-5381. Web site: http://licgweb.dos.state.fl.us/weapons/index.html

Applicant qualifications: Resident of the U.S.; 21 years or older; pass criminal record check; never convicted of a felony unless firearms rights have been restored; not convicted of violent or drug misdemeanor within last three years; not have adjudication withheld or sentence suspended on felony or misdemeanor of domestic violence unless three years have elapsed since probation or other conditions of the court have been fulfilled; not currently under injunction restraining applicant from committing acts of domestic violence or acts of repeated violence; not a chronic abuser of drugs or alcohol; not judged mentally incompetent or committed to a mental institution in last five years; no physical infirmity that would prevent safe handgun handling; complete a firearm training course.

Training course: Various including hunter training, NRA; must include a range course.

Places license holders may not carry: Law enforcement or detention facilities; courthouses or courtrooms; polling places; meetings of government bodies or school districts; school, college, or professional athletic events; schools, colleges or educational facilities; bars or places primarily used for the sale and consumption of alcohol; airports; federal property.

Reciprocity: Florida recognizes concealed-carry licenses from Arkansas, Georgia, Idaho, Indiana, Kentucky, Louisiana, Michigan, Mississippi, Montana, New Hampshire, North Dakota (if licensee is 21 years or older), Tennessee, and Wyoming. Florida licenses are honored by Arkansas, Georgia, Idaho, Indiana, Kentucky, Louisiana, Michigan, Mississippi, Montana, New Hampshire, North Dakota, Tennessee, and Wyoming. For latest information call, write, or check web site.

Licenses currently in use: 238,609 as of August 31, 1999.

License holders as a percentage of state population: 1.60.

## GEORGIA

Concealed-carry law took effect: Current law in 1968 but became more stringently interpreted as non-discretionary in 1989.

Administered by: Local probate courts.

License cost and duration: $45 for five years; renewal $15.

Apply to: The probate court in county of residence. For out-of-state inquiries, contact: Georgia Department of Public Safety, Legal Department, P.O. Box 1456, Atlanta, GA 30371-2303. Telephone: 404-624-7423. Georgia concealed-handgun law can be found on the Internet at: http://www.ganet.org/cgi-bin/pub/ocode/ocgsearch?number=16-11-128

Applicant qualifications: Pass criminal-record check; 21 years or older; not a fugitive from justice; not having been convicted of a felony or forcible misdemeanor; not currently charged with a felony or forcible misdemeanor; no drug convictions; not hospitalized for mental or alcohol/drug treatment in last five years.

Training course: Not required.

Places license holders may not carry: Public gatherings such as athletic or sporting events; churches or church functions; political rallies or functions; publicly owned or operated buildings; establishments selling alcohol for consumption on premises; within school safety zones, at school functions or on school property. "Schools" refers to any educational facilities including universities, colleges, technical and vocational schools.

Reciprocity: Georgia honors only the concealed-carry licenses from states which recognize its licenses. At present, these are Florida, Idaho, Indiana, Kentucky, Michigan, Montana, New Hampshire, and Tennessee. As of October 1999, Georgia recognized licenses from Texas, but that may change because Texas does not honor Georgia licenses. For latest information, call, write, or check web site.

Licenses currently in use: No statewide figures are kept.

## IDAHO

Concealed-carry law took effect: Non-discretionary system adopted in 1990.

Administered by: County sheriffs.

License cost and duration: $20, plus some administrative costs (in Ada County, administrative costs are $36 for a total of $56); license lasts for four years; renewal $12 plus (in Ada County $5) administrative costs.

Apply to: Sheriff in county of residence. Idaho concealed-weapons law may be found on the Internet at http://www.state.id.us/legislat/idstat.html Click on Concealed Weapons. Ada County Sheriff's Office in Boise can answer questions for out-of-state license holders planning to visit Idaho. Contact: Ada County Sheriff's Office, Attention: Concealed Weapons, 7200 Barrister Drive, Boise, ID 83704. Telephone: 208-377-6568.

Applicant qualifications: Legal resident of the U.S.; 21 years or older, but a sheriff has discretion to issue license to an applicant between 18 and 21; eligible to possess a firearm under federal and state law; not charged with, or convicted of, a felony; not a fugitive from justice; not an unlawful user or addict of drugs; not judged lacking mental capacity, mentally ill, gravely disabled, or incapacitated; not dishonorably discharged from the military; not judged guilty of a violent misdemeanor unless three years have elapsed since disposition or pardon; not subject of a withheld judgment that would disqualify; has not renounced U.S. citizenship; not awaiting trial, appeal or sentencing for a crime that would disqualify; not the subject of a protective order.

Training course: A sheriff may require proof of familiarity with a firearm by completion of any of a wide variety of training courses or other means.

Places license holders may not carry: Courthouses; juvenile detention facilities or jails; public or private schools, or school buses. May not carry while under the influence of alcohol or drugs.

Reciprocity: Idaho honors any valid concealed-carry license issued in another state provided the license holder carries the license any time he or she is carrying a weapon. Idaho licenses are honored by Florida, Georgia, Indiana, Kentucky, Michigan, and Montana.

Licenses currently in use: 30,892 as of August 30, 1999.

License holders as a percentage of state population: 2.51.

## INDIANA

Concealed-carry law took effect: 1935.

Administered by: Superintendent of the Indiana State Police.

License cost and duration: $25 for four years.

Apply to: Chief of police or county sheriff where applicant resides; if applicant is non-resident but works in Indiana, apply to sheriff in county of employment. For non-resident inquiries, call or write to: Indiana State Police, Firearms Section, 100 North Senate Avenue, Room 302, Indianapolis, IN 46204. Telephone: 317-232-8264. Indiana concealed-handgun laws can be found on the Internet at: http://www.state.in.us/legislative/ic/code/title35/ar47/

Applicant qualifications: Of good character and reputation; 18 years or older; not convicted of a felony; not convicted for resisting law enforcement in last five years; no unresolved indictments for a Class A or B felony or a violent felony; not an alcohol or drug abuser; not prone to violence or emotionally unstable conduct.

Training course: Not required.

Places license holders may not carry: School property, school functions or school buses.

Reciprocity: Indiana recognizes concealed-handgun licenses from all other states. Indiana licenses are honored by Florida, Georgia, Idaho, Kentucky, Michigan, and Montana.

Licenses currently in use: 295,428 as of December 31, 1998.
License holders as a percentage of state population: 5.01.

## KENTUCKY

Concealed-carry law took effect: October 1, 1996.
Administered by: Kentucky State Police.
License cost and duration: $60 for three years; renewals $60.
Apply to: Local sheriff in county of residence. For information contact: Kentucky State Police, Information
Services, 1250 Louisville Road, Frankfort, KY 40601.
Telephone: 502-227-8700. Web site:
http://www.state.ky.us/agencies/ksp/ccdw/ccdw.htm
Applicant qualifications: Resident of the state for six months;
21 years or older; eligible to possess a firearm under federal
law; not been committed to a drug treatment facility or
convicted of a misdemeanor relating to illegal drugs for last
three years; not a chronic abuser of alcohol; not been
judged mentally incompetent or committed to a mental
institution unless competency has been restored for at least
three years; not convicted of misdemeanor assault in the
fourth degree or of terroristic threatening; complete
firearms training and safety course.
Training course: Any approved firearms training and safety
course that includes instruction in handgun marksmanship principles, handgun safety and cleaning, laws
relating to firearms and use of deadly force, and a range
course of twenty rounds at a silhouette target at
seven yards.
Places license holders may not carry: Police stations or sheriffs' offices; detention facilities, prisons, or jails; courthouses or courtrooms; meetings of the governing bodies
of counties, municipalities, or special districts; meetings
of the General Assembly or its committees; anywhere
alcohol is served by the drink, except for restaurants that
make more income from the sale of food; schools,

child-care facilities, day-care centers, or certified family child-care homes; secure areas of airports; churches, synagogues, or houses of worship; places where carrying firearms is prohibited by federal law. Employers, managers, and property owners have the right to prohibit the carrying of firearms on their property.

Reciprocity: Kentucky honors all valid concealed-carry licenses issued in other states. Kentucky licenses are recognized by Arizona, Arkansas, Florida, Georgia, Idaho, Indiana, Louisiana, Michigan, Mississippi, Montana, Tennessee, West Virginia, and Wyoming.

Licenses currently in use: 52,191 as of September 17, 1999.

License holders as a percentage of state population: 1.33.

## LOUISIANA

Concealed-carry law took effect: September 20, 1996.

Administered by: Louisiana Department of Public Safety and Corrections.

License cost and duration: $100 for four years, plus an additional $50 for those who have not resided in the state for at least 15 years. Renewals: $100 for four years. Senior citizens aged 65 or older pay half fees for initial license and renewals.

Apply to: Louisiana State Police, Concealed Handgun Permit Section, P.O. Box 66375, Baton Rouge, LA 70896. Telephone 225-925-4867. Web site: http://www.dps.state.la.us/lsp/chips2.html.

Applicant qualifications: Legal resident of the state for at least six months; 21 years or older; pass approved handgun safety and training course or other evidence of handgun competence such as proof of military or law enforcement academy small arms training or possession of a current local concealed-carry permit; not suffering from mental or physical infirmity that prevents safe handgun handling; pass criminal-record check; not convicted of a felony; not committed to an institution for abuse of controlled dangerous substance or guilty of or charged with a misdemeanor relating to the abuse of controlled substance in preceding five years; not a chronic abuser of alcohol; not guilty of a violent misdemeanor unless five years have elapsed since court imposed conditions fulfilled; not guilty of or charged with any crime of violence or crime punishable by one year or more of imprisonment; not a fugitive from justice; not an addict or unlawful user of marijuana, depressants, stimulants, or narcotics; not judged mentally deficient or committed to a mental institution; not discharged from the military under other than honorable conditions; eligible to possess a firearm under federal law.

Training course: One of several approved handgun safety and training courses. The Department of Public Safety and Corrections course includes: one hour instruction on handgun nomenclature and safe handling procedures; one hour on ammunition knowledge and fundamentals of pistol shooting; one hour on handgun shooting positions; three hours on the use of deadly force and relevant laws; one hour on child access prevention; two hours of range shooting and proper handgun cleaning procedures including 12 rounds and a safe reload at each of six, ten, and fifteen feet.

Places license holders may not carry: Any facilities, buildings, locations, zones or areas in which firearms are banned by local, state or federal law; any law-enforcement offices, stations or buildings; detention facilities, prisons, or jails; courthouses or courtrooms; polling places; meeting places of governing authorities of political subdivisions; state Capitol building; secure areas of airports; churches, synagogues, mosques, or similar places of worship; government-permitted parades or demonstrations; any part of establishments licensed to sell alcohol for consumption on the premises; any school "firearm-free zones"; private residences unless the permittee first receives permission; any other properties or premises where access by those possessing concealed handguns is restricted by the property owner, lessee, or custodian.

Reciprocity: Louisiana has reciprocal agreements with the following states: Florida, Kentucky, Tennessee, and Texas. Other states honoring Louisiana licenses are Idaho, Indiana, Michigan, Montana, Utah, and Wyoming.

Licenses currently in use: 11,860 as of September 17, 1999.

License holders as a percentage of state population: 0.27.

## MAINE

Concealed-carry law took effect: Prior to 1977, but current law passed in 1989, with amendments in 1991 and 1993.

Administered by: Maine Department of Public Safety in 200 small towns and unorganized territories; and police departments in larger towns and cities.

License cost and duration: $35 for four years; $20 to renew; non-residential, $60, issued by Maine Department of Public Safety.

Apply to: Your local police department or Maine Department of Public Safety, Licensing and Inspections Unit, 164 State House Station, Augusta, ME 04333-0164. Telephone: 207-624-8775. Web site: http://janus.state.me.us/dps/alu/alu.htm

Applicant qualifications: A legal resident of the U.S.; 18 years or older; of good moral character; pass criminal-record check; not convicted of or currently charged with a felony; not convicted of or currently charged with a misdemeanor involving use of a dangerous weapon against another person; not a fugitive from justice; not a drug abuser; not mentally unstable or incapacitated; not

dishonorably discharged from the military in the last five years; not convicted in past five years of possession of a firearm on premises licensed for liquor consumption.
Training course: Applicants are required to demonstrate a knowledge of handgun safety by taking a course in last five years or by having received basic firearms training in the military.
Places license holders may not carry: Schools, colleges, and other educational facilities; wild life sanctuaries; at labor disputes; places licensed for on-premises consumption of liquor; in the Capitol area including the Legislature and state offices; on federal property.
Reciprocity: Maine has no agreements for concealed-carry license reciprocity with other states. It will not recognize out-of-state licenses, but it will issue Maine licenses to qualified applicants living in other states. Other states that honor Maine licenses are Idaho, Indiana, Kentucky, and Michigan. Wyoming will recognize a Maine license provided it was issued by the Maine Department of Public Safety.
Licenses currently in use: No statewide figures are kept because there are so many issuing authorities.

## MISSISSIPPI

Concealed-carry law took effect: July 1, 1991.
Administered by: Mississippi Department of Public Safety.
License cost and duration: $124 for four years; renewal $74.
Apply to: Mississippi Department of Public Safety, Firearm Permits Unit, P.O. Box 958, Jackson, MS 39205. Telephone: 601-987-1586. Web site: http://www.dps.state.ms.us/mhp/cib/firearm.html Application forms are available at any one of nine sub-stations of the Mississippi Highway Safety Patrol.
Applicant qualifications: Resident of the state for 12 months; 21 years or older; not suffering from a physical

infirmity preventing safe handling of a handgun; pass a criminal-record check; not convicted of a felony; not a habitual illegal drug or alcohol abuser in last three years; has not been judged mentally incompetent or committed to a mental institution or has waited five years since restoration of competency; has not been judged guilty of a felony where sentence suspended or withheld unless three years have elapsed since fulfillment of court conditions; not a fugitive from justice. License may be denied for conviction of violent misdemeanor if three years have not elapsed since completion of conditions set by the court.

Training course: Not required.

Places license holders may not carry: Law-enforcement facilities; prisons, jails, or detention facilities; courthouses or courtrooms; polling places; meeting places of any governmental entity including the legislature or its committees; public parks; school, college, or professional athletic events; bars where alcohol is served; schools, colleges, or universities; passenger terminals of airports; churches or places of worship; places where carrying handguns is prohibited by federal law; parades or demonstrations; premises where signs prohibiting firearms are posted by the management.

Reciprocity: Mississippi has reciprocity agreements with Florida, Kentucky, Tennessee, and Wyoming. In addition, Mississippi concealed-carry licenses are recognized in Idaho, Indiana, Michigan, and Montana. For latest information, call, write, or check web site.

Licenses currently in use: 17,000 as of September 1999.

License holders as a percentage of state population: 0.62.

## MONTANA

Concealed-carry law took effect: Montana has regulated carrying of concealed weapons since 1919; the law was changed to be non-discretionary in 1991.

Administered by: County sheriffs.

License cost and duration: $50 for four years; renewal $25.

Apply to: Sheriff of county in which applicant resides. For more information, contact: Montana Attorney General's Office, P.O. Box 201401, Helena, MT 59620. Telephone: 406-444-2026. Web site: http://www.doj.state.mt.us/ls/weapons.htm

Applicant qualifications: Eligible under state and federal law to possess a firearm; no unresolved felony charges; no felony or violent crime conviction; no conviction for carrying concealed under the influence or in a prohibited place in last five years; no warrant for arrest; not judged an unlawful abuser of drugs or alcohol and under state supervision; not judged mentally ill, defective, or disabled; not dishonorably discharged from the military; resident of the state for six months, a U.S. citizen; 18 years or older.

Training course: No particular course but applicant must demonstrate competency by completing firearms, hunter safety, or similar course.

Places license holders may not carry: Buildings leased or owned by state, federal, or local governments; banks or other financial institutions; rooms where alcohol is sold, dispensed, or consumed on the premises. Local governments can regulate the wearing of firearms at public assemblies, public buildings, parks, and schools.

Reciprocity: Montana honors concealed-carry licenses from all states that require a criminal-record check before issuing licenses. These are Alaska, Arizona, Arkansas, California, Colorado, Connecticut, Florida, Georgia, Idaho, Indiana, Iowa, Kentucky, Louisiana, Maryland, Massachusetts, Michigan, Minnesota, Mississippi, Nevada, New Jersey, New York, North Carolina, North Dakota, Oklahoma, Oregon, Pennsylvania, South Carolina, Tennessee, Texas, Utah, Virginia, Washington,

West Virginia, and Wyoming. Montana licenses are recognized by Florida, Georgia, Idaho, Indiana, Kentucky, and Michigan. For latest information, call, write, or check web site.
Licenses currently in use: 7,328 as of July 16, 1999.
License holders as a percentage of state population: 0.83.

## NEVADA

Concealed-carry law took effect: October 1, 1995.
Administered by: Local county sheriffs.
License cost and duration: Up to $60 for five years; renewal $25.
Apply to: Local sheriff's office in county of residence. For more information, contact: Nevada Attorney-General's Office, Criminal Division, 100 North Carson Street, Carson City, NV 89701. Telephone: 775-684-1266. Web site: http://www.state.nv.us/ag/
Click on Firearms in Nevada.
Applicant qualifications: Nevada resident; 21 years or older; demonstrated competence by passing a training course; pass a criminal record check; no outstanding warrant for arrest; not convicted of a felony; not convicted of a violent misdemeanor in last three years; not convicted of a crime involving domestic violence or stalking; not subject to a restraining or protective order to prevent domestic violence; not on probation or parole; not been subject in the last five years to any conditions set by a court in lieu of a felony conviction; not judicially declared incompetent or insane; not admitted to a mental health facility in last five years; not an abuser of alcohol or drugs.
Training course: Any approved training course that includes instruction in the use of the handguns to be carried and in Nevada laws governing the proper use of firearms. The make, model, and caliber of up to two guns can be listed on permit.

Places license holders may not carry: Law-enforcement facilities; prisons, jails, or detention facilities; courthouses or courtrooms; schools, colleges, or other educational facilities; any buildings owned or occupied by any level of government; any other places prohibited by state or federal law; any businesses posted as prohibiting the carrying of firearms on premises. Except for schools, colleges, and other educational facilities, prohibited places must have signs posted.

Reciprocity: Nevada does not honor concealed-handgun licenses from other states. Nevada licenses are recognized by Idaho, Indiana, Kentucky, Michigan, Montana, and Utah.

Licenses currently in use: Statewide figures not currently kept. However, between 1995 and the fall of 1999, the Criminal History Repository of the Nevada Highway Patrol checked the fingerprints of 14,034 applicants for concealed handgun licenses. The repository did not have figures for the percentage of applicants rejected but during the same period the Las Vegas Police Department received 10,827 applications and rejected 1,015 or 9.3 percent. Using this rate of rejection, it is likely that as of September 1999, about 12,720 licenses are current in the state.

License holders as a percentage of state population: 0.73.

## NEW HAMPSHIRE

Concealed-carry law took effect: Prior to 1977.

Administered by: Local police departments, mayors, and selectmen.

License cost and duration: $10 for four years. Non-residents $20 for four years, provided they have an unrestricted concealed-carry license in their own state. For Vermont residents a letter of approval from their local police chief is required.

Apply to: Local police department. For more information,
contact: New Hampshire State Police, Permits and
Licensing Unit, 10 Hazen Drive, Concord, NH 03305.
Telephone: 603-271-3575. As of September 1999, a web
site was planned to provide information about concealed
carry for out-of-state inquiries. Web site would be
reached through: http://www.state.nh.us/nhsp Click on
Permits and Licensing. New Hampshire firearms laws
can be found on the Internet at:
http://199.92.250.14/rsa/12/INDEX.HTM under Title
12, Public Safety and Welfare. Click on Chapter 159,
Pistols and Revolvers.

Applicant qualifications: A suitable person (no age limit);
not convicted of a felony; not convicted of a crime of
domestic violence; no pending charges; not a drug
abuser; not confined for mental disorder.

Training course: Not required.

Places license holders may not carry: Courtrooms or areas
used by courts; schools.

Reciprocity: New Hampshire has reciprocity agreements
with Florida and Georgia. In addition, New Hampshire
licenses are honored by Idaho, Indiana, Kentucky,
Michigan, and North Dakota.

Licenses currently in use: No statewide figures kept.


## NORTH CAROLINA

Concealed-carry law took effect: December 1, 1995.

Administered by: Local county sheriffs.

License cost and duration: $90 for four years; renewal $90.

Apply to: Sheriff in county of residence. For more information, contact: North Carolina State Bureau of
Investigation, Division of Criminal Information, 407
North Blount Street, Raleigh, NC 27601. Telephone: 919-
733-3171. Firearms laws may be found on the Internet
at: http://www.jus.state.nc.us/NCJA/guns.htm

Applicant qualifications: Resident of the state for at least 30 days; U.S. citizen; 21 years or older; eligible under state and federal law to possess a handgun; does not suffer from mental or physical infirmity preventing safe gun handling; completed a firearms training and safety course; not found guilty of a felony or some misdemeanors even if awarded a suspended sentence or prayer for judgment; no unresolved charges of a felony; not a fugitive from justice; not convicted of impaired driving in last three years; not an addict or user of illegal drugs; not dishonorably discharged from the military; not ruled mentally ill.

Training course: Firearms training and safety course required.

Places license holders may not carry: Law enforcement or correctional facilities; any offices or buildings occupied by state or federal employees; financial institutions; any premises posted as prohibiting firearms by person in control of the premises; educational property; areas of assemblies, parades, funerals, picket lines, and demonstrations; where alcohol is sold and consumed; state occupied property; state or federal courthouse; legislative buildings; any local government buildings, premises, or parks if the local government has posted signs prohibiting firearms; on school grounds.

Reciprocity: North Carolina does not honor concealed-carry licenses from other states. North Carolina licenses are recognized by Idaho, Indiana, Kentucky, Michigan, Montana, and Utah.

Licenses currently in use: 41,063 as of September 8, 1999.

License holders as a percentage of state population: 0.54.

## NORTH DAKOTA

Concealed-carry law took effect: Prior to 1977, but current law passed in 1985.

Administered by: Office of Attorney General, Bureau of
Criminal Investigation.

License cost and duration: $25 for three years.

Apply to: North Dakota Bureau of Criminal Investigation,
Attention: Firearms Permits, P.O. Box 1054, Bismarck,
ND 58502-1054. Telephone 701-328-5500. Firearms laws
of North Dakota may be found on the Internet at:
http://expedition.bismarck.ag.state.nd.us/ndag/
manuals/weapons.html

Applicant qualifications: Pass criminal record check—not
convicted of a felony involving violence or intimidation
in the last ten years; not convicted of a felony that did
not involve violence or intimidation in the last five years;
not convicted of a class A misdemeanor involving violence or intimidation while armed with a firearm or
other deadly weapon in the last five years; approval of
sheriff or police chief; 18 years or older; no history of
mental illness in last three years; pass written and shooting test.

Training course: Firearm safety and operation; law regarding
the license and use of deadly force; range qualification
course.

Places license holders may not carry: Licensed liquor establishments; gaming sites; athletic and sporting events;
schools and school functions; churches and church functions; political rallies or events; musical concerts; public
parks and public buildings; public gatherings.

Reciprocity: North Dakota honors concealed-carry licenses
from Florida (provided licensee is at least 21 years old),
New Hampshire, and Wyoming. North Dakota licenses
are recognized in Florida, Idaho, Indiana, Kentucky,
Michigan, Montana, and Wyoming. For the latest information, call, write, or check web site.

Licenses currently in use: 5,284 as of September 21, 1999.

License holders as a percentage of state population: 0.82.

## OKLAHOMA

Concealed-carry law took effect: January 1, 1996.

Administered by: Oklahoma State Bureau of Investigation.

License cost and duration: $100 for four years, plus a finger-printing fee paid to the local sheriff not to exceed $25; renewal $85.

Apply to: Oklahoma State Bureau of Investigation, Self-Defense Act Licensing Unit, P.O. Box 11497, Oklahoma City, OK 73136. Telephone 800-207-6724. Web site: http://www.osbi.state.ok.us/ Click on Self-Defense Act. Take completed applications to local sheriff.

Applicant qualifications: U.S. citizen and current legal resident of Oklahoma for at least six months; at least 23 years of age; complete training course; not convicted of a felony in any jurisdiction; not judged incompetent; not convicted of any of five misdemeanors relating to assault and battery, stalking, domestic abuse or illegal drugs; not attempted suicide or otherwise indicated mental instability within the previous ten years; not currently undergoing treatment for mental illness; not a habitual criminal; not ineligible to possess a pistol. A further list of conditions precludes residents from applying for a license for a specified period of time, usually three years.

Training course: An eight-hour course from an approved instructor for a fee not to exceed $60. Course to include pistol handling, safety and storage; dynamics of ammunition and firing; methods and positions for firing a pistol; laws relating to concealed carry and use of appropriate force; a practice shooting session; no weapon of a caliber larger than .45 may be used.

Places license holders may not carry: Bars or establishments where the sale and consumption of alcohol on the premises is the primary business; structures, buildings, or office space owned or leased by any city, town, county, state, or federal government authority for the purpose of doing business with the public; meetings of city, town, county, state, or federal officials, school board members, or other elected or appointed officials; prisons, jails, or detention facilities; elementary, secondary, vocational-technical schools, colleges, or universities; public or private school buses; sports arenas during professional sporting events; places where parimutuel betting is authorized. Business owners have the right to control the possession of weapons on their premises.

Reciprocity: Oklahoma has reciprocity agreements with Arkansas, Texas, Utah, and Wyoming. In addition, the following states honor Oklahoma concealed carry licenses: Idaho, Indiana, Kentucky, Michigan, and Montana.

Licenses currently in use: 30,406 to August 27, 1999.

License holders as a percentage of state population: 0.91.

## OREGON

Concealed-carry law took effect: Non-discretionary law adopted in 1990.

Administered by: County sheriffs.

License cost and duration: $65 for four years; renewal $50.

Apply to: Sheriff in county of residence. Oregon law can be found on the Internet at: http://www.leg.state.or.us/ors/166.html.
Relevant statutes are from 166.291 to 166.297.

Applicant qualifications: U.S. citizen or legal resident alien in the county of application who has declared in writing to the Immigration and Naturalization Service intent to acquire citizenship; 21 years or older; has a principal residence in the county of application; has no outstanding arrest warrants; is not free on any form of pretrial release; demonstrates competence with handgun; not convicted of a felony; not convicted of a misdemeanor within last four years; not committed to state mental health division;

not found mentally ill or prohibited from possessing a firearm as a result of that illness; not convicted of a misdemeanor of domestic violence.

Training course: Any of various handgun safety courses, or demonstrates competency through organized shooting competition or military service.

Places license holders may not carry: Courtrooms, jury rooms, judge's chambers, or adjacent areas; federal buildings; airport property; public or private property where firearms are prohibited by posted signs.

Reciprocity: Oregon does not honor out-of-state concealed-handgun licenses. States that recognize Oregon licenses are Idaho, Indiana, Kentucky, Michigan, and Montana.

Licenses currently in use: 96,540 as of September 3, 1999.

License holders as a percentage of state population: 2.94.

## PENNSYLVANIA

Concealed-carry law took effect: Pennsylvania changed from discretionary issue of permits to "shall issue" in 1989 except for Philadelphia; most recent change in the law, effective October 11, 1995, eased restrictions on residents of Philadelphia.

Administered by: Pennsylvania State Police.

License cost and duration: $19 for five years.

Apply to: Local sheriff or chief of police where applicant resides. For more information, contact: Pennsylvania State Police, Firearm Unit, 1800 Elmerton Avenue, Harrisburg, PA 17110. Telephone: 717-783-5598.

Applicant qualifications: Of good character and reputation; 21 years or older; legal resident of the U.S.; not charged or convicted of a felony or crime of violence; of sound mind and never committed to a mental institution; not an illegal drug user or habitual drunkard; not dishonorably discharged from the military; not a fugitive from justice; not prevented from possessing a firearm by state or federal law.

Training course: Not required.

Places license holders may not carry: Schools; school buses; educational establishments; state parks; courthouses where posted; federal property. In addition, game laws include some restrictions.

Reciprocity: Pennsylvania has no reciprocity agreements with other states and does not honor out-of-state concealed-handgun licenses. The following states honor Pennsylvania licenses: Idaho, Indiana, Kentucky, Michigan, and Montana.

Licenses currently in use: 636,232 as of September 23, 1999.

License holders as a percentage of state population: 5.30.

## SOUTH CAROLINA

Concealed-carry law took effect: August 24, 1996.

Administered by: South Carolina Law Enforcement Division.

License cost and duration: $50 for four years; renewal $50.

Apply to: Pick up application forms at any sheriff's office then mail the completed application to South Carolina Law Enforcement Division, Attention: Regulatory Department, P.O. Box 21398, Columbia, SC 29221-1398; Telephone 803-896-7014. As of November 1999, the South Carolina Law Enforcement Division planned to add concealed carry information to its web site at: http://www.sled.state.sc.us/

Applicant qualifications: A resident of the state for at least 12 months; 21 years or older; pass an approved training course; pass a criminal record check; not prohibited by state law from possessing a firearm.

Training course: Minimum eight-hour course to include instruction in law relating to handguns and the use of deadly force; handgun use and safety; proper storage with emphasis on preventing injury to children; range course.

Places license holders may not carry: Law enforcement offices or facilities; prisons, jails, or detention facilities or offices; courthouses or courtrooms; polling places on election days; offices or meetings of governing bodies of counties, public school districts, municipalities, or special purpose districts; school or college athletic events; day care or preschool facilities; wherever prohibited by federal law; churches or other established religious sanctuaries; hospitals, medical clinics, or doctors' offices or other medical facilities.

Reciprocity: South Carolina recognizes licenses from Arkansas, Tennessee, Utah, and Wyoming. South Carolina licenses are honored in Arkansas, Idaho, Indiana, Kentucky, Michigan, Montana, Tennessee, Utah, and Wyoming.

Licenses currently in use: 22,055 as of September 20, 1999.

License holders as a percentage of state population: 0.57.

## SOUTH DAKOTA

Concealed-carry law took effect: Prior to 1977 with most recent amendments in 1995.

Administered by: Local sheriffs and chiefs of police.

License cost and duration: $10 for four years.

Apply to: Sheriff of the county or chief of police of the municipality in which applicant resides. For more information, contact: South Dakota Attorney-General's Office, 500 East Capitol Avenue, Pierre, SD 57501-5070. Telephone: 605-773-3215. South Dakota firearms laws may be found on the Internet at: http://www.state.sd.us/state/legis/lrc/statutes/lrcmenu.htm Click on Statutes, Title List; click on Title 23, Law Enforcement; click on Chapter 7, Firearms Control.

Applicant qualifications: Resident of the county or municipality where applying for at least 30 days; U.S. citizen or legal resident for at least two years; 18 years or older;

neither pleaded guilty to, pleaded nolo contendere to, nor been convicted of a felony or crime of violence; not habitually in an intoxicated or drugged condition; has no history of violence; not found in last ten years to be a danger to self or others; not currently judged mentally incompetent; no weapons or drug violations in the past two years.

Training course: Not required.

Places license holders may not carry: Licensed establishments that derive more than half their income from the sale of alcohol; state capitol or county courthouses.

Reciprocity: South Dakota does not have reciprocity agreements with any other states and does not honor out-of-state licenses. States that recognize South Dakota concealed-handgun licenses are Idaho, Indiana, Kentucky, and Michigan.

Licenses currently in use: 43,783 as of September 22, 1999.

License holders as a percentage of state population: 5.93.

## TENNESSEE

Concealed-carry law took effect: A non-discretionary system was adopted in 1994 administered by local sheriffs; the law was amended to give administration to the state, effective October 1, 1996.

Administered by: Tennessee Department of Safety.

License cost and duration: $115 for four years; renewal fee $50.

Apply to: Local drivers' license office. For more information, contact: Handgun Carry Permit Office, Tennessee Department of Safety, 1150 Foster Avenue, Nashville, TN 37249-1000. Telephone: 615-251-8590. Web site: http://www.state.tn.us/safety/handguns.html

Applicant qualifications: Legal resident of Tennessee; 21 years or older; not convicted of a felony; not currently charged with a felony; not subject of a protection order that prohibits applicant from possessing or carrying a firearm; not a fugitive from justice; not addicted to alcohol or drugs; has not been hospitalized for mental illness, alcohol, or drug problems in last ten years; not judged mentally ill and/or had a conservator appointed by a court by reason of a mental defect; not been found by a court in the last seven years to pose an immediate substantial likelihood of serious harm because of mental illness; not convicted of a misdemeanor of domestic violence; not receiving social security benefits by reason of alcohol or drug dependence or mental disability; not convicted of stalking; not convicted of driving under the influence of an intoxicant twice or more in the last ten years and no such convictions in the last five years; pass approved training course.

Training course: Approved course involving classroom and range work.

Places license holders may not carry: Anywhere alcohol is sold or served; state parks, schools, churches; where prohibited by individuals, corporations, businesses, or local, state, or federal government entities on their premises when posted or announced.

Reciprocity: Tennessee has reciprocal agreements with the following states: Arkansas, Florida, Georgia, Kentucky, Louisiana, Mississippi, South Carolina, and Virginia. In addition, the following states honor Tennessee licenses: Idaho, Indiana, Michigan, Montana, Utah, and Wyoming. For the latest information, call, write, or check web site.

Licenses currently in use: 81,112 as of September 21, 1999.

License holders as a percentage of state population: 1.49.

## TEXAS

Concealed-carry law took effect: January 1, 1996.

Administered by: Texas Department of Public Safety.

License cost and duration: $140 for four years ($70 for senior citizens and indigents); renewal $70.

Apply to: Concealed Handgun Licensing Section, Texas
Department of Public Safety, P.O. Box 4143, Austin, TX
78765-4143. Telephone 512-706-7293/4. Web site:
http://www.txdps.state.tx.us/ Click on Concealed
Handgun Licensing.

Applicant qualifications: Pass criminal record check—not
convicted of, or currently charged with, a felony or with a
Class A or B misdemeanor in last five years; not a fugitive
from justice; 21 years or older; legal resident of Texas for
six months; not chemically dependent or of unsound
mind—capable of exercising sound judgement with
respect to the proper use and storage of a handgun; not
delinquent in paying child support, taxes, or student
loan; not currently under a spousal protective or restraining order; qualified under state and federal law to buy a
handgun; pass training course.

Training course: Ten to fifteen hours of classroom and
range instruction covering laws relating to weapons and
use of deadly force; handgun use, proficiency, and safety;
nonviolent dispute resolution; storage practices particularly regarding child safety; 50-round proficiency test
with semi-automatic or revolver of minimum .32 caliber. Applicants who qualify with a semi-auto may carry
either action, but those who qualify with a revolver may
carry a revolver only.

Places license holders may not carry: The premises or
buses of schools or educational institutes; polling
places; courtrooms or court offices; racetracks;
secured areas of airports; correctional facilities; businesses that derive 51 percent or more of their revenue
from the sale of alcohol for on-premises consumption; at high-school, collegiate, or professional sporting events. Provided they are properly signed,
hospitals, nursing homes, amusement parks, churches,
or places of worship, meetings of governmental enti-

ties, and private businesses. Premises do not include parking areas.

Reciprocity: Texas has reciprocal agreements with Arizona, Arkansas, Louisiana, and Oklahoma. In addition, the following states recognize Texas concealed-handgun licenses: Idaho, Indiana, Kentucky, Michigan, Montana, Utah, and Wyoming. For the latest information, call, write, or check web site.

Licenses currently in use: 198,010 as of September 30, 1999.

License holders as a percentage of state population: 1.00.

## UTAH

Concealed-carry law took effect: May 1, 1995.

Administered by: Department of Public Safety.

License cost and duration: $59 for five years; renewal $10.

Apply to: Utah Department of Public Safety, Bureau of Criminal Identification, 3888 West 5400 South, Taylorsville, UT 84118. Telephone 801-965-4445. Web site: http://www.bci.state.ut.us/ Click on Concealed Firearms Permit.

Applicant qualifications: Pass criminal record check—not convicted of a felony or crime involving violence, alcohol, narcotics, moral turpitude; 21 years or older; legal resident of the U.S.; not judged mentally incompetent; pass a firearms familiarity course.

Training course: Handling and safety of firearms; laws concerning use of deadly force, self-defense; transportation and concealment of firearms.

Places license holders may not carry: Secure areas of airports and federal government property. Any secure areas in which firearms are prohibited and that are posted. This includes courthouses, courtrooms, mental health, and correctional facilities. It is illegal to carry a handgun while intoxicated.

Reciprocity: Utah will honor concealed-carry licenses from Alaska, Arizona, Arkansas, Hawaii, Louisiana, Nevada,

North Carolina, Oklahoma, South Carolina, Tennessee, and
Texas. The following states will recognize Utah licenses:
Arizona, Arkansas, Idaho, Indiana, Kentucky, Michigan,
Montana, Oklahoma, South Carolina, and Wyoming. For
latest information, call, write, or check web site.
Licenses currently in use: 26,835 as of August 30, 1999.
License holders as a percentage of state population: 1.28.

## VERMONT

Vermont is the only state that allows its residents to carry
handguns for protection in the open or concealed without a permit or license. However, some of the larger cities
have local ordinances regulating the use and carrying of
loaded and/or concealed handguns in their jurisdictions.
Residents must be 16 years or older to possess a firearm
unless they have permission from parent or guardian.
Places where firearms may not be carried: On the premises
or grounds of state institutions; schools, if a student.

## VIRGINIA

Concealed-carry law took effect: 1988 with amendments
July 1, 1995.
Administered by: Virginia State Police and local circuit courts.
License cost and duration: Not to exceed $50 for five years.
Apply to: Clerk of local circuit court of county or city in
which applicant resides. For more information, contact:
Virginia State Police, Firearms Transaction Center, P.O.
Box 85608, Richmond, VA 23285-5608. Telephone:
804-674-2292. Web site: http://www.vsp.state.va.us/
Click on Complete Web Site Contents then Concealed
Weapons Permits.
Applicant qualifications: Pass criminal record check;
21 years or older; eligible under state and federal law to
possess a handgun; not released from commitment to a

mental institution within five years; not had mental competency restored in last five years; not subject to a restraining or protective order; not convicted of two misdemeanors within last three years if one was a Class 1 misdemeanor; not an unlawful user or distributor of drugs; not a habitual drunkard; a legal resident of the U.S.; not having been dishonorably discharged from the military; not a fugitive from justice; not facing a pending charge or conviction for a felony or, within the last three years, a violent misdemeanor; not convicted of a drug charge in the last three years and no such charge pending; not convicted of a stalking charge in the last three years and no such charge pending; not received mental health or substance abuse treatment in a residential setting in past five years.

Training course: Circuit court may require proof that applicant has demonstrated competence with a handgun by completion of a hunter education or safety course, or firearms safety or training course.

Places license holders may not carry: Businesses or special events for which licenses have been granted by the Virginia Alcoholic Beverage Control Board to serve alcohol for on-premises consumption; private property where posted or prohibited by the owner; places of religious worship; school property.

Reciprocity: Virginia has a reciprocity agreement with Tennessee. In addition, Virginia licenses are honored in Idaho, Indiana, Kentucky, Michigan, and Montana.

Licenses currently in use: 91,900 as of July 9, 1999.

License holders as a percentage of state population: 1.35.

## WASHINGTON

Concealed-carry law took effect: The law changed from discretionary issue of permits to "shall issue" in 1961; the most recent changes went into effect June 6, 1996.

Administered by: State of Washington, Department of
  Licensing, Firearms Program, P.O. Box 9649, Olympia,
  WA 98507-9649. Telephone: 360-753-2803. Web site:
  http://www.wa.gov/dol/bpd/firfront.htm
License cost and duration: $60 for five years; renewal $32.
Apply to: Local police chief in incorporated areas, otherwise
  local sheriff. A non-resident may apply to any police
  chief or sheriff.
Applicant qualifications: Resident of the state; 21 years or
  older; eligible to possess a handgun under state law; pass
  criminal record check; no convictions or unresolved
  charges for felonies or domestic violence misdemeanors;
  not subject to a court order or injunction regarding
  firearms; never committed to mental institution.
Training course: Not required.
Places license holders may not carry: Schools, school vehicles, and facilities being used by schools; law-enforcement
  facilities; courts; jails; mental institutions; bars.
Reciprocity: Washington does not honor licenses from any
  other state. Washington licenses are honored by the
  following states: Idaho, Indiana, Kentucky, Michigan,
  and Montana.
Licenses currently in use: 234,274 through July 1999.
License holders as a percentage of state population: 4.12.

## WEST VIRGINIA

Concealed-carry law took effect: Non-discretionary law
  adopted in 1989; latest amendments effective 1998.
Administered by: Local county sheriffs.
License cost and duration: $75 for five years.
Apply to: Sheriff of county of residence.
Applicant qualifications: Legal resident of West Virginia; 18
  years or older; not addicted to or an illegal user of alcohol or drugs; not convicted of a felony or an act of violence involving the misuse of a deadly weapon; not

dishonorably discharged from the military; physically and mentally competent; qualified to shoot and handle firearms by having completed one of various firearms safety and training courses.

Training course: Any one of various firearms safety and training courses is required.

Places license holders may not carry: School premises or school buses; courts; the property controlled by anyone who prohibits the carrying of firearms.

Reciprocity: West Virginia has reciprocity with Kentucky. In addition, a West Virginia concealed-carry license is honored in Idaho, Indiana, Michigan, and Montana.

Licenses currently in use: statewide figures not available.

## WYOMING

Concealed-carry law took effect: October 1, 1994.

Administered by: Attorney General, Division of Criminal Investigation.

License cost and duration: $75 for five years; renewal $50.

Apply to: Local county sheriff. For more information, contact: Wyoming Division of Criminal Investigation, Attn: Concealed Firearms Permits, 316 West 22nd Street, Cheyenne, WY 82002. Telephone: 307-777-7181. Web site: http://www.state.wy.us/~ag/dci/cw.html

Applicant qualifications: Pass criminal record check—no felony or drug convictions; 21 years or older; resident of Wyoming for at least six months; does not suffer from a physical infirmity that would preclude safe handgun handling; not a chronic abuser of alcohol; has not been judged incompetent or committed to a mental institution; demonstrate familiarity with firearm. Violent misdemeanor convictions in last three years may be grounds for denial of license.

Training course: Various.

Places license holders may not carry: Law enforcement facilities; detention facilities or jails; courtrooms; meetings of governmental or legislative entities; school, college, or professional athletic events; bars; churches or places of worship; schools or college facilities; anywhere carrying firearms is prohibited by state or federal law.

Reciprocity: Wyoming honors all out-of-state licenses provided they are issued by a state, rather than a local, government. These are Alaska, Arizona, Arkansas, Connecticut, Delaware, Florida, Kentucky, Louisiana, Maryland, Mississippi, New Jersey, North Dakota, Oklahoma, Rhode Island, South Carolina, Tennessee, Texas, and Utah. The following states honor licenses from Wyoming: Florida, Idaho, Indiana, Kentucky, Michigan, Mississippi, Montana, North Dakota, Oklahoma, and South Carolina.

Licenses currently in use: 5,714, as of September 17, 1999.

License holders as a percentage of state population: 1.19.

# AFTERWORD

Now that you have reached the end of this book, you should have a good idea of the rights and responsibilities of carrying a handgun. Stay out of trouble when you can, but stay in practice for when you can't. Live up to the responsibilities and guard the rights of keeping and bearing arms.

We live in a society where social order is breaking down and the number of violent crimes in which guns, particularly handguns, are used is very high. However, guns are not the cause of violent crime. Both Switzerland and Israel have well-armed civilian populations yet suffer little violent crime.

Unfortunately, it is all too easy for politicians to blame our high crime rate on inanimate objects—guns—rather than address more complex problems, such as lack of discipline, the breakdown of the family, kids without adequate supervision or education, or trash television. Politicians looking for something to ban are aided and abetted by members of the news media, most of whom know little about guns and are afraid of them.

I have been a handgun shooter and enthusiast for more than four decades. When I grew up in England, it was possible, but difficult, to own and shoot a handgun or rifle. When I migrated to Canada in the 1960s there were few restrictions on owning rifles and shotguns. There was more red tape to owning a handgun, but it was still possible. For a time in the late-1960s I lived in Australia and found a similar situation there.

Recently I have been appalled to see how restricted gun ownership and particularly handgun ownership has become in those countries. In 1996, a lunatic armed with legally-owned handguns gunned down a group of school kids in Scotland. In a knee-jerk response the government outlawed handguns. As a result, all handguns owned by law-abiding British civilians have been confiscated. Only the military and police have handguns in a country where the police used to pride themselves on being unarmed. Britain's Olympic pistol competitors have to practice in other countries.

Also in 1996, another mental case opened fire with a semi-automatic rifle on a crowd of tourists in Tasmania. Using the excuse that it will cut down violent crime, the Australian government banned all semi-automatic rifles and all semi-automatic and pump-action shotguns. Since the ban, violent crime has skyrocketed. In Canada, the government has spent hundreds of millions of dollars trying to set up a bureaucracy to register all seven million long guns in the country. Handguns are already registered and strictly controlled. The next step, of course, will be confiscation.

Here in the United States most of us are still able to enjoy the possession of arms, provided we don't live in one of the country's three largest and most dangerous cities—New York, Chicago, or Los Angeles. We are even making headway in many states in the battle to bear arms for self defense. But it will take only one massacre of the Killeen type by a licensed handgun carrier to turn the tide. We cannot afford to give the news media any cause for legitimate criticism. Therefore, I urge you to act responsibly, not just to preserve your right to bear arms, but so others may continue to enjoy the rights envisaged by the founding fathers. I also urge you to join the National Rifle Association, without which I am sure we would have lost those rights already.

Finally, may you never have to use your gun in self defense, but if you do I hope you will acquit yourself well. If you become involved in an armed confrontation, and if you found the information in this book of help or hindrance, please let me know.

# GLOSSARY

**auto-loader, auto-loading pistol.** *See* semi-automatic.

**ball.** Usually used to refer to military ammunition loaded with round-nosed bullets.

**barrel.** Tube attached to a handgun through which the bullet passes when fired from the cartridge.

**belly band.** A belt about four inches wide, usually made of elastic and nylon, that is worn under a shirt above the waist band and contains a built-in holster.

**bullet.** Projectile fired by a handgun or rifle.

**butt.** Where the gun is gripped. The lower part of the frame to which the stocks are attached.

**caliber.** Measurement in decimal fractions of an inch or millimeters of the internal diameter of a gun barrel.

**cartridge.** A piece of ammunition consisting of a case, primer, powder, and bullet.

**case, casing.** The cylinder-shaped container with one closed end into which primer, powder, and bullet are inserted to form a cartridge or round of ammunition.

**centerfire.** Refers to a gun that fires a cartridge containing a primer in the center of the base of the cartridge case.

**chamber.** Cylinder into which a cartridge is put. A semi-automatic pistol contains one chamber that forms the rear end of the barrel. A revolver contains several chambers arranged in a circle in the cylinder.

**clip.** Sometimes used inaccurately as a synonym for magazine.

**crane.** The yoke that attaches a revolver's cylinder to its frame.

**cross draw.** A way of carrying a handgun in a belt holster on the side of the body opposite the shooting hand. A right-handed shooter would carry a cross-draw holster on the left side of his belt. Drawing from a cross-draw holster requires the shooting arm to cross the chest to reach the holstered gun.

**cylinder.** A metal cylinder set in the frame of a revolver in which several chambers are drilled to contain cartridges.

**cylinder latch.** The latch, usually located on the left side of the frame, that holds a revolver cylinder closed.

**double action.** Originally a term that indicated a handgun could be fired in two ways: by cocking the hammer manually and squeezing the trigger or by a long, heavy pull on the trigger that cocks the hammer and lets it fall. It has come to mean shooting a handgun using the long, self-cocking pull and to refer to handguns designed to be fired in this way.

**draw.** The process of taking a handgun from a holster and bringing it into a firing position.

**ejection port.** A slot machined into the slide of a semi-automatic pistol through which the fired case is ejected from the gun.

**firing pin.** A pin that when rapped by the hammer hits the primer, which ignites the powder and fires the bullet. Some revolvers have the firing pin attached to the hammer, others are spring loaded in the frame. Semi-automatics usually have the firing pin set in the slide.

**frame.** The body of a handgun, to which all other parts are attached.

**front sight.** Used in conjunction with the rear sight to aim a handgun, it is usually located on the muzzle-end of the barrel or slide. Can be ramp or post shaped, or in older guns even semi-circular.

**grain.** A measure used to describe the weight of a bullet or the powder in a cartridge. There are seven thousand grains in a pound.

**grip.** The position of the hands in holding a handgun. Has also come to be used to describe the butt or part of the gun that is gripped.

**grip safety.** A safety lever in the butt which is depressed when the gun is gripped correctly.

**grips.** Has come to be used as a synonym for stocks.

**hammer.** A moving part of a handgun's action that is tripped by the trigger and drives the firing pin into the primer, firing the cartridge.

**handgun.** A gun designed to be fired with one hand. Most modern self-defense handguns are revolvers or semi-automatics.

**hip draw.** To draw a handgun from a holster located on the belt in the area of the hip on the side of the shooting hand. The holster holds the gun butt to the rear.

**hollow point.** A bullet that has a cavity in its front end designed to make it expand when it hits flesh.

**holster.** A pouch, usually made of leather or nylon, designed to hold a handgun being worn on the person.

**magazine.** A narrow box that contains cartridges and usually fits into the butt of a semi-automatic. It contains a follower and a spring.

**magazine well.** The slot in the butt of a semi-automatic into which the magazine is inserted.

**misfire.** When the firing pin hits the primer of a cartridge but the round fails to fire. Can be caused by a weak firing pin spring or defective primer.

**muzzle.** The end of a gun barrel where the bullet emerges when the gun is fired.

**powder.** The propellant which provides the energy to drive the bullet out of the barrel and to the target.

**primer.** A small metal cap in the base of a cartridge that contains the detonating compound that ignites the powder.

**rack.** To pull the slide of a semi-automatic back and let it go. Used in loading, unloading, and clearing malfunctions.

**rear sight.** Used in conjunction with front sight to aim the handgun, it is usually located on the rear end of the slide or frame. It usually takes the form of a rectangular-shaped notch between horizontal shoulders.

**recoil.** The kick experienced by a shooter when the weapon fires.

**revolver.** A multiple-shot handgun that carries usually five or six cartridges in a revolving cylinder.

**rimfire.** A cartridge or weapon that fires a cartridge with the detonating compound inside the rim of the case.

**rifling.** The twisting grooves cut in the barrel of a gun designed to put a spin on the bullet to make it more stable in flight.

**round.** A cartridge.

**safety.** A small lever that prevents a gun being fired.

**semi-automatic, semi-auto.** Short for semi-automatic or self-loading pistol. Fires one shot for each pull of the trigger. Uses energy from the fired cartridge to eject the spent case and recharge the chamber with a fresh round from the magazine.

**semi-wadcutter.** A bullet with a truncated-cone-shaped nose.

**single action.** A handgun that can be fired only after the hammer is cocked manually.

**slide.** The top part of a semi-automatic that usually contains the barrel and on which the sights are mounted.

**speedloader.** A device used for reloading a double-action revolver. It holds five or six rounds in a cylindrical pattern.

**stopping power.** The ability of a cartridge to stop an adversary. It is an imprecise calculation that takes into account bullet shape, weight, and speed.

**stovepipe.** A malfunction in a semi-automatic in which a fired cartridge case is not ejected but gets stuck vertically in the ejection port and resembles a stovepipe.

**strong hand.** The hand you normally shoot with when shooting one handed; the right hand of a right-handed shooter.

**trigger.** The lever that fires the gun, usually pressed by the forefinger.

**trigger guard.** A partial hoop of metal attached to the frame that prevents the trigger from being pulled inadvertently.

**weak hand.** The supporting hand. Opposite of strong hand; left hand of a right-handed shooter.

**wadcutter.** A flat-nosed bullet with a sharp shoulder designed to cut clean holes in a paper target.

**yoke.** Another name for crane. It is the yoke that holds the cylinder of a revolver to the frame.

# BIBLIOGRAPHY

Applegate, Col. Rex. *Kill or Get Killed: Riot Control Techniques, Manhandling, and Close Combat for Police and the Military.* Harrisburg, Penn.: Stackpole, 1961.

Askins, Col. Charles. *The Pistol Shooter's Book.* Harrisburg, Penn.: The Stackpole Company, 1961.

Ayoob, Massad F. *In the Gravest Extreme, the Role of the Firearm in Personal Protection.* Concord, N.H.: Police Bookshelf, 1980.

_____. *StressFire, Gunfighting for Police: Advanced Tactics and Techniques, vol. 1.* Concord, N.H.: Police Bookshelf, 1984.

_____. *The Truth about Self-Protection.* New York: Bantam Books, 1983.

Bloodworth, Trey, and Mike Raley. *Hidden in Plain Sight: A Practical Guide to Concealed Handgun Carry.* Chapel Hill, N.C.: Professional Press, 1995.

Cassidy, William L. *Quick or Dead.* Boulder, Colo.: Paladin Press, 1993.

Cirillo, Jim. *Guns, Bullets, and Gunfights: Lessons and Tales from a Modern-Day Gunfighter.* Boulder, Colo.: Paladin Press, 1996.

Cooper, Jeff. *Principles of Personal Defense.* Boulder, Colo.: Paladin Press, 1989.

_____. *To Ride, Shoot Straight and Speak the Truth.* Paulden, Ariz.: Gunsite Press, 1990.

Cramer, Clayton E., and David B. Kopel. *"Shall Issue": The New Wave of Concealed Handgun Permit Laws.* Golden, Colo.: Independence Institute, 1994.

Enos, Brian. *Practical Shooting: Beyond Fundamentals.* Clifton, Colo.: Zediker Publishing, 1990.

Fairbairn, Capt. William E., and Capt. Eric A. Sykes. *Shooting to Live, with the One Hand Gun.* Boulder, Colo.: Paladin Press, 1987.

Farnam, John S. *The Farnam Method of Defensive Handgunning.* Boulder, Colo.:DTI Publications, 2000.

Gaylord, Chic. *Handgunner's Guide.* New York: Hastings House, 1960.

Jenkins, John H., and H. Gordon Frost. *"I'm Frank Hamer": The Life of a Texas Peace Officer.* Austin and New York: Pemberton Press, 1968.

Jordan, William H. *No Second Place Winner.* N.p., 1965.

Keith, Elmer. *Sixguns by Keith.* Harrisburg, Penn.: The Stackpole Company, 1961.

Kleck, Gary. *Targeting Guns: Firearms and Their Control.* New York: Aldine de Gruyter, 1997.

Kopel, David B. *The Samurai, the Mountie, and the Cowboy: Should America Adopt the Gun Controls of Other Democracies?* Buffalo, N.Y.: Prometheus Books, 1992.

Lake, Stuart N. *Wyatt Earp: Frontier Marshal.* Boston and New York: Houghton Mifflin, 1931.

LaPierre, Wayne. *Guns, Crime and Freedom.* Washington: Regnery Publishing, 1994.

Lott, John R., Jr. *More Guns, Less Crime: Understanding Crime and Gun Control Laws.* Chicago: University of Chicago Press, 1998.

McGivern, Ed. *Fast and Fancy Revolver Shooting and Police Training.* Chicago: Follett, 1938.

O'Connor, Jack, Roy Dunlap, Alex Kerr, and Jeff Cooper. *Complete Book of Shooting: Rifles, Shotguns, Handguns.* New York: Harper & Row, 1965.

Plaxco, J. Michael. *Shooting from Within.* Clifton, Colo., Zediker Publishing, 1991.

Quigley, Paxton. *Armed & Female.* New York: E. P. Dutton, 1989.

Rauch, Walt. *Real-World Survival: What Has Worked For Me.* Lafayette Hill, Penn.: Rauch & Company, 1998.

Rosa, Joseph G. *They Called Him Wild Bill: The Life and Adventures of James Butler Hickok.* Norman, Okla.: University of Oklahoma Press, 1974.

Siddle, Bruce K. *Sharpening the Warrior's Edge.* Millstadt, Ill.: PPCT Research Publications, 1995.

Taylor, Chuck. *The Complete Book of Combat Handgunning.* Boulder, Colo.: Paladin Press, 1982.

# INDEX

# Order Form

Call toll free and order now.
- Telephone orders: 1-888-700-4333. Have your VISA or MasterCard ready.
- Fax orders:  210-308-9676.
- Postal orders: Privateer Publications, P.O. Box 29427, San Antonio, TX 78229, USA.
- Telephone: 210-308-8191.

Please send _____ copies of *The Concealed Handgun Manual* at $17.95 each.          Total:          $_____

Please add 7.75% for books shipped
    to Texas addresses.          Sales tax:          $_____

Shipping: $4.00 for first book;
    each additional, add $1.00.  Shipping:          $_____

Total Payment: $_____

Credit card: ___VISA ___MasterCard          or ___Check
Card number: _____
Name on card: _____Exp. Date: _____/_____
Signature:_____

SHIP TO:
Your company name: _____
Name: _____
Address: _____
City: _____ State: _____ Zip: _____
AC/Telephone: _____

I understand that I may return any books for a full refund for any reason, no questions asked.

Please phone for information on quantity discounts.

## Order Form

Call toll free and order now.
- Telephone orders: 1-888-700-4333. Have your VISA or MasterCard ready.
- Fax orders: 210-308-9676.
- Postal orders: Privateer Publications, P.O. Box 29427, San Antonio, TX 78229, USA.
- Telephone: 210-308-8191.

Please send ____ copies of *The Concealed Handgun Manual* at $17.95 each.     Total:          $_____

Please add 7.75% for books shipped to Texas addresses.     Sales tax:     $_____

Shipping: $4.00 for first book; each additional, add $1.00.  Shipping:     $_____

                                  Total Payment: $_____

Credit card: ___VISA ___MasterCard      or ___Check
Card number: _____
Name on card: _____Exp. Date: _____/____
Signature:_____

SHIP TO:
Your company name: _____
Name: _____
Address: _____
City: _____ State: ____ Zip: _____
AC/Telephone: _____

I understand that I may return any books for a full refund for any reason, no questions asked.

Please phone for information on quantity discounts.